V. JOHNSEN

W9-CKL-323

GROWING WITH SPORTS

A Parent's Guide to the Young Athlete

GROWING WITH SPORTS

A Parent's Guide to the Young Athlete

**Ernest M. Vandeweghe, M.D.
& George L. Flynn**

Prentice-Hall, Inc., Englewood Cliffs, New Jersey

Growing With Sports: A Parent's Guide to the Young Athlete,
by Ernest M. Vandeweghe, M.D., and George L. Flynn

Copyright ● 1979 by Ernest M. Vandeweghe and George L. Flynn
All rights reserved. No part of this book may be reproduced in any form or by any means, except for the inclusion of brief quotations in a review, without permission in writing from the publisher.
Printed in the United States of America
Prentice-Hall International, Inc., London/Prentice-Hall of Australia, Pty. Ltd., Sydney/
Prentice-Hall of Canada, Ltd., Toronto/Prentice-Hall of India Private Ltd., New Delhi/
Prentice-Hall of Japan, Inc., Tokyo/Prentice-Hall of Southeast Asia Pte. Ltd., Singa-
pore/Whitehall Books Limited, Wellington, New Zealand
10 9 8 7 6 5 4 3 2

Library of Congress Cataloging in Publication Data

Vandeweghe, Ernest M.
   Growing with sports.

   1. Physical education for children.
2. Physical fitness.   3. Sports—Accidents and
injuries.   I. Flynn, George L., joint author.
II. Title.
GV443.V34   613.7'042   78-26011
ISBN 0-13-367813-X

Dedicated to Colleen Kay Hutchins

ACKNOWLEDGEMENT

I want to thank all those who through their love of athletics and concern for their young athletes influenced my thinking and understanding of "GROWING WITH SPORTS." My personal coaches— Father Herbert J. McElroy, Edward J. Flynn (Oceanside High School), Karl Lawrence (Colgate University), and Joe Lapchick (New York Knicks).

To thank the great athletes I have had the privilege to meet and work with—Carl Braun, Bob Cousy, Donna deVarona, Marty Glickman, and Jerry West.

Special thanks to the many coaches who have shared their vast knowledge with me—Vince Lombardi, Bud Wilkinson, John McKay, and John Wooden.

To my mother and dad – I was their young athlete, and to our own four children who had to suffer through my best efforts.

CONTENTS

INTRODUCTION

As an athlete, parent and doctor, Ernie Vandeweghe has been involved with sports and youngsters nearly all his life. When he was four, living in Canada, he played golf with his father, using his dad's clubs. When learning to shoot, he used his grandfather's 20-gauge shotgun. So as a child, he grew up using adult equipment. When the Vandeweghe family moved to Long Island, the ten-year-old Ernie plunged into the year-round sports of America. He was very successful at all of them and still is today.

Dr. Vandeweghe has definite ideas on raising children and using sports to keep them healthy and active. Today his pediatric practice with the Prairie Avenue Medical Group in Los Angeles brings many opportunities to heal, help, and counsel young athletes as well as their parents. Additionally, he has four very active young athletes at home where he and his wife, Colleen, a former Miss America, can see the results of these ideas. The oldest child, Kiki, is a starting forward on the UCLA basketball team, and before turning to basketball, Kiki held California records in swimming. Tauna is also at UCLA, a member of their swimming team and represented the United States in the Montreal Olympics of 1976. Heather, in high school, is an outstanding tennis player, and Bruk, the youngest, is just coming into his own as a basketball player and is already an excellent golfer.

Obviously, genes played an important role in the natural talents of the Vandeweghe children, but Dr. Vandeweghe feels that it really was exposure to sports at a young age for all the children that contributed more to their development. Colleen Vandeweghe, herself a top swimmer in college and an outstanding athlete, had the children swimming by the time each was three years old. They were swinging tennis rackets and golf clubs by four, and riding bikes, skiing and horseback riding at five. Basketball, football, baseball, and soccer followed.

Ernie knew he wanted to be a doctor early in life and went to Colgate for pre-med. He was All-America in both basketball and soccer. He never expected to play professional basketball because of his medical studies at Columbia University. Some professional football players had studied to be doctors while playing football—Danny Fortman, M.D., another Colgate graduate, studied for his M.D. while becoming a Hall of Fame guard for the Chicago Bears in the early forties. But the time demands of professional football are much less than those of professional basketball. The football player has only one game a week, short practice sessions, and a lot of free time. The pro basketball player travels constantly, plays at least three games a week and can be away from home for weeks at a time. It seemed that that kind of schedule and the demands of medical school would never permit Ernie Vandeweghe to think about a career in basketball while studying to be a doctor.

But Joe Lapchick, coach of the New York Knicks, wanted him and agreed that Ernie could practice and play with the Knicks whenever it did not interfere with his medical studies. The decision as to when and where he would play was strictly up to Ernie Vandeweghe.

As a result, Ernie had five years of fun playing for the Knicks. And for the Knicks, they had the best "sixth" man in pro basketball. Today, the "sixth" man has been popularized by such outstanding players as Frank Ramsey and John Havlicek of the Boston Celtics. But it was Ernie Vandeweghe who started it all. Often, he'd arrive as the game was starting and warm-up running underneath the stands.

And like today's game, the players were fast, talented, and rough. One night in Philadelphia, Ernie drove to the basket and he left his feet as he went in for the shot. Philadelphia had a center called "Big Ed" Sadowsky, standing about 6'9', weighing close to 280 pounds. He liked to protect the area around the basket from people like the driving Vandeweghe. As Ernie drove to the basket, Big Ed moved over and put a large hip into Ernie's legs as he flew by. Vandeweghe did a cartwheel, landed on his head and shoulders, and lay there. His teammate, Dick McGuire, ran over, looked at him and said; "Don't touch him. I think he's dead." But Ernie recovered and went on to play several more seasons before injuries and his schedule finally forced him to retire.

Basketball fans today are amazed at the size and grace of today's player. There are a few players who are 7 feet or taller and a number ranging in the 6 foot plus area. They are not beanpoles, but well muscled, coordinated athletes. In the days Ernie Vandeweghe played, he had teammates like Walter Dukes and Ray Felix, who were both seven-footers. His backcourt partner was Carl Braun, at 6'6", and with Ernie at 6'4", they presented a very tall backcourt, as sizable and as talented as any playing today.

Vandeweghe's greatest talent as an athlete was his quickness. In a game like basketball, speed is not as important as quickness, both of foot and hand. And he had both. Perhaps the greatest guard to ever play the game, as a playmaker, scorer, ballhandler and passer, was Bob Cousy. Nobody ran a fast break like the Celtics' Cousy. Yet Vandeweghe defensed Cousy better than any other guard in the league. He was taller than Bob, had longer arms and very quick hands that were often able to dart in and steal the ball. In one game, Vandeweghe had stolen the ball from Cousy a couple of times in succession and the steals had led to Knick baskets. Next time coming down the floor, Red Auerbach yelled to Cousy to pass the ball to someone else. Quite a compliment to Vandeweghe's quickness and defensive talents.

But Ernie would be the first to admit that it was Bob Cousy who made pro basketball exciting for the fans. Before Cousy, the game was dominated by George Mikan and the Minneapolis Lakers. Mikan was huge, 6'10" and weighed about 260 pounds. He would rebound, throw the ball out, and then lumber down the floor, setting himself at the key. The Lakers would wait for him and then pass the ball into Big George. He'd back in on the defensive center—there wasn't any center in the league strong enough to stop him—and when he felt he was in close enough, he'd sweep around that player for a hook shot. Mikan was a great shooter in close, a powerful rebounder, and he dominated the game. But it was pattern basketball, predictable and dull. Then along came Cousy, and the running game came to pro basketball. The fans came out to see this little guy (little by basketball standards at 6'2") and his passing, dribbling, and ball handling. He entertained them and more and more people came to see Cousy and the Celtics. Ernie Vandeweghe thinks Bob Cousy was the most exciting player to have ever played the game. There were, and are, better shooters, better leapers with fabulous slam-dunk shots and all of that, but for pure excitement on the court, Ernie thinks that nobody was as great as Cousy.

"Over the years, the size of the athlete has not really changed much," says Ernie. "The big change has been in physical capabilities." There is so much more playing time available to athletes today, as well as many more programs and facilities. Twenty years ago, most athletes in high school played football, basketball and baseball, each in its own season. Now, they can play tennis, soccer, be on the swimming, golf, and hockey teams. These sports are now recognized at the high school level, and the facilities are furnished by the school system or local community. So our young athlete today, as well as the parent, can play sports and develop year round, and not worry about making the varsity. With this increase in activity there has been an increase in the physical capabilities of today's athlete. They are bigger, stronger, and faster than the athlete of twenty years ago. With the increased awareness of proper diet, better training, coaching, and supervision in schools and in the communities, and the availability of more opportunities and facilities for sports, today's athlete should be expected to grow and develop more than his predecessor.

Sports, such as skiing, tennis, track and field, swimming, and golf have had a tremendous growth. So with the increase in the physical capabilities of the athlete and the boom in the physical plants providing more opportunity for participation in sports, there has developed a greater awareness of the importance of fitness, conditioning, training, and handling injuries.

Having been involved in sports all his life, Dr. Vandeweghe has some very enlightening things to say about sports and youngsters. He believes in competition, in participation, and in winning. And he believes in starting children at a very young age. Talking with other athletes, he knows what separates the great from the near great, and having been there himself, he can translate that to other parents and to the young athlete. Being a parent, he knows what it takes to interest the youngster in sports, to sustain the child through the drudgery of practice and the hurt of failure, and to maintain his equilibrium after achieving success. As a doctor, he knows all about the physical as well as the mental stresses placed on the young athlete's body and mind.

Ernie Vandeweghe believes in participation and he believes in winning. He knows that winning is a lot better than losing and he devotes little time in discussing sports with those who put down the emphasis on competition and success. It is a tough world out there, and to Ernie Vandeweghe, one of the best ways to prepare for the competition of life is to participate in competition in sports. He recognizes that few will ever attain the professional level, but that does not mean that those young athletes are failures. Just having competed is an accomplishment. And the more one competes, the greater the chance of success. And with success will come that confidence that is so much a part of successful living.

The Vandeweghe family is very competitive with one another and they are also very close. When Tauna is in a swimming meet, the whole family is sure to get there and cheer her on. They do the same when Kiki and the UCLA basketball team is playing. Colleen still plays tennis well enough to give Heather a tough game and when Kiki and Ernie go at it on the courts, the play is hard, fast, and excellent.

It takes a great deal of commitment on the part of any athlete to be successful—he must sacrifice outside fun for training and conditioning; he must put up with long hard practice sessions and the loneliness of running or swimming laps, shooting baskets or hitting the backhand. And it takes just as much commitment for the parent to make sure the children get to practice on time, to the game, prepare that special meal, supervise their studies, and be the driver, cheerleader, counselor and confidant. Very few athletes make it without the help and encouragement of their parents.

Over the years, Ernie Vandeweghe has been asked repeatedly questions on diet, training programs, exercises, motivation, injuries, rehabilitation, and many others. These questions have led to the writing of this book. Ernie is the right man to take on this kind of book. Ernie Vandeweghe, an outstanding athlete in college, and as a professional, is still a fine golfer, tennis player, horseman, and skier. You would be advised not to be against him in a one-on-one game in the back yard against anyone. He's a member of the President's Counsel on Physical Fitness, a member of the President's Commission on Olympic Sports, Director of the National Athletic Health Institute, an Associate Professor of Pediatrics at UCLA, and former team physician for the Los Angeles Lakers.

This book, GROWING WITH SPORTS: A PARENT'S GUIDE TO THE YOUNG ATHLETE, represents much of what he has learned as an athlete, doctor, and parent.

George L. Flynn
Oakland, N. J.

GROWING
WITH SPORTS
A Parent's Guide to the Young Athlete

1

HOW IT
HAPPENED TO ME

My last class for the day at Columbia Presbyterian Medical Center was over. It was already 4:30 P.M. and our basketball game in Syracuse against the Nats was scheduled for 8 o'clock. I had called the Knicks earlier, telling them I'd play that night, but when I got outside, it was cold, rainy, and overcast, a typical February evening in New York. I thought the planes were probably grounded so I grabbed a cab to the 125th Street railroad station and caught the Broadway Limited to Syracuse. I didn't have a reservation and all the compartments were taken. But Marty Glickman and his wife were on the train. Marty was going to Syracuse to broadcast the game back to New York. They offered me space in their compartment so I could rest on the way, and, as I recall, they sat on the chairs so I could stretch out on the bed.

   I often traveled with Marty Glickman in those days. My medical school schedule kept me from practicing with the Knicks. My classes usually ended late in the afternoon, and I'd rush to the airport or train station to go with Marty to the game. After the game the two of us would grab the first plane to New York—me to get some sleep and study for my classes the next day and Marty to be back in time for his morning radio sports show.

   Traveling to and fro with Marty was a great experience for me. Marty had a much broader spectrum of interest than just basketball, and

1

he helped me unwind from the tensions of my studies so I was in a good mental state when we got to the arena. And coming back at night together, he helped me get my mind off the game so I'd be ready for school in the morning. The rest of the team would sack in until morning before returning to New York or going on to the next city we'd be playing in.

I remember that night in 1951 because of something Marty asked me that I could not answer. Maybe now I can through this book. Marty asked me how he could get his son interested in sports. I thought the question was a strange one, since Marty was a top sportscaster, had easy access to athletes and the games, and had been a world class athlete himself.

Marty Glickman grew up in Brooklyn and the only way a young boy without the money for a ticket could get to see his beloved Brooklyn Dodgers was to be faster and quicker than the other boys getting any baseball that was knocked over the right field fence. Free admission came to the boy who returned the ball. Some cynics said the Dodgers did this so they would not have to buy new baseballs. In any event, it was from chasing baseballs on the streets of Brooklyn that Marty developed that speed and quickness an athlete must have. Later at Syracuse University, Marty became a world class sprinter and he was a member of the United States 1936 Olympic track team. Marty, being Jewish, was one of the athletes singled out by the crippled minds of Hitler's Third Reich for special pressure during those Games in Berlin.

Later, as a broadcaster in New York, Marty covered the Knicks, the football Giants, and many other sports events. His children met the greats of the world of sports. The locker rooms of Yankee Stadium, the Polo Grounds, and Madison Square Garden were open to them, and they knew and talked to Frank Gifford, Mickey Mantle, Kyle Rote, and the other athletes of those days. Yet he was asking my advice on how to interest his son in sports. All I could tell Marty was how it had happened to me.

Sports have been a part of my life as long as I can remember. My parents were good athletes, as were most of my relatives. I was born in St. John, New Brunswick, Canada, and we had a house on the river, so at an early age I played hockey, from October to May on the frozen river, and in the summer I swam, canoed, and fished. Dad belonged to the country club and he'd take me golfing with him quite often. I remember that he'd let me use his 4-wood to hit my shots, and to this day, when I have a difficult long shot, I'll use the 4-wood and it usually saves me. Dad did not believe in letting me play with children's clubs, so I learned on his.

When I was ten, we moved to Oceanside, Long Island, New York.

My grandfather owned a house on the shore along with a big lot next to it. We built our home on the other side of the lot. Grandad and my father fixed up that lot so there was a baseball diamond for the summer, a football field for the fall, and since both of them had been soccer players, they also marked out a soccer field. At one end of the field there was a basketball court, and when winter came they would flood part of the field so we had a fairly good-sized hockey-skating rink. Of course, the whole neighborhood played there, so we always had some kind of game going, often more than one.

I joined the C.Y.O. in town and Fr. Hubert McElroy helped make organized sports a big part of my life. I had never played any organized basketball until that time, and the first night of tryouts I showed up without sneakers, so I played in my stocking feet. I made the team and we were pretty good, winning the C.Y.O. title for that area. Fr. McElroy also had a C.Y.O. baseball team in the summer, and even though I had never played baseball, I joined the team. Hitting was not a problem for me because of all the golf I had played. I remember that when he asked me what position I played, I said, "right field," not knowing that's where the worst player usually played. Soon I was the center fielder. So between the C.Y.O. program and the field by my house, I played sports from dawn to dusk.

In high school the same thing happened, only now I was an end on the football team, was starting guard on the varsity basketball team, and played on the baseball team, ran for the track team, and participated in the field events. When I was not playing for the high school team, there would be pick-up games all over the area and I had the chance to test myself against players who were older and from schools that we did not play in the regular season.

Looking back, it might seem that all we did was play sports. But I knew early in life that studies were just as important, and I learned a very interesting trick about studying that would later help me in medical school. My mother would not allow anything in my room when I went to study—no radio, no phonograph, no visitors. There was no television then. In the quiet of my room I could concentrate so completely that I could absorb my lessons in about one-third of the normal time. Simply by shutting myself off from every outside influence, my concentration became so directed and intense that I could zip through my homework and be finished in time to go out and play some more ball. Even today, when I have to prepare for a lecture or speech, cutting myself off and concentrating as intensely as I can for a brief period allows me to get the necessary preparation done quickly.

I find it interesting today that parents seem surprised to find out that

I was a professional athlete. They think that my going to medical school would have made it impossible for me to participate at that level. And behind their surprise I can sense that old adage about the "dumb athlete." That old cliché dies hard.

Now I'm not saying that all athletes are Nobel laureates, but most athletes, by the nature and demand of their sport, have to be intelligent. The young athlete should know that school work will have a great deal more influence on his success in the world than the number of points he scored against Central High. Later in life, beating Central High makes for good conversation but it does not put bread on the table.

Almost without exception, the good athlete can be a good student, assuming the school doesn't pamper him with easy courses and guaranteed grades. That does happen, but not as frequently as critics of sports would have us believe. And I know from personal experience as an athlete and a parent, that youngsters involved in sports or other outside activities tend to be better organized in their study habits because of the heavy demands on their time.

Growing up playing sports, all sports, I always wanted to win. I was never just pleased with having played well if I wasn't a winner. Today it seems fashionable to criticize those who stress winning, but I never knew any really successful athlete who did not burn with the desire to win. The great football coach Vince Lombardi supposedly said, "Winning is the only thing." I happen to believe that Vince Lombardi was right. I've played a great deal in my career and never found losing better than winning. This does not mean winning at any price, however. What Lombardi meant was that making the effort to win is the most important thing. Nobody wins all the time, but if you don't strive to do the best you can, then you are letting yourself down, as well as your teammates, coaches, parents, friends, and fans.

The critics of the "winning" syndrome seem to want everyone to end up in a tie, no winners or losers. But life is not like that and neither is sports. Whatever one does in sports, there is eventually one winner; one person or one team will finish first. This happens to be true of cake sales, bridge, bingo, selling insurance, and algebra class.

In my conversations with great athletes about the motivation to succeed, it is interesting to note that not one could put a finger on just what it was in their makeup that drove them to be the best. Not Mickey Mantle, Jerry West, Elgin Baylor, or any of the greats could say exactly what it was that made each so dedicated to being successful. It is a certain something in an athlete, deep inside, and almost every successful athlete has it.

This certain something cannot be force-fed into an athlete. However, it can be cultivated by success, by encouragement, and by parental guidance. In all my conversations with the great athletes, at some point each will make mention of something his parents did along the way that helped him. And in most cases, the parents of these great athletes were not outstanding athletes themselves. Their interest, encouragement, and advice, and their just being there, were more than enough.

When I was teaching my children sports, I always tried to make it fun for them in addition to teaching them the fundamentals of the sport. If it was golf, whenever we were by ourselves on the course, I'd let them tee up a ball on the fairway, take a running start of twenty feet away, and see how far they could hit the ball. They really enjoyed that, so the drudgery of practice and the patience that are necessary for golf were broken up by the fun of whacking a ball as hard and as far as they could. And when we'd get to a waterhole, I'd let them hit old balls and see if they could knock them across from the regular tee. They couldn't wait to get to the waterholes.

In tennis, I always let them hit a ball as high in the air as they could and then try to catch the ball on the racket as it came down. They loved this and it helped teach them good hand-and-eye coordination. They may have been somewhat interested in practicing their ground strokes, but the real fun was hitting and catching those high shots.

For an athlete to be successful and to maintain interest and drive himself further, there must be a "fail-win" situation. In other words, the parents should see that their children win some and lose some. In winning, they become more interested and motivated. When losing, they know that if they do better, they'll win. Bud Wilkinson, the former great coach at Oklahoma, never let a practice end without every player having experienced some opportunity to win. Even the worst player knew that he'd have his chance at winning something during practice. Also, coaches who have those summertime clinics always make sure that each day, each youngster has a chance to win something.

I went to Colgate University because I wanted to be a doctor and because my father had gone there. In fact, he's considered the greatest soccer player to have ever played for Colgate. I had planned to play football because I felt it was my best sport and I loved the game. But my last lab of the day did not end until after 4 P.M. and practice began at 3 P.M., so it soon became apparent that I was going to have to give up one. I dropped football. However, those fall afternoons in New England demand that you play something. One day I saw the soccer team practicing. Since they did not begin until late in the afternoon, I went out for the team and made it.

Although I made All-America for four years at soccer, I never was the player my dad was. I was chosen to be on the United States Olympic Soccer team in 1948 but I did not accept their invitation because I was sure that I'd be playing on our Olympic basketball team. I had made All-America in basketball the year before as a sophomore and knew that I'd repeat in my junior year, so I passed up soccer to try out for the basketball team. What nobody told me, or anyone else for that matter, was that the Olympic committee had decided that the team would be made up of six members of that year's NCAA basketball champions and six members of the AAU championship team. When Kentucky won the NCAA and Phillips 66 won the AAU, six players from each became our twelve-man Olympic team, and the rest of us could only stand by and root for them. They did win the Gold Medal. I never represented our country, but my daughter Tauna has carried the Vandeweghe banner to the Olympics. Tauna was a member of the United States Women's Swimming team in 1976 and competed at Montreal.

I graduated from Colgate in 1950, and even though I had made the All-America team again, I had no intention of playing professional basketball. I wanted to be a doctor and I had been accepted at Columbia Presbyterian Hospital in New York. Studying to be a doctor precluded any chance to be a professional player because of the demands of school and the problems of traveling and practicing that a pro player faces. I thought I'd play amateur ball for the New York Athletic Club and try out for our Olympic team in 1952. In the pro draft that year I was supposed to be the number one choice of the Rochester Royals, but they knew, as did everyone in the NBA, that I was going to medical school. So they drafted someone else.

That summer, before I began at Columbia, I was playing golf out on Long Island and I saw Coach Joe Lapchick of the New York Knicks in the clubhouse after the round of golf. We were old friends. When I was a senior in high school, Coach Lapchick was coaching at St. John's and he had recruited me. After meeting my family and understanding my desire for a medical career, he had recommended that I go to Colgate. In my freshman year at Colgate, Coach Lapchick was selected to coach the Eastern College All-Stars against a team of stars from the West. Even though I was a freshman, he selected me and, though only seventeen, I started for the East at Madison Square Garden and had one of those days an athlete dreams about. I was named Most Valuable Player in the game.

In the clubhouse that afternoon, Coach Lapchick asked me if I would consider playing for the Knicks. I told him about medical school. He said he knew all about that, but that he'd work it out with the Knicks that I did not have to practice with the team if it interfered with school and I could play whenever I felt my studies would permit. There never was a contract like that before in the NBA and I jumped at the chance. But before I signed, I discussed the idea with my advisor, Dr. Frank Stinch-field. He thought it was a tremendous idea, and the Dean of the Medical School, Dr. Severinghouse, agreed. So I joined the New York Knicks and began medical school at the same time.

I made one rule: I would never cut a class to play for the Knicks. I never did. All I had to do as far as the team was concerned was to call them the day of the game to let them know if I was going to play. Since I was not practicing with the team, I had to stay in shape some other way. There was a small gym in Bard Hall of the medical school and after studies or labs or rounds, while the other students went out for a beer or a movie, I'd go down to the gym and shoot baskets and run around. And to keep in shape during the day, I decided never to use the elevators to get from class to class but to run up and down the stairs. One year my Anatomy class was on the eighteenth floor and the class before that was on the first. Running up those eighteen flights of stairs helped keep the legs in shape. And since medical school was my life, playing pro basket-ball was my fun and relaxation. Other students used the weekends to relax; I'd be in the Garden or in Boston or Chicago or Milwaukee playing ball and having a great time.

About the third year I was with the Knicks I hurt my knee playing in Philadelphia. But I did not take time off because I was an intern at Bellevue and just could not take the time to rest the leg and take proper care of it. A year later I finally retired, and with rest and exercise such as tennis, the knee healed. I was almost finished with my residency at Bellevue and had been away from pro basketball for a year when I got a call one night from the Knicks. Both guards had been hurt and they were desperate for help. They had a couple of games with the Celtics over the weekend and asked me to help out.

So after my rounds on Friday afternoon, I caught the train to Philadelphia, where the Knicks were playing the Celtics in the first game of a doubleheader. The Knicks were terrible that year but we beat the Celtics for the first time all year. I came back that night, worked the late shift at the hospital, caught a train to Syracuse for another night game against the Celtics, and again we won. Sunday was an off day for me at the hospital so I stayed with the team and we came back the next day for our final game against the Celtics. In those days, opponents would sometimes play each other two or three nights in a row in different cities.

I had been away from the game almost two seasons. This last game in Madison Square Garden not only ended my career in pro basketball, it almost ended me. Late in the fourth quarter the Celtics were leading by seven points and there were only two minutes to go. I got lucky, hit a short jumper, stole the ball from Bob Cousy, fed Harry Galatin, who scored. I stole the ball again at half court, drove down and scored, and almost passed out. We had come from seven down to just one down in less than fifteen seconds; the fans were going wild and that old Garden was shaking. The Celtics called time out and I didn't think I could make it to the bench. I was woozy, completely out of breath, and knew I'd never run anymore that day.

It had finally caught up with me; away from competition for a year, then three tough games in less than three days, plus working at the hospital. As I sat there with my whole body in pain from that last physical explosion, I knew it was all over for me. I had nothing left and the coach knew it just by looking at me. The knee was gone again, and as the Knicks went back onto the court, I knew I'd never come this way again.

So much for my athletic career. As a doctor, I've worked with youngsters from all over the country and at every level, from grammar school age to the professionals. As a parent, I've always encouraged my children to participate and be the best they can be. My wife and I make sure that at least one of us is at every event or game the children play. We find this a great way to keep us young and stay close to them.

Looking back, I see that the day-by-day attention devoted to the children has usually fallen more on the shoulders of their mother. The fact that my wife Colleen is a fine athlete has had a great deal to do with whatever success our children have enjoyed. Exposure to sports is very important to children as they grow. Because my medical practice demanded a great deal of my attention, it was Colleen who got the children to whatever event they were participating in, and she stayed to encourage them.

This book is organized to help you, the parent, understand and help your young athlete. I have given you some of my background as an athlete and a parent. In the next chapter we'll go into what others as well as myself think it takes to become an athlete. From there, we'll discuss training and conditioning, then specific exercises for individual sports. Following that is a very important chapter on injuries; there we'll look at what happens to the body with an injury, how to care for the injury, and how to establish a good rehabilitation program. The next two chapters are devoted to nutrition and general health, and the final chapter is a "summing up."

I have tried to keep the medical information as simple as possible. In the chapter on injuries there will necessarily be a certain amount of medical terminology, but the charts and graphs should adequately explain the location of the different muscles and bones. And throughout the book, we'll hear from other athletes and coaches describing their experiences in the hopes that what they did to become successful will be helpful to you and your young athlete.

Sports have been and are so much a part of my life and the life of my family that I can't be dispassionate when it comes to affirming the benefits that come to us from sports. But there will be no preaching; rather, when you have finished this book, I hope you'll understand what sports can mean to your child and to you.

2

WHAT IT TAKES TO BE AN ATHLETE

Most of us think of the athlete as handsome, well-muscled, graceful, tall, and modest. He is the All-American boy, a Jack Armstrong, and in today's terms, a Bart Starr or a Jerry West or a Bruce Jenner. To some extent, that picture is not too far from reality. Yet if you were to look at Hall of Fame baseball player Yogi Berra, or at Kareem Abdul-Jabbar, who is 7 foot 4, or at Willie Shoemaker, who is 5 foot 4, or at Valery Alexai, the world's strongest man, you would note that none of them is the picture of the ideal athlete.

But all of them have the physical and mental capabilities that go to make up the athlete.

The physical skills required are speed, strength, endurance, hand-eye coordination, power, agility, quickness, good vision, and muscular suppleness. The mental characteristics of the successful athlete are mental quickness, confidence, patience, concentration, self-control, discipline, sacrifice, enthusiasm, humility, desire, mental toughness, alertness, and commitment. These skills and attitudes are what go into the making of the successful athlete. And these attributes do not come with birth; they are developed and grow as success comes to the athlete. Obviously, the skill of throwing a baseball or hitting a golf ball or kicking a football are the final results of the coordination of the use of the basic physical skills.

Of all these skills, probably the most important is speed. It is vital to

10

success in almost every sport. Bud Wilkinson, the former great coach at Oklahoma, considers speed to be the single most important skill for a football player. Yet many great athletes have succeeded without great speed. Paul Hornung of the Green Bay Packers did not have the blinding speed of some others, but he knew how to run with power and control, and because of his natural abilities and the fact that he could pass as well as run, he made the famed Lombardi Sweep a devastating offensive weapon. Frank Gifford, who was a triple-threat halfback with Southern California and the New York Giants, lacked that great speed also, but made up for it with smart running, good power, and a natural instinct for running. Speed in a running back is necessary, but even in the case of great runners like O. J. Simpson, Gayle Sayers, and Jimmy Brown, speed came on only after their power and agility got them past the line of scrimmage.

At the football level played by our youngsters, speed often makes one player superior to another; that is good because usually the faster athletes are smaller, and if they did not have speed they would not be able to play. But it is interesting to note that, say in professional baseball, the great base stealers are not only fast but, more important, quick. Maury Wills and Lou Brock are the best base stealers of modern times, and although they both had good speed, it was their quickness in getting away from the base that made them so successful. So the skill of quickness for them was more valuable than just sheer speed.

Thus speed, one of the basic requirements for success in sports, must be joined by the development of the other skills such as strength, power, agility, and quickness. All the skills can be developed and improved through a proper training and conditioning program.

One way parents can tell if their child is athletic and is interested in sports is, of course, by watching them at the recreation field, playing Little League baseball or football, swimming, running, and engaging in all the activities of youngsters. Also, there are specific tests that can help parents find out how their youngsters compare with the national average in the basic areas of speed, power, endurance, and strength. In addition to showing the youngsters' abilities in the fundamental skills required for athletic competition, this test can also help identify the areas in which training and conditioning are needed. We have provided you with a fairly simple fitness test that has been suggested by the President's Council on Youth Fitness and developed by the American Association for Health, Physical Education and Recreation. These seven tests can be given by the parent, and it is a lot of fun for the youngster as well as the parents. Many schools give this test in their physical education classes, so you might check to see if the test is available through their facilities.

DIRECTIONS AND NORMS
FOR THE AAHPER YOUTH FITNESS TEST*_____

Pull-up (Boys)_____

Equipment: A metal or wooden bar approximately 1½ inches in diameter is preferred. A doorway gym bar can be used, and if no regular equipment is available, a piece of pipe or even the rungs of a ladder can also serve the purpose.

Description: The bar should be high enough so that the pupil can hang with his arms and legs fully extended and his feet free of the floor. He should use the overhand grasp. After assuming the hanging position, the pupil raises his body by his arms until his chin can be placed over the bar, and then lowers his body to a full hang as in the starting position. The exercise is repeated as many times as possible.

Rules: 1. Allow one trial unless it is obvious that the pupil has not had a fair chance.
2. The body must not swing during the execution of the movement. The pull must in no way be a snap movement. If the pupil starts swinging, check this by holding your extended arm across the front of the thighs.
3. The knees must not be raised, and kicking of the legs is not permitted.

Scoring: Record the number of completed pull-ups to the nearest whole number.

Table 2.1 Pull-Up for Boys (Percentile Scores Based on Age, Test Scores in Number of Pull-Ups) _____

Percentile	Age								Percentile
	10	11	12	13	14	15	16	17	
100th	16	20	15	24	20	25	25	32	100th
95th	8	8	9	10	12	13	14	16	95th
90th	7	7	7	9	10	11	13	14	90th
85th	6	6	6	8	10	10	12	12	85th
80th	5	5	5	7	8	10	11	12	80th
75th	4	4	5	6	8	9	10	10	75th
70th	4	4	4	5	7	8	10	10	70th
65th	3	3	3	5	6	7	9	10	65th
60th	3	3	3	4	6	7	9	9	60th
55th	3	2	3	4	5	6	8	8	55th
50th	2	2	2	3	5	6	7	8	50th
45th	2	2	2	3	4	5	6	7	45th
40th	1	1	1	2	4	5	6	7	40th
35th	1	1	1	2	3	4	5	6	35th
30th	1	1	1	1	3	4	5	5	30th
25th	0	0	0	1	2	3	4	5	25th
20th	0	0	0	0	2	3	4	4	20th
15th	0	0	0	0	1	2	3	4	15th
10th	0	0	0	0	0	1	2	2	10th
5th	0	0	0	0	0	0	0	1	5th
0	0	0	0	0	0	0	0	0	0

Flexed-Arm Hang (Girls)_____

Equipment: A horizontal bar approximately 1½ inches in diameter is preferred. A doorway gym bar can be used; if no regular equipment is available, a piece of pipe can serve the purpose. A stopwatch is needed.

Description: The height of the bar should be adjusted so it is approximately equal to the pupil's standing height. The pupil should use an overhand grasp. With the assistance of two spotters, one in front and one in back of pupil, the pupil raises her body off the floor to a position where the chin is above the bar, the elbows are flexed, and the chest is close to the bar. The pupil holds this position as long as possible.

Rules: 1. The stopwatch is started as soon as the subject takes the hanging position.

2. The watch is stopped when (a) pupil's chin touches the bar, (b) pupil's head tilts backwards to keep chin above the bar, (c) pupil's chin falls below the level of the bar.

Scoring: Record in seconds to the nearest second the length of time the subject holds the hanging position.

Table 2-2. Flexed-Arm Hang for Girls (Percentile Scores Based on Age, Test Scores in Seconds)_____

Percentile				Age					Percentile
	10	11	12	13	14	15	16	17	
100th	66	79	64	80	60	74	74	76	100th
95th	31	35	30	30	30	33	37	31	95th
90th	24	25	23	21	22	22	26	25	90th
85th	21	20	19	18	19	18	19	19	85th
80th	18	17	15	15	16	16	16	16	80th
75th	15	16	13	13	13	14	14	14	75th
70th	13	13	11	12	11	13	12	12	70th
65th	11	11	10	10	10	11	10	11	65th
60th	10	10	8	9	9	10	9	10	60th
55th	9	9	8	8	8	8	8	9	55th
50th	7	8	6	7	7	8	7	8	50th
45th	6	6	6	6	6	6	6	7	45th
40th	6	5	5	5	5	6	5	6	40th
35th	5	4	4	4	4	4	4	4	35th
30th	4	4	3	3	3	3	3	4	30th
25th	3	3	2	2	2	2	2	3	25th
20th	2	2	1	2	1	1	1	2	20th
15th	2	1	0	1	1	0	1	0	15th
10th	1	0	0	0	0	0	0	0	10th
5th	0	0	0	0	0	0	0	0	5th
0	0	0	0	0	0	0	0	0	0

*Test material is reprinted with permission of the American Association for Health, Physical Education and Recreation, 1201 Sixteenth St., N.W., Washington, D.C.

14   *What It Takes to Be an Athlete*

Sit-Up

Equipment: Mat on floor.

Description: The pupil lies on his back, either on the floor or on a mat, with legs extended and feet about 2 feet apart. His hands are placed on the back of the neck with the fingers interlaced. Elbows are retracted. A partner holds the ankles down, the heels being in contact with the mat or floor at all times. The pupil sits up, turning the trunk to the left and touching the right elbow to the left knee, returns to starting position, then sits up turning the trunk to the right and touching the left elbow to the right knee. The exercise is repeated, alternating sides.

Rules: 1. The fingers must remain in contact behind the neck throughout the exercise.

2. The knees must be on the floor during the sit-up but may be slightly bent when touching elbow to knee.

3. The back should be rounded and the head and elbows brought forward when sitting up as a "curl" up.

4. When returning to starting position, elbows must be flat on the mat before sitting up again.

Scoring: One point is given for each complete movement of touching elbow to knee. No score should be counted if the fingertips do not

Table 2-3. Sit-Up for Girls (Percentile Scores Based on Age, Test Scores in Number of Sit-Ups)

Percentile	10	11	12	13	14	15	16	17	Percentile
100th	50	50	50	50	50	50	50	50	100th
95th	50	50	50	50	50	50	50	50	95th
90th	50	50	50	50	50	50	50	50	90th
85th	50	50	50	50	50	50	50	50	85th
80th	50	50	50	50	49	42	41	45	80th
75th	50	50	50	50	42	39	38	40	75th
70th	50	50	50	45	37	35	34	35	70th
65th	42	40	40	40	35	31	31	32	65th
60th	39	37	39	38	34	30	30	30	60th
55th	33	34	35	35	31	29	28	29	55th
50th	31	30	32	31	30	26	26	27	50th
45th	30	29	30	30	27	25	25	25	45th
40th	26	26	26	27	25	24	24	23	40th
35th	24	25	25	25	23	21	22	21	35th
30th	21	22	22	22	21	20	20	20	30th
25th	20	20	20	20	20	19	18	18	25th
20th	16	19	18	19	18	16	16	16	20th
15th	14	16	16	15	16	14	14	15	15th
10th	11	12	13	12	13	11	11	12	10th
5th	8	10	7	10	10	8	7	9	5th
0	0	0	0	0	0	0	0	0	0

maintain contact behind the head, if knees are bent when the pupil lies on his back or when he begins to sit up, or if the pupil pushes up off the floor from an elbow. The maximum limit in terms of number of sit-ups should be: 50 sit-ups for girls, 100 sit-ups for boys.

Table 2-4. Sit-Up for Boys (Percentile Scores Based on Age, Test Scores in Number of Sit-Ups)

| Percentile | Age | | | | | | | | Percentile |
	10	11	12	13	14	15	16	17	
100th	100	100	100	100	100	100	100	100	100th
95th	100	100	100	100	100	100	100	100	95th
90th	100	100	100	100	100	100	100	100	90th
85th	100	100	100	100	100	100	100	100	85th
80th	76	89	100	100	100	100	100	100	80th
75th	65	73	93	100	100	100	100	100	75th
70th	57	60	75	99	100	100	100	100	70th
65th	51	55	70	90	99	100	99	99	65th
60th	50	50	59	75	99	99	99	85	60th
55th	49	50	52	70	77	90	85	77	55th
50th	41	46	50	60	70	80	76	70	50th
45th	37	40	49	53	62	70	70	62	45th
40th	34	35	42	50	60	61	63	57	40th
35th	30	31	40	50	52	54	56	51	35th
30th	28	30	35	41	50	50	50	50	30th
25th	25	26	30	38	45	49	50	45	25th
20th	23	23	28	35	40	42	42	40	20th
15th	20	20	25	30	36	39	38	35	15th
10th	15	17	20	25	30	33	34	30	10th
5th	11	12	15	20	24	27	28	23	5th
0	1	0	0	1	6	5	10	8	0

Shuttle Run

Equipment: Two blocks of wood, 2 inches by 2 inches by 4 inches, and stopwatch. Pupils should wear sneakers or run barefooted.

Description: Two parallel lines are marked on the floor 30 feet apart. The width of a regulation volleyball court serves as a suitable area. Place the blocks of wood behind one of the lines. The pupil starts from behind the other line. On the signal "Ready? Go!" the pupil runs to the blocks, picks one up, runs back to the starting line, and *places* the block behind the line; he then runs back and picks up the second block, which he carries back across the starting line.

Rules: Allow two trials with some rest between.

Scoring: Record the time of the better of the two trials to the nearest tenth of a second.

Table 2-5. Shuttle Run for Girls (Percentile Scores Based on Age, Test Scores in Seconds and Tenths)

| Percentile | Age | | | | | | | | Percentile |
	10	11	12	13	14	15	16	17	
100th	8.5	8.8	9.0	8.3	9.0	8.0	8.3	9.0	100th
95th	10.0	10.0	10.0	10.0	10.0	10.0	10.0	10.0	95th
90th	10.5	10.2	10.2	10.2	10.3	10.3	10.2	10.3	90th
85th	10.8	10.6	10.5	10.5	10.4	10.5	10.4	10.4	85th
80th	11.0	10.9	10.8	10.6	10.5	10.7	10.6	10.5	80th
75th	11.0	11.0	10.9	10.8	10.6	10.9	10.8	10.6	75th
70th	11.1	11.0	11.0	11.0	10.8	11.0	10.9	10.8	70th
65th	11.4	11.2	11.2	11.0	10.9	11.0	11.0	11.0	65th
60th	11.5	11.4	11.3	11.1	11.0	11.1	11.0	11.0	60th
55th	11.8	11.6	11.5	11.3	11.1	11.2	11.2	11.1	55th
50th	11.9	11.7	11.6	11.4	11.3	11.3	11.2	11.2	50th
45th	12.0	11.8	11.8	11.6	11.4	11.5	11.4	11.4	45th
44th	12.0	12.0	11.9	11.8	11.5	11.6	11.5	11.5	40th
35th	12.1	12.0	12.0	12.0	11.7	11.8	11.8	11.6	35th
30th	12.4	12.1	12.1	12.0	12.0	11.9	12.0	11.8	30th
25th	12.6	12.4	12.3	12.2	12.0	12.0	12.0	12.0	25th
20th	12.8	12.6	12.5	12.5	12.3	12.3	12.2	12.0	20th
15th	13.0	13.0	12.9	13.0	12.6	12.5	12.5	12.3	15th
10th	13.1	13.4	13.2	13.3	13.1	13.0	13.0	13.0	10th
5th	14.0	14.1	13.9	14.0	13.9	13.5	13.9	13.8	5th
0	16.6	18.5	19.8	18.5	17.6	16.0	17.6	20.0	0

Table 2-6. Shuttle Run for Boys (Percentile Scores Based on Age, Test Scores in Seconds and Tenths)

Percentile	Age								Percentile
	10	11	12	13	14	15	16	17	
100th	9.0	9.0	8.5	8.0	8.3	8.0	8.1	8.0	100th
95th	10.0	10.0	9.8	9.5	9.3	9.1	9.0	8.9	95th
90th	10.2	10.1	9.8	9.8	9.5	9.3	9.1	9.0	90th
85th	10.4	10.3	10.0	9.9	9.6	9.4	9.2	9.1	85th
80th	10.5	10.4	10.2	10.0	9.8	9.5	9.3	9.2	80th
75th	10.7	10.5	10.3	10.1	9.9	9.6	9.5	9.3	75th
70th	10.8	10.7	10.5	10.2	9.9	9.7	9.5	9.4	70th
65th	10.9	10.8	10.6	10.3	10.0	9.8	9.6	9.5	65th
60th	11.0	10.9	10.7	10.4	10.0	9.8	9.7	9.6	60th
55th	11.0	11.0	10.9	10.5	10.2	9.9	9.8	9.7	55th
50th	11.2	11.1	11.0	10.6	10.2	10.0	9.9	9.8	50th
45th	11.4	11.2	11.0	10.8	10.3	10.0	10.0	9.9	45th
40th	11.5	11.3	11.1	10.9	10.5	10.1	10.0	10.0	40th
35th	11.6	11.4	11.3	11.0	10.5	10.2	10.1	10.0	35th
30th	11.8	11.6	11.5	11.1	10.7	10.3	10.2	10.1	30th
25th	12.0	11.8	11.6	11.3	10.9	10.5	10.4	10.4	25th
20th	12.0	12.0	11.9	11.5	11.0	10.6	10.5	10.6	20th
15th	12.2	12.1	12.0	11.8	11.2	10.9	10.8	10.9	15th
10th	12.6	12.4	12.4	12.0	11.5	11.1	11.1	11.2	10th
5th	13.1	13.0	13.0	12.5	12.0	11.7	11.5	11.7	5th
0	15.0	20.0	22.0	16.0	16.0	16.6	16.7	14.0	0

Standing Broad Jump

Equipment: Mat, floor, or outdoor jumping pit, and tape measure.

Description: Pupils stand with the feet several inches apart and the toes just behind the takeoff line. Preparatory to jumping, the pupil swings the arms backward and bends the knees. The jump is accomplished by simultaneously extending the knees and swinging forward the arms.

Rules: 1. Allow three trials.

2. Measure from the takeoff line to the heel or other part of the body that touches the floor nearest the takeoff line.

3. When the test is given indoors, it is convenient to tape the tape measure to the floor at right angles to the takeoff line and have the pupils jump along the tape. The scorer stands to the side and observes the mark to the nearest inch.

Scoring: Record the best of three trials in feet and inches to the nearest inch.

Table 2-7 Standing Broad Jump for Girls (Percentile Scores Based on Age, Test Scores in Feet and Inches)

Percentile	Age								Percentile
	10	11	12	13	14	15	16	17	
100th	7' 0"	7'10"	8' 2"	7' 6"	7' 4"	7' 8"	7' 5"	7' 8"	100th
95th	5' 8"	6' 2"	6' 3"	6' 3"	6' 4"	6' 6"	6' 7"	6' 8"	95th
90th	5' 6"	5'10"	6' 0"	6' 0"	6' 2"	6' 3"	6' 4"	6' 4"	90th
85th	5' 4"	5' 8"	5' 9"	5'10"	6' 0"	6' 1"	6' 2"	6' 2"	85th
80th	5' 2"	5' 6"	5' 8"	5' 8"	5'10"	6' 0"	6' 0"	6' 0"	80th
75th	5' 1"	5' 4"	5' 6"	5' 6"	5' 9"	5'10"	5'10"	5'11"	75th
70th	5' 0"	5' 3"	5' 5"	5' 5"	5' 7"	5' 9"	5' 8"	5'10"	70th
65th	5' 0"	5' 2"	5' 4"	5' 4"	5' 6"	5' 7"	5' 7"	5' 9"	65th
60th	4'10"	5' 0"	5' 2"	5' 3"	5' 5"	5' 6"	5' 6"	5' 7"	60th
55th	4' 9"	5' 0"	5' 1"	5' 2"	5' 4"	5' 5"	5' 5"	5' 6"	55th
50th	4' 7"	4'10"	5' 0"	5' 0"	5' 3"	5' 4"	5' 4"	5' 5"	50th
45th	4' 6"	4' 9"	4'11"	5' 0"	5' 1"	5' 3"	5' 3"	5' 3"	45th
40th	4' 5"	4' 8"	4' 9"	4'10"	5' 0"	5' 1"	5' 2"	5' 2"	40th
35th	4' 4"	4' 7"	4' 8"	4' 8"	5' 0"	5' 0"	5' 0"	5' 0"	35th
30th	4' 3"	4' 6"	4' 7"	4' 6"	4' 9"	4'10"	4'11"	5' 0"	30th
25th	4' 2"	4' 4"	4' 5"	4' 6"	4' 8"	4' 8"	4'10"	4'10"	25th
20th	4' 0"	4' 3"	4' 4"	4' 4"	4' 6"	4' 7"	4' 8"	4' 9"	20th
15th	3'11"	4' 1"	4' 2"	4' 2"	4' 3"	4' 6"	4' 6"	4' 7"	15th
10th	3' 9"	3'11"	4' 0"	4' 0"	4' 1"	4' 4"	4' 4"	4' 5"	10th
5th	3' 6"	3' 9"	3' 8"	3' 9"	3'10"	4' 0"	4' 0"	4' 2"	5th
0	2' 8"	2'11"	2'11"	2'11"	3' 0"	2'11"	3' 2"	3' 0"	0

Table 2-8. Standing Broad Jump for Boys (Percentile Scores Based on Age, Test Scores in Feet and Inches)

Percentile	10	11	12	13	14	15	16	17	Percentile
100th	6' 8"	7' 0"	7'10"	8' 9"	8'11"	9' 2"	9' 1"	9' 8"	100th
95th	6' 1"	6' 3"	6' 6"	7' 2"	7' 9"	8' 0"	8' 5"	8' 6"	95th
90th	5'10"	6' 0"	6' 4"	6'11"	7' 5"	7' 9"	8' 1"	8' 3"	90th
85th	5' 8"	5'10"	6' 2"	6' 9"	7' 3"	7' 6"	7'11"	8' 1"	85th
80th	5' 7"	5' 9"	6' 1"	6' 7"	7' 0"	7' 6"	7' 9"	8' 0"	80th
75th	5' 6"	5' 7"	6' 0"	6' 5"	6'11"	7' 4"	7' 7"	7'10"	75th
70th	5' 5"	5' 6"	5'11"	6' 3"	6' 9"	7' 2"	7' 6"	7' 8"	70th
65th	5' 4"	5' 6"	5' 9"	6' 1"	6' 8"	7' 1"	7' 5"	7' 7"	65th
60th	5' 2"	5' 4"	5' 8"	6' 0"	6' 7"	7' 0"	7' 4"	7' 6"	60th
55th	5' 1"	5' 3"	5' 7"	5'11"	6' 6"	6'11"	7' 3"	7' 5"	55th
50th	5' 0"	5' 2"	5' 6"	5'10"	6' 4"	6' 9"	7' 1"	7' 3"	50th
45th	5' 0"	5' 1"	5' 5"	5' 9"	6' 3"	6' 8"	7' 0"	7' 2"	45th
40th	4'10"	5' 0"	5' 4"	5' 7"	6' 1"	6' 6"	6'11"	7' 0"	40th
35th	4'10"	4'11"	5' 2"	5' 6"	6' 0"	6' 6"	6' 9"	6'11"	35th
30th	4' 8"	4'10"	5' 1"	5' 5"	5'10"	6' 4"	6' 7"	6'10"	30th
25th	4' 6"	4' 8"	5' 0"	5' 3"	5' 8"	6' 3"	6' 6"	6' 8"	25th
20th	4' 5"	4' 7"	4'10"	5' 2"	5' 6"	6' 1"	6' 4"	6' 6"	20th
15th	4' 4"	4' 5"	4' 8"	5' 0"	5' 4"	5'10"	6' 1"	6' 4"	15th
10th	4' 3"	4' 2"	4' 5"	4' 9"	5' 2"	5' 7"	5'11"	6' 0"	10th
5th	4' 0"	4' 0"	4' 2"	4' 5"	4'11"	5' 4"	5' 6"	5' 8"	5th
0	2'10"	1' 8"	3' 0"	2' 9"	3' 8"	2'10"	2' 2"	3' 7"	0

50-Yard Dash

Equipment: Stopwatch, preferably one with a split-second timer.

Description: It is preferable to administer this test with two parents. Have student take position behind the starting line. The starter will use the commands "Are you ready?" and "Go!" The latter will be accompanied by a downward sweep of the starter's arm to give a visual sign to the timer, who stands at the finish line.

Rules: The score is the amount of time between the starter's signal and the instant the pupil crosses the finish line.

Scoring: Record in seconds to the nearest tenth of a second.

Table 2-9. 50-Yard Dash for Girls (Percentile Scores Based on Age, Test Scores in Seconds and Tenths)

Percentile	Age								Percentile
	10	11	12	13	14	15	16	17	
100th	6.0	6.0	5.9	6.0	6.0	6.4	6.0	6.4	100th
95th	7.0	7.0	7.0	7.0	7.0	7.1	7.0	7.1	95th
90th	7.3	7.4	7.3	7.3	7.2	7.3	7.3	7.3	90th
85th	7.5	7.6	7.5	7.5	7.4	7.5	7.5	7.5	85th
80th	7.7	7.7	7.6	7.6	7.5	7.6	7.5	7.6	80th
75th	7.9	7.9	7.8	7.7	7.6	7.7	7.7	7.8	75th
70th	8.0	8.0	7.9	7.8	7.7	7.8	7.9	7.9	70th
65th	8.1	8.0	8.0	7.9	7.8	7.9	8.0	8.0	65th
60th	8.2	8.1	8.0	8.0	7.9	8.0	8.0	8.0	60th
55th	8.4	8.2	8.1	8.0	8.0	8.0	8.1	8.1	55th
50th	8.5	8.4	8.2	8.1	8.0	8.1	8.3	8.2	50th
45th	8.6	8.5	8.3	8.2	8.2	8.2	8.4	8.3	45th
40th	8.8	8.5	8.4	8.4	8.3	8.3	8.5	8.5	40th
35th	8.9	8.6	8.5	8.5	8.5	8.4	8.6	8.6	35th
30th	9.0	8.8	8.7	8.6	8.6	8.6	8.8	8.8	30th
25th	9.0	9.0	8.9	8.8	8.9	8.8	9.0	9.0	25th
20th	9.2	9.0	9.0	9.0	9.0	9.0	9.0	9.0	20th
15th	9.4	9.2	9.2	9.2	9.2	9.0	9.2	9.1	15th
10th	9.6	9.6	9.5	9.5	9.5	9.5	9.9	9.5	10th
5th	10.0	10.0	10.0	10.2	10.4	10.0	10.5	10.4	5th
0	14.0	13.0	13.0	15.7	16.0	18.0	17.0	12.0	0

Table 2-10. 50-Yard Dash for Boys (Percentile Scores Based on Age, Test Scores in Seconds and Tenths)

Percentile	10	11	12	13	14	15	16	17	Percentile
100th	6.0	6.0	6.0	5.8	5.8	5.6	5.6	5.6	100th
95th	7.0	7.0	6.8	6.5	6.3	6.1	6.0	6.0	95th
90th	7.1	7.2	7.0	6.7	6.4	6.2	6.1	6.0	90th
85th	7.4	7.4	7.0	6.9	6.6	6.4	6.2	6.1	85th
80th	7.5	7.5	7.2	7.0	6.7	6.5	6.3	6.2	80th
75th	7.6	7.6	7.3	7.0	6.8	6.5	6.3	6.3	75th
70th	7.8	7.7	7.5	7.1	6.9	6.6	6.4	6.3	70th
65th	8.0	7.8	7.5	7.2	7.0	6.7	6.5	6.4	65th
60th	8.0	7.8	7.6	7.3	7.0	6.7	6.5	6.5	60th
55th	8.1	8.0	7.8	7.4	7.0	6.8	6.6	6.5	55th
50th	8.2	8.0	7.8	7.5	7.1	6.9	6.7	6.6	50th
45th	8.3	8.0	7.9	7.5	7.2	7.0	6.7	6.7	45th
40th	8.5	8.1	8.0	7.6	7.2	7.0	6.8	6.7	40th
35th	8.5	8.3	8.0	7.7	7.3	7.1	6.9	6.8	35th
30th	8.7	8.4	8.2	7.9	7.5	7.1	6.9	6.9	30th
25th	8.8	8.5	8.3	8.0	7.6	7.2	7.0	7.0	25th
20th	9.0	8.7	8.4	8.0	7.8	7.3	7.1	7.0	20th
15th	9.1	9.0	8.6	8.2	8.0	7.5	7.2	7.1	15th
10th	9.5	9.1	8.9	8.4	8.1	7.7	7.5	7.3	10th
5th	10.0	9.5	9.2	8.9	8.6	8.1	7.8	7.7	5th
0	12.0	11.9	12.0	11.1	11.6	12.0	8.6	10.6	0

Softball Throw for Distance_____

Equipment: Softball (12-inch), small metal or wooden stakes, and tape measure.

Description: A football field marked in conventional fashion (5-yard intervals) makes an ideal area for this test. If this is not available, it is suggested that lines be drawn parallel to the restraining line, 5 yards apart. The pupil throws the ball while remaining within two parallel lines, 6 feet apart. Mark the point of landing with a small stake. If his second or third throw is farther, move the stake accordingly so that, after three throws, the stake is at the point of the pupil's best throw.

Rules: 1. Only an overhand throw may be used.

2. Three throws are allowed.

3. The distance recorded is the distance measured at right angles from the point of landing to the restraining line.

Scoring: Record the best of the three trials to the nearest foot.

Table 2-11. Softball Throw for Girls (Percentile Scores Based on Age, Test Scores in Feet.)

| Percentile | Age | | | | | | | | Percentile |
	10	11	12	13	14	15	16	17	
100th	167	141	159	150	156	165	175	183	100th
95th	84	95	103	111	114	120	123	120	95th
90th	76	86	96	102	103	110	113	108	90th
85th	71	81	90	94	100	105	104	102	85th
80th	69	77	85	90	95	100	98	98	80th
75th	65	74	80	86	90	95	92	93	75th
70th	60	71	76	82	87	90	89	90	70th
65th	57	66	74	79	84	87	85	87	65th
60th	54	64	70	75	80	84	81	82	60th
55th	52	62	67	73	78	82	78	80	55th
50th	50	59	64	70	75	78	75	75	50th
45th	48	57	61	68	72	75	74	74	45th
40th	46	55	59	65	70	73	71	71	40th
35th	45	52	57	63	68	69	69	69	35th
30th	42	50	54	60	65	66	66	66	30th
25th	40	46	50	57	61	64	63	62	25th
20th	37	44	48	53	59	60	60	58	20th
15th	34	40	45	49	54	58	55	52	15th
10th	30	37	41	45	50	51	50	48	10th
5th	21	32	37	36	45	45	45	40	5th
0	8	13	20	20	25	12	8	20	0

Table 2-12. Softball Throw for Boys (Percentile Scores Based on Age, Test Scores in Feet)

Percentile	10	11	12	13	14	15	16	17	Percentile
100th	175	205	207	245	246	250	271	291	100th
95th	138	151	165	195	208	221	238	249	95th
90th	127	141	156	183	195	210	222	235	90th
85th	122	136	150	175	187	204	213	226	85th
80th	118	129	145	168	181	198	207	218	80th
75th	114	126	141	163	176	192	201	213	75th
70th	109	121	136	157	172	189	197	207	70th
65th	105	119	133	152	168	184	194	203	65th
60th	102	115	129	147	165	180	189	198	60th
55th	98	113	124	142	160	175	185	195	55th
50th	96	111	120	140	155	171	180	190	50th
45th	93	108	119	135	150	167	175	185	45th
40th	91	105	115	131	146	165	172	180	40th
35th	89	101	112	128	141	160	168	176	35th
30th	84	98	110	125	138	156	165	171	30th
25th	81	94	106	120	133	152	160	163	25th
20th	78	90	103	115	127	147	153	155	20th
15th	73	85	97	110	122	141	147	150	15th
10th	69	78	92	101	112	135	141	141	10th
5th	60	70	76	88	102	123	127	117	5th
0	35	14	25	50	31	60	30	31	0

600-Yard Run-Walk

Equipment: Track or any open area marked for 600 yards, and stopwatch.

Description: Pupil uses a standing start. At the signal "Ready? Go!" the pupil starts running the 600-yard distance. The running may be interspersed with walking.

Rules: Walking is permitted, but the object is to cover the distance in the shortest possible time.

Scoring: Record in minutes and seconds.

Table 2-13. 600-Yard Run-Walk for Girls (Percentile Scores Based on Age, Test Scores in Minutes and Seconds)

Percentile	Age								Percentile
	10	11	12	13	14	15	16	17	
100th	1'42"	1'40"	1'39"	1'40"	1'45"	1'40"	1'50"	1'54"	100th
95th	2' 5"	2'13"	2'14"	2'12"	2' 9"	2' 9"	2'10"	2'11"	95th
90th	2'15"	2'19"	2'20"	2'19"	2'18"	2'18"	2'17"	2'22"	90th
85th	2'20"	2'24"	2'24"	2'25"	2'22"	2'23"	2'23"	2'27"	85th
80th	2'26"	2'28"	2'27"	2'29"	2'25"	2'26"	2'26"	2'31"	80th
75th	2'30"	2'32"	2'31"	2'33"	2'30"	2'28"	2'31"	2'34"	75th
70th	2'34"	2'36"	2'35"	2'37"	2'34"	2'34"	2'36"	2'37"	70th
65th	2'37"	2'39"	2'39"	2'40"	2'37"	2'36"	2'39"	2'42"	65th
60th	2'41"	2'43"	2'42"	2'44"	2'41"	2'40"	2'42"	2'46"	60th
55th	2'45"	2'47"	2'45"	2'47"	2'44"	2'43"	2'45"	2'49"	55th
50th	2'48"	2'49"	2'49"	2'52"	2'46"	2'46"	2'49"	2'51"	50th
45th	2'50"	2'53"	2'55"	2'56"	2'51"	2'49"	2'53"	2'57"	45th
40th	2'55"	2'59"	2'58"	3' 0"	2'55"	2'52"	2'56"	3' 0"	40th
35th	2'59"	3' 4"	3' 3"	3' 3"	3' 0"	2'56"	2'59"	3' 5"	35th
30th	3' 3"	3'10"	3' 7"	3' 9"	3' 6"	3' 0"	3' 1"	3'10"	30th
25th	3' 8"	3'15"	3'11"	3'15"	3'12"	3' 5"	3' 7"	3'16"	25th
20th	3'13"	3'22"	3'18"	3'20"	3'19"	3'10"	3'12"	3'22"	20th
15th	3'18"	3'30"	3'24"	3'30"	3'30"	3'18"	3'19"	3'29"	15th
10th	3'27"	3'41"	3'40"	3'49"	3'48"	3'28"	3'30"	3'41"	10th
5th	3'45"	3'59"	4' 0"	4'11"	4' 8"	3'56"	3'45"	3'56"	5th
0	4'47"	4'53"	5'10"	5'10"	5'50"	5'10"	5'52"	6'40"	0

Table 2-14. 600-Yard Run-Walk for Boys (Percentile Scores Based on Age, Test Scores in Minutes and Seconds)

Percentile	Age 10	11	12	13	14	15	16	17	Percentile
100th	1'30"	1'27"	1'31"	1'29"	1'25"	1'26"	1'24"	1'23"	100th
95th	1'58"	1'59"	1'52"	1'46"	1'37"	1'34"	1'32"	1'31"	95th
90th	2' 9"	2' 3"	2' 0"	1'50"	1'42"	1'38"	1'35"	1'34"	90th
85th	2'12"	2' 8"	2' 2"	1'53"	1'46"	1'40"	1'37"	1'36"	85th
80th	2'15"	2'11"	2' 5"	1'55"	1'48"	1'42"	1'39"	1'38"	80th
75th	2'18"	2'14"	2' 9"	1'59"	1'51"	1'44"	1'40"	1'40"	75th
70th	2'20"	2'16"	2'11"	2' 1"	1'53"	1'46"	1'43"	1'42"	70th
65th	2'23"	2'19"	2'13"	2' 3"	1'55"	1'47"	1'45"	1'44"	65th
60th	2'26"	2'21"	2'15"	2' 5"	1'57"	1'49"	1'47"	1'45"	60th
55th	2'30"	2'24"	2'18"	2' 7"	1'59"	1'51"	1'49"	1'48"	55th
50th	2'33"	2'27"	2'21"	2'10"	2' 1"	1'54"	1'51"	1'50"	50th
45th	2'36"	2'30"	2'24"	2'12"	2' 3"	1'55"	1'53"	1'52"	45th
40th	2'40"	2'33"	2'26"	2'15"	2' 5"	1'58"	1'56"	1'54"	40th
35th	2'43"	2'36"	2'30"	2'17"	2' 9"	2' 0"	1'58"	1'57"	35th
30th	2'45"	2'39"	2'34"	2'22"	2'11"	2' 3"	2' 1"	2' 0"	30th
25th	2'49"	2'42"	2'39"	2'25"	2'14"	2' 7"	2' 5"	2' 4"	25th
20th	2'55"	2'48"	2'47"	2'30"	2'19"	2'13"	2' 9"	2' 9"	20th
15th	3' 1"	2'55"	2'57"	2'35"	2'25"	2'20"	2'14"	2'16"	15th
10th	3' 8"	3' 9"	3' 8"	2'45"	2'33"	2'32"	2'22"	2'26"	10th
5th	3'23"	3'30"	3'32"	3' 3"	2'47"	2'50"	2'37"	2'40"	5th
0	4'58"	5' 6"	4'55"	5'14"	5'10"	4'10"	4' 9"	4'45"	0

In about 1956 President Eisenhower received a report from the military that a great many of the young men who were coming into the services from high school were not able to pass the basic physical fitness tests. Further, a report showed that America's youth were nowhere near as fit as their European counterparts. President Eisenhower, a former athlete himself, was shocked to learn that over 57 percent of our youth could not pass the Krause-Weber fitness test, whereas only 8.7 percent of the European children failed the same tests. Yet twenty years after that report to the President, our physical education programs still emphasized the individual and skill-learning concepts of sports. Russia and other East European countries had changed the stress of their physical education programs from success in individual sports to group activities. They also placed a strong emphasis on national goals, very understandable in a controlled society. But they did develop more generally fit youngers.

Research indicates that a good program of conditioning and training leads to a tremendous improvement in the physical fitness of young children, notably in the areas of muscle development, strength, and endurance. Additionally, a strong physical fitness program can produce self-discipline, improved posture, reduction in tensions, increase in poise, improved grace of movement, better control of body weight, increased resistance to illness and injury, growth of confidence, ability to accept criticism, and development of leadership abilities. A good physical fitness program also teaches the youngster to cooperate with other people and broadens his associations. All of these benefits that come from fitness and a good school program are very important in developing the athlete.

The physical capabilities of the child have a great deal to do with the kind of sport he or she selects. One prime consideration should be on the physical demands of any particular sport. The following chart is useful for selecting a sport based upon the advantages of body height and weight. However, this chart is not gospel; heavy boys and girls do ski.

Naturally, different sports make different physical and mental demands on the individual. The "toughest sports" are those that make the most demands on the body and the mind. In his book *Fitness, Health, and Work Capacity,* Dr. Paul Hunsicker of the University of Michigan developed a chart that analyzed 31 different sports from the point of view of demands made on the athlete. He used a scale of 0 to 3, with 0 meaning no involvement, 1 meaning mild involvement, 2 being moderate involvement, and 3 meaning heavy demand. The tests covered ten areas of athletic stress and demand: strength, endurance, body type (tall, heavy, etc.) flexibility, coordination, speed, agility, balance, intelligence, and creativity.

Height	Weight	Sport	
		Boys	**Girls**
Tall	Heavy	Boxing	Field hockey
		Football	Soccer
		Wrestling	Lacrosse
	Medium	Track and field	Dancing
		Basketball	Softball
		Baseball	Volleyball
	Light	Track and field	Tennis
		Tennis	Basketball
		Fencing	Softball
		Cross country	
Medium	Heavy	Football	Bowling
		Hockey	Archery
	Medium	Swimming	Swimming
		Golf	Field hockey
		Bowling	Golf
	Light	Distance running	Fencing
		Baseball	Softball
		Boxing—light	
Short	Heavy	Baseball	Softball
		Hockey	Soccer
		Weight lifting	Field hockey
	Medium	Gymnastics	Diving
		Diving	Figure skating
		Handball	Skiing
		Water polo	
	Light	Soccer	Dancing
		Figure skating	Gymnastics
		Riding	

Sport	Strength	Endurance	Body	Flexibility	Coordination	Speed	Agility	Balance	Intelligence	Creativity
Archery	1	0	1	1	2	0	0	1	1	0
Badminton	1	2	1	1	3	2	3	1	1	1
Baseball	2	1	1	1	3	2	2	1	1	1
Basketball	2	3	3	2	3	3	3	2	1	1
Biking	2	3	2	1	1	2	0	1	1	0
Bowling	1	1	0	1	1	0	0	1	0	0
Distance running	1	3	3	1	1	1	1	1	1	0
Fencing	2	3	1	2	3	3	3	2	1	1
Fishing, deep sea	2	3	1	1	1	1	1	1	1	0
Fishing, lake	1	1	1	1	1	1	1	1	1	0
Football	3	2	3	1	2	3	2	1	1	0
Golf	1	1	1	1	3	1	1	1	1	0
Gymnastics	3	2	3	3	3	1	2	3	0	0
Handball	2	2	1	2	3	2	2	1	1	0
Hiking	1	2	1	1	1	0	0	0	0	0
Judo	3	2	1	2	2	3	3	2	1	1
Mountain climbing	2	3	1	2	2	1	2	2	2	1
Ping-pong	1	2	1	1	2	2	2	1	1	0
Rowing	3	3	3	2	1	1	1	1	1	0
Rugby	3	3	3	2	1	1	1	1	0	0
Scuba	1	2	1	1	2	0	1	1	2	1
Skiing, cross country	2	3	2	2	3	2	2	2	1	0
Soccer	2	3	2	2	3	3	3	2	1	0
Sprints	2	1	3	1	1	3	1	1	1	0
Squash	2	2	1	2	3	2	2	1	1	0
Swimming, distance	2	3	2	2	1	0	0	0	1	0
Swimming, sprints	3	1	2	2	1	2	0	0	0	0
Tennis	2	3	1	1	3	2	2	2	1	0
Water skiing	2	1	1	1	2	0	2	3	1	0
Wrestling	3	3	1	3	2	3	3	2	1	1
Yoga	1	2	2	3	2	1	1	3	1	1

Of the five toughest sports, Dr. Hunsicker rates basketball as the most demanding, followed by wrestling, fencing, soccer, and gymnastics. Interestingly enough, the glamour sports of baseball and football are not in the top five. The same can be said of tennis, golf, and swimming. If you look at the chart, you will see that the five toughest get their highest marks in endurance, speed, and agility—recalling the ancient days of Greece.

It would be worthwhile, in our consideration of what it takes to be an athlete, to look to some of the great athletes and find out what helped them to become successful and what it was that moved them as young-sters toward the sport in which they became successful. All too often, we marvel at the skills of the super professionals yet never think of the days and years of training, conditioning, practice, and determination they put in to reach their level of excellence. Throughout this book you will read about successful athletes and what it took for them to be successful. I use the term "successful" rather than "winning" because there have been many great athletes who never played on a championship team. The athletes that we will meet cover a wide spectrum of the sports world, from professional to Olympic champion.

The Boston Celtics have been called the greatest basketball team ever put together. They have dominated professional basketball since the mid-Fifties. One of the reasons for their greatness was Bill Sharman. Among the people who are part of basketball, Bill Sharman is considered the greatest shooter to have played the game. Others have scored more points over their careers, but from a pure shooting standpoint, either from the floor under pressure from a defender, or at the free throw line, Sharman is without peer. Teaming with Bob Cousy, Sharman was part of the best back court tandem in basketball history. He was a fine athlete in other sports, as well: he played college baseball at Southern California, and later for the Brooklyn Dodgers; he was an outstanding golfer and tennis player, and a high school football star. After his basketball playing days were over, Bill Sharman went into coaching; he won world cham-pionships in the American Basketball Association, then led the Los Angeles Lakers to their first National Basketball championship.

Bill Sharman_____

The first games I remember where there were pressure and com-petition was marbles. I don't know if marbles was a big sport around the rest of the country, but it was in the schools on the West Coast. There used to be marble tournaments and I'd play before school, at recess, at lunch time, and after school. If you were good, you'd win most of the marbles and then you could start trading for aggies, and that was something special. That was my first experience in competition.

I don't remember not being able to play any sport. I guess I had the natural ability to play anything and do it well because I recall it all came easy to me. And I guess that this would apply to anyone in any profession or endeavor. If you're successful at doing something, then you enjoy it more, your confidence grows, and so does your success.

And I think I have always been a dedicated person, as far back as the marble tournaments. If I got into something, I wanted to win at it, always wanted to be the best. I was lucky that I had the build and ability to be good. I enjoyed winning and I enjoyed practicing whatever sport I was playing at the time.

In junior high school we played a lot of softball and it was in seventh grade that I began playing basketball. There was a small league in the school and we would play at lunch time and after school. As soon as I joined one of the teams and went home to tell my parents, my dad went out and put up a basket in the back yard, which probably happens to kids all over the country. I talked my dad into putting up a light so I could practice at night also.

Basketball is a sport that you can practice by yourself. So many other sports require other players, such as baseball, football, or tennis. But basketball lets you practice alone if you want. I think that was probably the main reason I stayed with basketball and worked harder at it than at the other sports.

When I got to high school, I played all the sports. I played football in the fall, basketball in the winter, baseball in the spring, and tennis in the spring; in my senior year I lettered in five sports. One Saturday in the spring I participated in three different sports: There was a tennis match, which I won; at a track meet that morning I threw the discus and the shot put and ran the hurdles; and that afternoon we had a baseball game.

When I was in the ninth grade I was not allowed to play football, because the doctor who gave the physicals found that I had a slight heart murmur. But the next year Dad changed jobs and we moved to Porterville, California. There the doctor did not find anything wrong, so I played football along with the other sports.

The coaches then did not emphasize physical fitness for the athlete as they do now, and there were no off-season programs as there are today. Today's programs are very organized, but we just went from sport to sport and that activity kept us in tremendous condition. Because I played so many sports, I did a great deal of running. I also took up cross country, which helped my endurance and stamina. But we did not do the stretching exercises that they do today. I've been a great believer in stretching since my coaching days. Also, in my last two years with the Celtics, stretching helped me overcome some pulled muscles.

I was very lucky in my athletic career in never having a major injury, outside of a lot of stitches in the face from basketball and some fingers bent out of shape from baseball. I never needed a knee operation or broke any major bones or had a head injury.

During my ten years with the Celtics we did some calisthenics, but not too much stretching. We did do a lot of running; because we were such a fast-break team, we had to be in shape to run full speed all the time.

When I look back on how I got into sports and why I had some success, I think that my having a good build for sports and my being fairly quick and strong were very important. But the big thing was that I had success at an early age and so I stayed with sports because of the enjoyment it brought to me. Later, as a professional, I was not so tall for a basketball player and probably a little too tall as a baseball player. Apparently, my physical qualities were ideal for sports when I was young, but that was not the case when I was at the professional level. By that time, however, my skills had developed to the extent that being less than ideal physically was not a handicap.

I was also lucky that I had good coaching at the junior and senior high school levels. That can be so important to the young athlete. And the biggest help to me were my parents. My dad was a fine athlete. He never played pro ball but he was a very good semipro baseball player. He loved sports and would take me to sports events. He bought me baseball mitts, basketballs, and all the other equipment I needed. When I started basketball, he put up that backboard and basket. Today, you can go to the store and buy one already put together with a pole. Back then, Dad had to build the whole thing himself, and then he hooked up the lights so I could practice at night.

I remember that I won the Valley tennis tournament, then the county tournament, and qualified for the national championships that were to be played in Kalamazoo, Michigan, that year. This was during the war and there were no funds to transport the players to the tournament. So Dad came up with the money to get me there.

He would play catch with me in the back yard, but he was such a hard-working man that he really did not have the time to work with me on all the sports. Mom always attended the games and was a great support to me too.

Looking back, I was lucky. My parents gave me great support, I had good coaching at a young age, and I had the physical ability to participate and to have some success. Practice was always fun, even at the professional level, and that is important. Today, the equipment and coaching have improved, and so have the facilities. But the fun of sports and the benefits it offers are the same now as when I was playing.

A member of the Black Hall of Fame for athletes, Willye White has represented the United States in many international track and field events. She was a member of five United States Olympic teams and won two Silver Medals. She has also been a member of four United States teams in the Pan American Games and is a former Pan American champion. Representing this country, Willye White has performed in more than 150 countries on thirty different international teams.

Willye White

I remember beginning my athletic career when I was ten years old. By the time I was sixteen, I was on the 1956 Olympic team as a sprinter and in the long jump. I'd always been sort of a tomboy and played football and baseball and other sports with the boys. If you wanted to play with the boys, you had to be able to run and jump as well as they did, so I guess that's how I developed my abilities. I knew I had a lot of natural ability, but I never thought much about it. I was just having fun.

I never had a coach when I was growing up and it was not until I got to Tennessee State that I got some coaching. Before that, I would read books about jumping and watch the good runners and copy their techniques.

Later on I traveled a lot and sports gave me the chance to see the world. I did not have the money to travel, so I paid my way through rigorous training, staying in shape, and constant practice, so that when the next international competitions took place I'd be ready to make the team and see the world. You can put up with a lot of pain in training if you know that soon you'll be in Paris or on the French Riviera or in Rio or any of the other wonderful places in this world. You suffer the pain today for the pleasure tomorrow.

My advice to parents of a young girl or boy who is interested in sports is to let them play whatever sport they want, and I don't care if it is a girl and she wants to be a boxer. Encourage her and help her any way you can, because if you don't you may find yourself going down to jail to get her out or trying to help her off drugs or liquor. It is a way for her to occupy her time, and so many girls do not have anything to occupy their time. Sports is an outlet for the energies of the young; even a rough sport like football or basketball, in the long run, will be better for a girl than sitting around with nothing to do because "girls don't play boys' sports."

After school, from 4 to 7 P.M. I was on the athletic field, working out and trying to improve my speed and power. I could have easily gone to somebody's apartment, smoked a little pot or dropped some pills or something like that. But instead, I chose sweat and run and practice. Even now, people on the drug scene that I know ask me why I still want to go out and run around a track or play basketball or racquet ball. I don't need drugs or alcohol. I can get high running with the wind in my face, getting all sweaty, and then going home and taking a shower. I think it's the best feeling in the world, and I feel sorry for those who were never allowed to take part in athletics. They have really missed out on a beautiful part of their life.

American swimming teams over the last twenty years have dominated international competition. In the women's diving competition we have had superiority because of one woman: Micki King. Out of the University of Michigan, Micki King has been a Gold Medal winner for the United States in three Olympics. She came on the sport scene in the Sixties and has been the best woman diver in the world for at least a decade. Now retired from active competition, Micki King is a coach and teacher to the young divers in this country.

Micki King

My folks started me swimming at age three. I started diving when I was ten and my first meet was when I was fifteen. Actually, my first diving was off my father's shoulders at the lake in Michigan near our home. It was at the local YWCA in Pontiac, Michigan, that I actually began diving. They had a regulation board and that's where it all started.

When I entered my first meet at fifteen, I won, and I enjoyed winning so much that I decided diving was what I wanted to do. But we did not have that many opportunities for competition, because swimming and diving in Michigan is not a big high school sport and chances for good matches were few. But I had some good coaches in high school who made opportunities for me, and I kept winning. As a result, when I got to college, I had a fair reputation around the Michigan area.

In those days, women did not compete too often. Even my own peer group in high school did not understand all the practicing and the traveling I would go on just to compete. My parents understood, though, and that was all that mattered.

When I got to the University of Michigan, women were not even allowed in the men's swimming pool. We had a women's pool and a men's pool. The athletic director was adamant against women using the men's pool; whenever I was in that pool practicing with the other divers, I'd go and hide whenever he came in. Now, of course, they love me at the school, but at the time I was going there it was very difficult to be a woman athlete.

I had grown up competing against the boys and never against girls. Then, when I was fifteen, I went to my first match and there were other girls there. They were good, and I was scared and surprised. I thought I was the only girl diver in the world! And this spurred me on so that I could show that I was the best woman diver.

Today the young girl or boy who wants to get into diving can go to a summer camp and learn. There were no such things when I began, and it was not until my junior year in college that I heard of a swimming camp. I attended, and it was great fun and helpful, too. Today there are excellent camps and instructors everywhere, and these summer camps are best for learning and training.

I was a late starter in diving. Today, there is so much competition and so many programs that the parents should really start their children when they are very young. Today, competitive divers at the age of fifteen are doing routines that I did in Olympic competition.

I would suggest that the parents get their children into other activities such as scouting or playing a musical instrument. They should be exposed to a broader spectrum of activities to see where their interests lie before they become specialized. Once you become specialized in a sport, you have to devote 100 percent of your time to it. So, even though I don't think you can wait too long before picking a sport, I think you should have a broad area from which to choose.

As far as my own children are concerned, I want them to be athletes, but I don't care if they are divers or swimmers or what, just as long as they play some sport which they enjoy.

Being a diver, I've had my share of injuries. My eardrums were broken twice, and I've had shin splints and badly bruised arms and hands from hitting the water improperly. Sinus problems can develop when you dive deep. Of course, I've hit the diving board with my heels while executing some of the more difficult dives. By and large, though, diving is not a dangerous sport.

Bill Toomey won the Gold Medal for the decathlon in the 1968 Olympics. By so doing, he became known as the world's greatest athlete. In 1968–1969 he won the Sullivan Award as the best amateur athlete in the country and the Maxwell Award as the best male athlete in the country. He still is a top athlete and now works in television broadcasting track meets for the networks. In college, Bill Toomey had a fair reputation as a runner but he was not a world class runner. After college, he wanted to stay in track and so began to concentrate on the decathlon. Sometime after his victory in Mexico City in the 1968 Olympics, Bill was in New York for an awards dinner. Also being feted was Vince Lombardi. Before the dinner, when the award winners were having cocktails with the committee, Lombardi walked up to Bill Toomey, introduced himself, and said,

"You are my favorite athlete." That tells you something about Bill Toomey.

Bill Toomey

In college, I did a lot of different events, hoping to be good in a number of them. But I was not being realistic, so when I got out of college I had to make a choice, either to concentrate on a running event or do the decathlon. To evaluate myself, I entered a decathlon and set up a certain standard which I had to meet. If I got 6,000 points, I would do it. If not, I'd work at being a distance runner. Now I had a direction, whereas before I'd gone from one thing to another. I began to plan better, to be more efficient in my workouts, and to establish goals.

Looking back, I think it is important for a young person getting into sports to try a lot of different things, rather than concentrating too early on one sport. The important thing about sports at a young age is that it is part of one's education; becoming too specialized may cause problems. However there are certain sports that require an early commitment if the athlete is going to reach the level of world class in that sport. Gymnastics is one, swimming another, and certain events in track and field are others.

But I think that one of the most important factors in choosing a sport is what the child wants to do. If he or she wants to specialize at an early age, then maybe it is not so bad. But it must be the *child's* decision; otherwise the parents could have problems and the child may develop a lack of interest in the future.

I won the decathlon when I was 29 years old. I did not start my training as a decathlon athlete until I was 24, an age when many decathlon athletes are near retirement. Bob Mathias won the decathlon when he was 17 and won again in the next Olympics when he was 21. In those days, nobody specialized in the decathlon as they do now. Bob captured the Gold Medal as a fine, all-round athlete who was a good track and field performer. Today, that would be impossible because the athletes are much more specialized and train year round to win the decathlon in the Olympics.

Every year the standards for the decathlon go up. My advice to any youngster who wants to participate in the decathlon is to get a good training program in all the events and work hard to improve those areas in which he is weakest. It is a long and rigorous program but the rewards are worth it. I know.

In the four and a half years that Donna deVarona swam in world class competition, she broke eighteen world records. She started swimming at the age of ten and had her first competitive meet under an AAU sponsorship at twelve. Later she joined the YMCA and practiced with many of the best swimmers. At thirteen, Donna broke her first record, winning the individual medley in the AAU meet in Indianapolis. She was on our women's swimming team in the 1960 Olympics, and in 1964 she won the Gold Medal in the individual medley and was a member of the 4 by 100 freestyle team that won the Gold for America. Today she is a successful member of the sports broadcasting team with the ABC television network.

Donna deVarona

I got into sports because I had an older brother who was quite active and my father was an All-America football player and a rower. Dad wanted to try out for the Olympics in 1940, but the war came and he did not get the chance. So he always had my brother and me in sports programs. I remember that I had to study and take ballet, learn diving and tumbling, and in the summer Dad got us passes to the swimming pool. My brother was now into Little League baseball and, since I could not play baseball with him in the summer, I started swimming at the pool and having races with the other kids. I was part of a little program they formed, and through that I heard about the AAU swimming program.

I tried to join the Berkeley Women's Swimming Club but I was told I was too old to swim and my Mother could not afford their dues. So I joined the YMCA and began competing there. I was looking for some sport that I could compete in, and since baseball was ruled out for me because I was a girl, swimming gave me that chance. Looking back, I feel that I got into swimming because it was the only thing open to me. Had I been allowed to play baseball, maybe I'd have become the first woman to make it to the major leagues.

My father wanted us to be active, but it was very hard for me as a girl to play many sports. So they made a lot of sacrifices for me when I got into competitive swimming. In fact, we moved from the San Francisco area to southern California because there was a greater opportunity there for me to swim year round and in better programs.

I tell youngsters that they should not just stress their sport and participate in only that. Even though I was a world class competitor in high school, I ran for school offices, acted in the school plays, and whenever I was part of one of our international teams, I made an effort to meet the other athletes and find out about the other sports. I've seen athletes who had limited their lives to just one sport when they were young. That can be devastating. If that child does not win all the time, then he or she has little to fall back on. The parents can be very helpful in encouraging their children to take an interest in things other than the one sport. The same thing goes for the coach; the coach must make sure young athletes do not limit their horizons and must encourage a broad-based education.

I was lucky. I had a program for my energies, I had parents who encouraged me, and I had a very fine coach. But I did have the talent, and I found the sport that was right for me. One of the problems in our sports scene in America is that a lot of youngsters get into a sport for which they have little talent; then when they fail, they are soured on sports and activity.

I think the most important way parents can help youngsters is to let them get a knowledge of themselves. And the only way they can do that is through life experiences. We live in a competitive society and a lot of the values that help children grow as people can be found in sports. It is not the only place. Performance in any endeavor helps children grow. But sports does offer a great opportunity for growth and maturity.

My parents gave me the freedom to find out for myself how good I could be. They encouraged me in sports at a time when it was not fashionable to be an athlete. They gave me their time. And I tell parents today that their youngsters need their encouragement and affection and help. These are the most important things parents can give their children.

In today's world of professional athletes, the great all-round performer is almost a relic. There are no longer the triple-threat halfbacks of football; baseball pitchers don't have to hit in the American league; and basketball at the professional level is filled with players who can shoot but can't do much else, can't play defense, dribble well, pass well, rebound well, and also score. Rick Barry is the exception. Not only is he the top scorer for the Golden State Warriors, he's their leader in assists, he's a strong rebounder at both ends of the court, he leads the team in "steals," and he is one of the finest all-round players that the game has ever seen. At 6 foot 7, Rick is big enough to handle any forward in the league, and he is considered to be one of the best defensive players in the National Basketball Association. Ever since he came into pro basketball, Rick Barry has been on the All-Star team.

Rick Barry_____

I learned the game of basketball from my father, who played semipro ball. He was a strict fundamentalist, so when he taught me, he insisted that I learn the fundamentals of the game. All youngsters should learn everything they can about the basics that make up the game they will be playing. I always tell youngsters that the knowledge of the fundamentals of the game is the foundation on which they construct their game and their growth in the game. I liken it to a skyscraper. I tell them that you can't build a tall building with a weak foundation and the same thing holds true in sports.

If you're lucky to have a father or older brother to teach you the fundamentals of the sport, that's fine. If not, then I think it is important to go to a good camp and have professional coaches teach you. And along with good instruction in the basics of the game, I tell the youngsters that they have to practice and that practice should never be a duty or a chore, but must be fun.

I loved to practice. I remember that as a youngster in New Jersey I'd pack myself a lunch, leave the house about 8 A.M., go over to the recreation field and play basketball all day, come home at night for dinner, and, in the summertime, go back to the field to play some more. And if nobody was around, I'd just shoot and dribble and practice by myself. I'd play in the rain and in the wintertime. We'd sweep off the courts, clearing the snow away so there was a place to dribble and run, and sometimes my hands would be so numb from the cold and the wind that shooting was almost impossible. Bu I went out and played no matter what the weather. At that age it never really seemed like work; it was just too much fun.

Another thing I tell the kids is to practice all phases of the game. Don't just go out and shoot a basketball; practice defense, practice dribbling, passing, and rebounding. The same thing in football: practice throwing and catching, learn what the linemen have to do, punt the ball, and even practice field goals so you learn all the facets of the sport. Youngsters should be able to play every position on a team, because the demands on them at that age are not the special demands they will face in college and, if they are good enough, at the pro level.

I'm one of the few basketball players who still shoots foul shots in the underhand position. My father taught that to me because that was the way he shot them, and the way all the players did then, even at the pro level. Today almost everyone shoots one-handed, but I still do it the way my dad taught me and I'm still leading the NBA in free-throw shooting accuracy. My dad had me practice one whole summer shooting free throws the underhanded way, and I found out that the more I practiced, the better I became. That has stayed with me throughout my career.

So my thoughts about what the youngsters should do in developing their skills in a sport are to practice, learn the fundamentals of the sport, play as many different positions on the team as you are allowed, and practice, practice, and practice. Once you have that feeling that you are learning your sport and becoming better at it, then you're on your way to a great deal of fun, and, I hope, success.

Today Jerry West is the rookie coach of the Los Angeles Lakers of the National Basketball Association. In 1961, as a rookie player with the Los Angeles Lakers, Jerry West was named to the second team of NBA All-Stars. Every year after that until he retired in 1974, he was on the first team of NBA All-Stars. Many experts consider him the greatest clutch player in the history of the game. Whenever the Lakers needed a basket to win or tie a game, they almost always went to West and he delivered. Had it not been for the Boston Celtics, Jerry West and the Lakers would have dominated pro basketball in the sixties and early seventies.

West was tall for a guard, 6 foot 4, with long arms that gave him an advantage in jump shooting or driving toward the basket against smaller guards. He also was an outstanding rebounder for a guard. But it was his shooting that made West the great player he was.

In addition to his basketball powers, Jerry West is a fine all-round athlete. He's a scratch golfer and excellent at almost any sport he tries.

Jerry West

When I was eight years old I wanted to play basketball with the other guys, but I was so small that I could not get enough power behind the ball to get it to the basket. So all I ever got to do was throw the ball to the bigger players. And I have always remembered the advantage the bigger kids had over the smaller, younger ones.

I dreamed about being a big star someday. I'd look at the star of the high school team and dream that someday I would be just as good. I had no idea that I'd even make my junior high school team, but I did make that team. Then I made the high school team and I thought that was the end for me. But I was offered an athletic scholarship to West Virginia University and I went on to play college ball, to play on our 1960 Olympic basketball team, and to spend fourteen years as a pro. So my dreams came true, and I believe any child who wants some career badly enough can have his or her dreams come true. Mine did.

Television gives children today a great advantage in learning how to play a sport. Nobody taught me how to play basketball. Today, kids can watch the best players in all the sports at the college and professional level, and can copy the moves and techniques they see. That is always a great way to learn—copy somebody who is good. And even further, kids today, if their parents can afford it, can go to many different camps and be coached by performers who really know the game.

Where I grew up there was an outdoor court, but it had a dirt floor, which made dribbling hard. I remember playing on the dirt court in the snow. In the summertime I played at a hoop put up on a telephone pole. I would stay out at night and shoot by the light that came from the porch next door. The woman would turn off the light just to get me to go home, and then turn it back on after I left.

I had a tremendous desire to play basketball and I never considered that all I had to go through to play was a problem. Maybe if I had been raised in a different environment I might not have worked so hard, but I'll never know. And all that practice was fun, and that's what sports should be.

I would advise any boy or girl to play a sport they like, even if it is not one of the glamour sports like basketball or football or baseball. In my case, the coaches did not want me to play football because I was so small. There was little organized baseball then. My physical stature made basketball a difficult sport for me, too, but I loved it and that's why I stayed with it.

I did not grow until I was a junior in high school. Almost overnight I grew about eight inches, and suddenly I was tall. It was a tremendous adjustment for me, both psychologically and physically. I was so skinny that I was embarrassed to be seen in the uniform. I wore a T-shirt under the jersey so no one would see how skinny I was. Of course, that was just for my benefit; it never made any difference to the players or the fans.

This growth spurt of mine left me much taller but weak. I was 6 foot 2 and weighed less than 150 pounds. And even though I averaged 38 points a game in a good basketball area, I knew that to play in college I'd have to put on weight. I played well in college but never felt as strong as I thought I should. It was not until I was 27 and had been a pro for six years that I felt I reached my physical peak.

As my play improved, so did my jumping ability. I had very long arms and I was getting quicker. I could feel myself improving every day. I never worked on any jumping devices, strengthening apparatus, or stretching devices. Today, these things can be a tremendous help, but I was fortunate to have these abilities naturally.

I think that the reason I was so late in developing was that when I had the growth spurt, all the rest of my body took time to catch up, especially my strength. It took a long time before I developed. Many other athletes developed late in their teens. Bob Pettit could not make his church team in high school, but when he was a senior he was a high school All-America. So parents of children who seem to be slower or less developed than the other boys or girls should not worry, but just keep encouraging their children. Youngsters playing any sport need to be encouraged by their parents and their coaches.

O. J. Simpson_____

What I needed as I was growing up was support and encourage-ment from my mother and others. Mom used to come to the big games and I knew she was there cheering me on. That helped a great deal. The equipment and other things that she bought me were great, but her being there meant much more.

Two of my school teachers also were very helpful with their friendship and support. One was Mr. Erlichman and the other was Jack McBride, who was a teacher and the football coach. Mr. McBride taught me that "you have to pay the price" if you're going to succeed in anything. One day I skipped classes and was shooting craps in the basement of the school when he caught me. I thought that since we had a big game that night he'd forget about it, but he didn't. He talked to me on the bus going to the game that night and he told me: "O. J., you have to earn people's respect. They are not going to just give it to you. You have got to earn it. You have to pay a price for respect and for success, and if you're willing to do that, you can do anything. If not, you'll never amount to anything." And I really appreciated what he told me and what he did for me.

SUMMARY_____

From the famous athletes we have talked to in this chapter, there emerge three basic themes that are helpful to parents who want to get their children into sports and make them successful. One is that all had the help and encouragement of their parents; second, all the athletes enjoyed success, and with that success came the drive for more success; and third, all enjoyed practice.

Without the will to succeed, none of these athletes or any athlete can ever win. I have never known anyone who was successful in any endeavor who did not have that drive within him or her. So it is very important that our youngsters know that we want them to succeed and that we expect their best effort. If the parent does not care, then the athlete will find it easy to fail if the going is tough.

Furthermore, if there is a will to be successful, then the necessary practice and training, hard as they may be at first, will become second nature to our athlete. And from that determination to be good, to be successful, finally comes that success, and with it the desire for more.

To be an athlete requires skills and physical talent, as we have seen in this chapter. To be a successful athlete, the physical skills must be coordinated with the mental discipline necessary for winning. And the parents play a very important role here. Encourage our young athletes in any sport or activity, remembering that they will grow and mature and develop; the lack of talent they display when they begin will soon change, and all the qualities that go into making an athlete will someday be there in your child. As Willye White said, it is a beautiful part of their life.

3.

TRAINING AND CONDITIONING

You have heard the phrase, "in top shape." In sports, the athlete who is not in shape will seldom be a winner, no matter how physically talented he or she may be. Many times we have seen a player, or even a team, jump off to a big lead and then wilt late in the game and lose to an opponent who may not be as talented but is in better condition.

The great Green Bay Packer teams of Vince Lombardi were a perfect example of what conditioning meant. Teams playing against them would often be "sky-high" because of the challenge of beating the Packers. They would play two or three quarters of outstanding football, sometimes playing over their heads. But late in the game the Packers, who were still strong because of their superior physical condition, would usually come on to win.

The great UCLA basketball teams of John Wooden were another example. They won because they had fine players, because they were well coached, and also because they were in great condition. UCLA won more national championships than any other school in college basketball history, and they did it with many different types of teams. For example, Wooden's teams in the mid-sixties won with speed without size; those teams beat bigger and stronger teams because the Bruins developed their famed "zone press" and literally ran the other team off the court. The zone press requires stamina, speed, quickness, and talent, so those teams really had to be in shape.

Former Oklahoma coach Bud Wilkinson has said that the difference between a champion and the one who plays well but does not win the big event is that the fellow who almost wins slows up a little about ten yards from the end of a wind-sprint and the champion always finishes as strong as he started. The champion has no folding point.

And it is conditioning that often determines that folding point. It often tells the difference between winning and losing. Good conditioning is essential to successful competition.

Another prime reason for striving to be in top condition is that it makes the athlete less susceptible to injury. Fatigue reduces speed and agility, making the athlete more prone to injury.

A competitor's condition determines his ability to play, his mental attitude, his determination, and finally, the team's coordination and spirit. Many athletes fail to make the team because they are not willing to pay the price in pain and sweat to get into good condition. And that price is demanded not only from the body but also from the mind. Mental condition is a phase of the totally conditioned athlete that is too often overlooked. If an athlete wants to be great, then his mental condition is important to him as well as his physical condition.

In this chapter we will discuss those methods of training and conditioning that are basic to all athletics. The equipment and techniques have changed greatly over the centuries, but the basic premise and the fundamentals for getting in shape go far back into history.

In A.D. 131–201 a Roman citizen named Galen had much to say about the training of athletes. He was probably the first "team physician." He wrote that "exercise produces strength by hardening the organs, increasing the respiration and intrinsic warmth, producing better nutrition, metabolism, and elimination." So he was not far from our modern concept of the benefits of good training. Even back then, Galen wrote that "the athlete, in order to prepare himself for his labors in competition, must practice unmodestly, sometimes all day at their objectives." That parallels our feelings today that the athlete must train year round to be successful competitively. Even in Medieval times this concept held true. Knights trained year round at jousting and sword play, but, of course, that was training for combat and survival as well as for sport.

Since this book is about young athletes, I want to emphasize again the special value of exercise in the formative years. Young people need a well rounded program of physical exercise if they are to attain their best physical development.

Here is a list of benefits that accrue with a sound exercise program.

1. Exercise aids blood circulation.
2. Exercise increases the red corpuscles in the blood.

3. Exercise is an aid in elimination.
4. Exercise helps clear the skin.
5. Exercise obviously helps strengthen the muscle system.
6. Exercise aids digestion.
7. Exercise improves the muscle tone.
8. Exercise helps relieve internal congestion.
9. Exercise strengthens and develops the lungs.
10. Exercise strengthens the heart, which is a muscle.
11. Exercise improves the body's heat regulatory mechanism.

To the young athletes the end results of exercising are general improvement of health and an increased ability of the body to resist fatigue and to sustain effort. One of the fundamental laws of physiology is that the functional efficiency of any organ or system improves with use and decreases without use. The most important part of training for any sport is the actual performance of that sport. Actual performance promotes muscle memory and efficiency, and also develops endurance under gamelike conditions. In the off-season, it is also useful to play positions other than the one played during the regular season. This improves the athlete's all-around game and increases his or her versatility.

The exercises presented below deal with the basics of running, jumping, stretching, and strength development. The next chapter will contain specific exercises for specific sports, but here we will deal with the general exercises that form the core of all training and conditioning programs.

RUNNING

Probably the most basic exercise in the conditioning of an athlete is running. Running is such a natural activity that most of us never stop to see if we are doing it right. But, as with most activities, there is a right way and a wrong way to run.

Here are some hints to proper running.

1. Relax. The body must be supple to attain the best performance.
2. Point the toes straight ahead. At least a half-inch on each step can be lost if the toes are not pointed straight ahead; in a race, that can spell defeat.
3. Run in a straight line—the shortest distance between two points.
4. Develop the proper stride. The distance of average stride is the length of the body. After developing the proper running techniques, try to lengthen the stride, but be careful not to overstride.
5. The running angle is important. The body should be leaning

slightly forward with the head up and the ankles, hips, shoulders, and head in a straight line. Bending forward tends to slow the runner.

6. Arm action is important. Arms should be relaxed. Otherwise they become heavy and make running more difficult. The arms should be held so they form a little less than a 90-degree angle and should be brought forward in a pumping action with the hands moving toward the center of the body; as the arm comes back along the body, the hand should not pass beyond the hip.

How do you run? Running flat-footed is hard on the arches and so can lead to problems with the feet and the legs. Toe running is great for speed and short distances but it can strain the calf muscles if you are jogging or running for distances. The heel and toe method is the best for distance running and jogging. The weight of the body lands on the heel and then rolls onto the ball of the foot as you push forward. In running, remember that short sprints will develop speed and leg power and distance running will develop endurance. Running in tight circles or doing figure 8's backwards will develop the ankles, knees, hips, and back.

The safest places to run are on country lanes, bicycle paths, or running tracks. Open fields are dangerous because running on uneven ground can lead to a quick ankle injury. Sidewalks or streets are really not much better. Concrete and asphalt are very hard on the feet. If the only place you can run is in the street, protect your feet by wearing shoes that have a rubber, shock-absorbing sole. The shoes should also have good support for the arches and the balls of the feet.

It is surprising that many runners do not dress properly. When running on a warm day, wear shorts with a light T-shirt or one of the mesh or fishnet shirts to let the air cool the body. If the temperature is above 80 degrees, drink at least two 8-ounce glasses of water fifteen minutes before beginning. Running in warm weather for long distances can be very dangerous because rapid loss of water and salt through perspiration can cause heat exhaustion or heat stroke.

Here is a suggestion on how to begin a good running program and how to protect yourself. If working out by yourself, try to schedule the workout in the early morning or the evening, when it is usually cooler. If you must run during the heat of the day, make sure that there is water available to you. No matter what the weather, always start your program off with a warm-up period for both the upper and lower body. During the first few weeks of the running program, just use jogging or slow running. Try to increase distance instead of speed. Then, after you can run one mile with little difficulty, increase your speed rather than distance. By gradually increasing the speed at which you run the mile, you'll be getting maximum conditioning without increasing distances or the time spent in running.

Improving Speed_____

It used to be thought that a runner either was blessed with speed or was not. Now we know that speed can be improved in all runners. Maybe we won't all become world class sprinters, but there are techniques that can be used to improve speed.

First, practice running short sprints as fast as possible. Run perhaps twenty yards as fast as you can, then repeat. Then jog another twenty, then two more bursts for twenty yards each. Push for maximum speed.

Second, lie on your back, and raise your legs straight up in the air, and do the bicycle pedaling motion for rapid leg movement without resistance. Repeat this exercise for one minute, with twenty-second breaks to catch your breath. Third, run up an incline at top speed. Walk down and repeat several trips. The Russians and other European countries have had marked success in improving speed with "down the incline" technique. But running downhill puts tremendous stress on the knees and therefore is not recommended for young athletes.

Interval Training_____

Most Olympic athletes use the "interval training" method because it conditions their body to hard work and also benefits their heart and circulation.

For instance, great 400-meter track stars often train by alternately running and walking the 400 meters. First they run 400 meters in 60 seconds, then they walk it, then they repeat this sequence for a total of ten times.

Research shows that 90-second work periods followed by brief rest periods are ideal for general overall conditioning. Here is a suggested Interval Training schedule worked out by the American College of Sports Medicine.

SUGGESTED INTERVAL TRAINING SCHEDULE_____

Pre-Running Program First Week_____

1. Warm-up with stretching, twisting, and bending exercises—concentrate on muscles in the back of the legs and the inside of the thighs.

2. Walk 200 yards.
3. Touch toes, stretch legs, twist at the waist, and circle the arms.
4. Jog approximately 50 yards, walk approximately 50 yards (six times).
5. Do push-ups, sit-ups (knees bent), chest raising, and pull-ups.
6. Walk approximately 100 yards, jog 100 yards (three times).
7. Taper off by walking approximately 200 yards.

Second Week
1, 2, and 3 same as above.
4. Jog 50 yards, walk 50 yards (eight times).
5. Calisthenics as in first week.
6. Jog 100 yards, walk 100 yards (six times).

Third Week
1, 2, and 3, same as above.
4. Jog 50 yards, walk 50 yards (eight times).
5. Calisthenics as above.
6. Jog 100 yards, walk 100 yards (ten times).

By the end of the third week, muscles should begin to adapt to the amount of exercise needed to be done. The running program may be started at this time.

Running Program First Week
1. Warm-up.
2. Run 100 yards, walk 100 yards (five times).
3. Rest and calisthenics.
4. Run 50 yards, walk 50 yards (five times).
5. Walk 200 yards to taper off.

Second Week
1. Warm-up.
2. Run 100 yards, walk 100 yards (nine times).
3. Rest and calisthenics.
4. Run 300 yards.
5. Walk 200 yards to taper off.

Third Week
1. Warm-up.
2. Run 100 yards, walk 100 yards (nine times).
3. Rest and calisthenics.

4. Run 400 yards.
5. Walk 200 yards to taper off.

Fourth Week_____
1. Warm-up.
2. Run 100 yards, walk 100 yards (twelve times).
3. Rest and calisthenics.
4. Run 500 yards.
5. Walk 200 yards to taper off.

Fifth Week_____
1. Warm-up.
2. Run 150 yards, walk 100 yards (nine times).
3. Rest and calisthenics.
4. Run 600 yards.
5. Walk 200 yards to taper off.

Sixth Week_____
1. Warm-up.
2. Run 150 yards, walk 150 yards (twelve times).
3. Rest and calisthenics.
4. Run 700 yards.
5. Walk 200 yards to taper off.

Seventh Week_____
1. Warm-up.
2. Run 200 yards, walk 100 yards (ten times).
3. Rest and calisthenics.
4. Run 800 yards.
5. Walk 200 yards to taper off.

Final Running Program_____
The following program is a goal toward which the individual should be progressing.

1. Warm-up.
2. Run 440 yards (one quarter of a mile), walk 220 yards (five times).
3. Calisthenics.
4. Run one mile.
5. Taper off by walking 440 yards.

As you can see from this final interval program, extreme distances are not necessary to attain a high level of fitness.

From this point on, the purpose will be to increase running speed, instead of distance. Be sure that a warm-up always precedes the workout. You should attempt to work out as many times a week as possible; however, a minimum of three times a week should be maintained.

(The American College of Sports Medicine offers the foregoing information in an advisory capacity only, and cannot be responsible for the individual who undertakes a physical conditioning program without medical examination and subsequent advice from a licensed M.D. Heat, altitude and physical condition of the athlete must also be taken into consideration when undertaking any conditioning program.)

Second Wind

We have all heard athletes, sportswriters, or broadcasters talk about the athlete getting his "second wind." It does not mean that a new supply of oxygen has somehow been turned on in his body as a scuba diver would employ his auxiliary air tanks. Second wind has little to do with respiration or breathing. Rather, it is a sensation that signals the adjustment of the body to hard work.

What actually happens is that early in a workout or a game, there is a piling up of lactic and other metabolic acids. There is a corresponding lag in sweat production and the shifting of blood from the splanchnic (abdominal) vessels to the working muscles. As a result, the body is overheated, so the athlete finds the exercise difficult and painful and the athlete feels sluggish. Suddenly there is a sensation of relief because the body adjustment occurs to improve energy production and muscular work. A new level of body balance is reached which can now support strenuous exercise. The athlete relaxes and all systems of the body are go for maximum muscular effort.

JUMPING

The ability to jump with control is vital for most sports. In baseball, the fielder will often have to jump up to catch a line drive; in football, the receiver jumps to make that sideline catch or the tough one coming over the middle of the field; in basketball, jumping is necessary for rebounding and for the basic jump shot. Volleyball, soccer, and almost all sports require the ability to jump properly and in a coordinated manner.

Jumping is also an excellent conditioning maneuver and, combined with running, is one of the basic exercises for getting into top condition. The exercises in this section help develop the strength and coordination needed to jump properly. Of course, before beginning the jumping exercises, as with all training and conditioning programs, a brief warm-up is imperative. Otherwise, groin and calf muscles could be stretched.

One of the best warm-up exercises is the straddle-jump. The athlete stands erect with feet spread apart about the width of the shoulders, hands relaxed at the sides. On the count of one, the hands are brought overhead, touching, as the athlete jumps in the air and brings the feet together. Then on the count of two, the feet are spread as the athlete returns to the floor, and the hands are brought back to the side. This is repeated about 25 times at a speed that is comfortable.

The following exercises are for increasing jumping ability.

1. Mark on a wall or backboard a spot about two inches higher than the spot you can touch jumping up. Then jump to reach that spot and continue until you have touched it. After you have touched that spot a few times, mark another about two inches higher and continue jumping until that is touched.

2. Find a bench or chair. Step up on it first with one leg, then bring the leg down, and step up with the other. Repeat until you have done 25 with each leg.

3. *Squat jump.* From a squat position, jump straight up in the air and try to land softly. Repeat for a total of ten times, rest a minute, and do it again for two more sets of ten. If possible, have dumbbells or some other kind of weights in your hands.

4. *Drop jump.* Stand on a bench at least two or three feet high, and jump down to the floor as softly as you can. As soon as you land on the floor, spring straight into the air as high as you can. Repeat at least ten times and then rest. Do two more sets of ten with rest in between.

5. *No-resistance jumping.* For more advanced training, stand in water deep enough to cover the shoulders when you are in a crouched position. Then jump as high as possible and as rapidly until you have done ten jumps. Rest and repeat ten more as many times as you can. Jumping in water has become a very successful technique for increasing the jumping ability of athletes. In water, there is less resistance against the upward movement of the body. With this reduced resistance, the muscles are capable of contracting faster, producing a more sudden discharge of power. This technique can improve the nerve-muscle coordination system, so that more muscle fibers contract at once, producing more power in the jump and allowing the athlete to jump higher. This is a great exercise for basketball and volleyball players.

The muscles in the abdomen, pelvis, and upper and lower legs all play an important part in jumping ability and power. There are exercises that can be done to develop these muscles and thus increase jumping ability.

A sound program of regular sit-ups will develop the abdomen and pelvic muscles and help the jumping ability, as well as help tone these muscles for other needs in sports.

Leg muscles can be strengthened by proper use of weight training. The Universal and Nautilus gyms have excellent leg strengthening exercises. Running up or hopping up stairs at home or school can greatly strengthen leg muscles. Hopping on one leg at a time increases the work load and improves strength. With greater muscle tone a stretching program is necessary.

The lower leg or the calf area can also be developed with some simple exercises. Stand on the edge of a step so that only the toes are on the step. Let your weight shift to the heels, thus stretching the tendons there and strengthening them as well. Keep arms out in front for balance. Repeat ten times.

Next, after stretching the tendons, do slow toe rises, do not bounce: Standing on the edge of the step, with just the toes on the step, put your arms out straight so they are parallel to the step. Slowly raise your body up, using just the toes to lift you. Repeat 25 times, rest, then repeat. This can be done in the shower, on the floor of your room, or anywhere. If there is no step available, just raise and lower your heels off the floor, making sure the heels never touch the floor during the exercise. This will really develop the calf muscles. Remember, do this exercise slowly.

Another good exercise to develop the lower extremities for jumping is the bicycle ride. Lie on your back, raise your torso, and support it with your hands under your hips. Using the same motion you would riding a bicycle, move the feet and legs as rapidly as possible for a count of 40. Rest and repeat as many times as you want.

STRETCHING

Whenever we see an athlete who moves with grace and power without seeming effort, we are watching one of the more beautiful aspects of sports and athletics. We see this same grace and fluidity in a dancer or a cat. We use many terms to describe such movements—effortless, graceful, smooth, easy, catlike. What we are describing is the flexible person.

In sports, bodily movement of any kind depends on the ability of the muscles to move the joints in a manner that the brain dictates. Those muscles and joints that have a full and proper range of movement improve the quality of the movement. What is happening is that there is a coordination of flexibility with strength and power.

The flexible athlete is physically more adaptable to any game situation. He is able to change direction more quickly and easily. There is less chance that he will be injured because he is able to fall properly or take a blow more easily. And the flexible athlete is almost always the one who is totally relaxed when in competition.

It is important to be aware that a decrease in athletic injuries can be attained through increased flexibility. When there is greater movement range within the joints, the ligaments and other tissues are not easily stretched or torn. Increased flexibility also aids the body in reducing the shock of impact in contact sports and provides the athlete greater freedom of movement in all directions.

Stretching is the best way to increase muscle and tissue flexibility. It helps release tensions, leading to muscle relaxation and muscle rejuvenation. The increase in flexibility allows the athlete to move with greater ease and therefore improves athletic performance.

Stretching exercises are now routine for most college and professional teams. When I came up as a pro, I did these exercises, but few if any of the other pros did them. Now they all do. So do all the Olympic athletes. Many believe that the injury ratio has been kept lower through a regular system of stretching exercises. Also, rehabilitation of injured athletes is quickened with stretching programs.

With the exercises that follow, you can set up a stretching program that can be done anywhere. These exercises should be performed as follows:

1. *Statically.* Exercise without bouncing motion. Allow the entire body to remain relaxed throughout all movement, not tense or strained.

2. *Under control.* All actions should be executed in a deliberate, unhurried manner, never "quick" or "sudden."

3. *To the end point.* Move to a point of initial sensation where you can feel the muscles stretching, and go no further. Hold that point as long as desired then slowly return to position.

4. *Individually.* Each person should progress at his or her own rate of speed and adjust the stretching exercises to individual needs.

Note: See the muscle charts at the end of this chapter to identify the muscles referred to in the exercises.

Pull-down (for arms and shoulders)_____

Grasp a fence or ledge so that the hands are approximately an inch above shoulder height. Spread your legs to shoulder width and move away from the fence, sufficiently to allow the arms to be fully extended and in a "locked" position. The legs should be kept straight and directly under the hips to offer maximum support, as illustrated in position A.

Keeping the arms fully extended and "locked," permitting the head to "hang" naturally, shift the weight of the body back and downward, creating a pull-down effect as seen in position B. This movement produces a stretch of the latissimus dorsi, tricep, and spinal column. Hold a comfortable stretch, relax, and repeat the movement once again.

To alter this stretch, assume position B. "Break" the elbows, shifting the body weight forward; this results in the formation of a "sway" in the vertebral column. This shifting of the body weight forward accentuates the stimulation of the tricep, deltoid, trapezius, and thoracic areas. At this point, the head may be lifted, producing an added stretch in the low back region.

A   B

Reverse Elbow Pull (for arms and shoulders)_____

Place left hand behind head at the base of the neck. Reach across the top of the head with the right hand and grasp left elbow, as demonstrated in position C.

Slowly, "pull' elbow toward the right shoulder, as illustrated in position D, stopping at the point of initial sensation. Hold comfortable stretch, slowly relax, and repeat the movement once again.

This movement has a direct stretching effect on the deltoid and tricep muscles of the shoulder involved. This exercise *must* be performed in a deliberate manner, and with extreme care, in order to avoid injury to the shoulder!

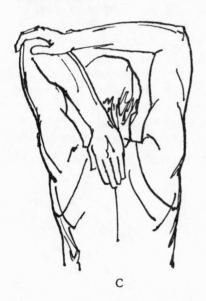

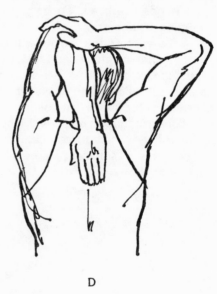

C   D

Standing Side Bend (for spinal column)_____

For many, the standing side bend is a familiar movement; however, we offer this stretch with a slight variation.

Spread the feet slightly wider than the shoulders. Standing tall to keep the spine aligned, place the left hand over the head and bend slowly to the right, as in position E, positioning the right hand anywhere along the leg to act as a brace. Continue to bend until a satisfactory stretch is achieved. Hold this stretch 15 to 20 seconds, then slowly return to the upright position.

Position F is more difficult and requires greater muscular control and flexibility. As before, start with a good base of support, but this time join hands overhead. To bend to the right, the right hand must be gripping the fingers of the left hand as pictured in diagram F.

To execute the movement, stand erect, keep the arms fully extended, then carefully bend to the right, using the right hand to slightly "pull" the left arm across. Bend far enough to obtain a stretch, even if only a slight sensation. Then slowly return to the upright position. Reverse the position of the hands (left holding the fingers of the right hand) and bend cautiously to the left, until a satisfactory stretch is realized.

It is advisable to continue to perform the movement pictured in position E until sufficient progress has been made to allow advancement to position F.

E   F

Bend and Hang (for quadriceps, hamstrings, lower legs)_____

The bend and hang is a natural movement that can be performed anytime and anyplace.

Stand with the feet shoulder width apart, legs remaining "locked" (no break in the knees), and bend down, allowing the head and arms to hang in a relaxed manner. Permit the force of gravity to "pull" the upper body toward the ground, as demonstrated in position G .

As always, move only to the point of comfortable stimulation. This sensation will be experienced in the hamstrings, low back, and gastrocnemius. Remember, no bouncing. Become sensitive to the needs of your body. Allow yourself to actually "feel" the relaxation of the muscles.

If in the "hanging" of the upper body, too great a pressure is created in the hamstrings, use the arms as a brace to support the weight of the torso. This posture is demonstrated in position H. Place the hands along the lower leg for support and control. As the muscles adjust and relax in this stationary position, the intensity of the stretch in the tissues will diminish. This phenomenon occurs within a matter of minutes. Then the hands may be carefully lowered to a position which once again triggers a comfortable stimulation of the collagenous tissues!

This is a tremendous stretch that can be executed several times daily—after prolonged sitting in a chair, or riding in a car, or anytime the individual wishes to rejuvenate his body.

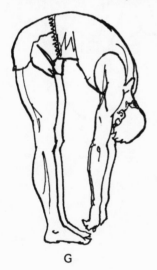
G

H

Hip flexor stretch (for groin and hip areas)_____

To effectively stretch the muscles of the entire groin and hip areas, the hip flexor stretch is an excellent exercise. Increased flexibility of the muscles of hip flexion and extension will allow the individual to increase the length of his running stride and thereby increase running speed.

The initial posture is similar to positioning oneself in the "starting blocks" for a footrace. As shown in diagram I, the right leg is extended to the rear, with the right knee resting on the ground and the left foot placed directly under the chest. (Be certain to maintain the left heel in contact with the ground.) Slowly shift the body weight forward until a satisfactory stimulation of the muscles of hip flexion is accomplished. Residual stimulation may be experienced in the Achilles tendon of the left leg. Hold a satisfactory stretch as long as desired, then slowly relax the tension.

I

Standing hurdle stretch (for quadriceps, hamstrings, lower legs)

An exceptional pregame/practice stretch, the standing hurdle stretch can be executed with a variety of available "equipment," such as bleacher seats, locker room baskets, and tabletops. This stretch is excellent for increasing the flexibility of the hamstring muscles. It is imperative to start at a height that falls within your capabilities. Starting from too great a height will result in tension in the muscles and may cause injury to the tissues.

After establishing the proper height for you, face forward squarely, with the toes pointed directly to the front (as if running). This foot positioning will aid in isolating the stretch in the hamstring muscles. Use your arms to lift the leg onto the ledge and stand erect as demonstrated in position J . If an adequate stretch is obtained in this position, hold as long as desired, then gently lower the leg to the floor.

To increase the stimulation in the hamstring muscles, bend forward at the waist slowly, until the desired sensation is realized. Be certain to use your hands to guide and control the forward movement, as shown in position K.

J   K

The gastrocnemius stretch (for quadriceps, hamstrings, lower legs)

This stretch is a highly effective movement designed to stimulate the gastrocnemius muscle of the lower leg, with residual effect on the Achilles tendon. The only "equipment" needed is a wall, locker, or fence.

To stretch the right gastrocnemius, stand facing the wall, two to three feet away, with toes pointed directly to the front. It is important to keep the right leg fully extended and "locked" (no bending) and the right heel in contact with the floor at all times.

Lean forward, placing the hands on the wall and positioning the left foot at the base of the wall as illustrated in position L. As always, if this specific position produces a satisfactory stretch of the gastrocnemius, then hold as long as desired.

To increase the stimulation of the gastrocnemius: simultaneously, (1) bend the left knee, (2) "break" the elbows and place the forearms flush against the wall, and (3) slowly move the hips forward, keeping the right leg fully extended and "locked," with the right heel in contact with the floor as pictured in position M. Then reverse and stretch the left gastrocnemius.

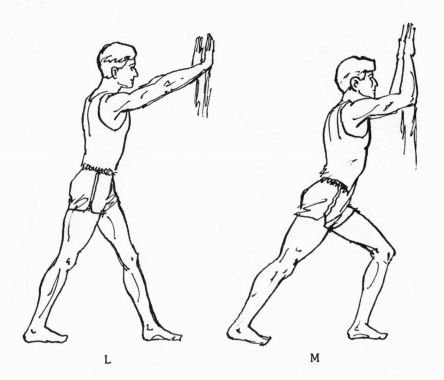

L   M

Knee to chest (for spinal column)_____

The knee to chest stretch is an excellent therapeutic movement for those who suffer from an unusually tight lumbar area, and for those who have a history of low back problems. This is a tremendous wake-up stretch for the morning.

Lie on your back, then flex the hip and slowly lift the right leg toward the chest. Interlace the fingers of your hands and grasp the leg just below the knee cap, to help control the movement. Position N demonstrates the proper form. With deliberate care, slowly "pull" the leg toward the chest as shown in position O. Hold a comfortable stretch as long as you wish, then gradually return the leg to full extension. Relax a moment, then repeat the movement with the opposite leg.

For an additional stretch of the low back area, simultaneously lift both legs toward the chest. Interlock your arms around the legs. Lift the head and "tuck" it into the chest and hold that position. Then rock gently forward and backward; this results in a "massaging" of the muscles along the spinal column.

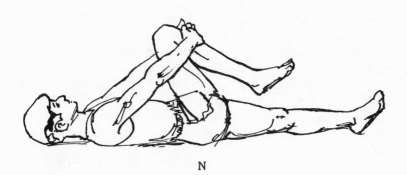

N

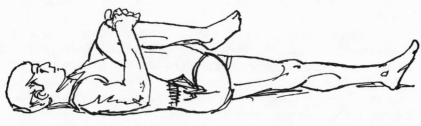

O

STRENGTH_____

Strength is vital in almost every athletic endeavor. I'm not talking here about brute strength, as in weight lifting or football or wrestling. What I mean is the necessary physical strength to accomplish the goals the athlete sets for himself. This strength can be in the legs, for running, basketball, and soccer; or in the upper torso, for football, baseball, and wrestling; or just overall strength for every sport.

Increased strength is generally the result of experience in handling the work load. Strength increases when repetitive exercise is performed against heavy resistance. At first the athlete tends to overmobilize his muscular effort, but after several repetitions the neuromuscular coordination system learns exactly how much effort is needed and the exercise is then performed with the precise degree of contractions necessary. The athlete discovers the use of momentum and incorporates it into the exercise program with all the mechanical advantages it offers to make the best use of the available power.

Athletes inexperienced in weight training exercises tend to concentrate on those parts of the body which they consider underdeveloped and to ignore those which they believe to be up to standards. Ideally, though, the beginner should start a general overall body building program for a few months and then add extra exercises to develop muscles he feels are not up to his goals. For significant results, the individual must work out according to specific guidelines and keep in mind exactly what he is trying to accomplish.

It is important to remember that extensive weight training is not done during the time that the athlete is in active training. The energy output demanded by two training programs is too high to be sustained; the athlete will become fatigued and will lose weight and strength rather than gain them.

Weight training can be just as beneficial to girls as to boys. Done with proper guidance, weight training for girls will not develop bulging, unattractive muscles. Rather, young women who use resistive exercise as a part of their preparation for athletics will find their figure becoming more lithe and vibrant.

Weight training, like any other form of activity, should not be carried to an extreme. I do not recommend weight lifting alone. Rather, it should be part of an overall training program. The only way to develop muscle mass is by strain. Whether the boy is trying to rebuild a weakened muscle from an injury or to develop other muscles, he must strain his muscles to the ultimate to build muscle mass. The exercises that are prescribed here are designed to keep the muscles properly balanced in the body and to develop strength in the flexor and extensor muscle groups. These muscles help prevent injuries to the bone and joints as well as to the muscles themselves.

In general, the rules of weight lifting are as follows: Breathe in deeply when lifting, exhale while lowering the weights. Always start with a weight that can be comfortably handled, usually 80 percent of the weight the youngster can lift. Then lift or exercise in a series of ten repetitions three times. Also, it is important to warm up before any weight training program. A simple straddle-jump done 25 times is fine. And a weight training program is more effective if it is done every other day rather than every day.

Here are some exercises to develop certain muscles and abilities. In all of these exercises with weights, each movement should be done slowly.

Calf raise, to develop spring, and ankle and lower leg strength. Place the barbell on the back of the neck, spread feet eight to ten inches apart, keep body straight, and rise up on the toes as far as possible. Repeat ten times, rest, repeat ten times, rest, repeat, and rest.

Bench press, to develop the upper body, shoulders, chest, and arms. Lying flat on the back on a bench, with feet on the ground or floor, grasp the bar on the ends inside the weights, elbows wide along the line of the bar. Lower weight to chest while exhaling, then inhale and raise bar straight up with full extension of elbows. Repeat ten times, rest, and repeat the series again.

Leg extension, to develop the quadriceps—muscles in the thigh— place weight on the foot or use an iron boot. Sit on the edge of a table with the knee bent, lift foot straight out, lower slowly, and repeat the series. Do not use a swing motion. Repeat using other leg.

Leg flexor, to strengthen the hamstrings. With iron boot or weight on the foot, lie on stomach, raise the leg so it is at a right angle to the floor. Do sequence ten times, rest and repeat three series.

Overhead press, to build up shoulders. Raise barbell to top of the chest, then lift the weights over the head with full extension of arms, exhale and lower to chest level. Repeat in series.

Ladder walk, to build stronger shoulders. If a horizontal ladder is available, grasp one rung with both hands, hanging straight down, then "walk" hand over hand to the end of the ladder. Rest and repeat.

Arm curl, to develop the biceps. Stand straight with the barbell held comfortably, palms facing out. Hold the bar at waist level then inhale and raise to the shoulders; exhale as it is lowered to the waist. Repeat ten times, rest, and repeat.

Following is a group of isometric and isotonic exercises. Each is to be done to the count of ten.

Head and neck muscles: Lie on your back and have someone put a hand on your forehead. Try to force your head up against the resistance of the hand. After a count of ten, roll over and have the assistant put a hand on the back of your head. Try to raise your head against that resistance for a count of ten. Repeat three times. These exercises will strengthen the neck muscles sufficiently to provide support and prevent injury.

Arm exercises: Extend the arm from the body at right angles, first in front, then to the side, then to the rear. Have someone apply pressure, trying to force the arm down. For the isotonic exercise, with weight in hand, raise and lower the arm ten times in those three positions. Repeat with other arm.

Hand exercises: There are many hand-grippers on the market but they usually require excessive amounts of force and do not allow for pliability and motion. I find a good hand exercise for developing flexibility and strengthening the fingers is to get a glob of silly putty, about the size of a tennis ball, and continually roll and compress it in the hand. Another excellent exercise to strengthen the hand is to take a section of the newspaper, usually about ten pages thick, and try to crumple the paper in one hand and roll it into a ball. Then throw the ball or wad of paper into the wastebasket, practicing your hand and eye coordination.

Upper arm exercises: Bend the elbow so that the palm is facing up. Then with the other hand, grab the palm and hold it while you try to raise your hand upward. The pressure is applied for the count of ten and should be done in a series of three. This exercise strengthens the biceps. To exercise the triceps, the same position is assumed but the palm is facing down and the pressure is to force the hand down.

For the isotonic exercise for upper arm and elbow, hold a weight in your hand while you flex and lower the arm ten times. Rest and repeat two more times. To strengthen the triceps in an isotonic exercise, lie face down on a table or bed with your arms hanging over the side. Grasp the weight and straighten the arm at the elbow to full extension. The isotonic exercises are done in a slow, rhythmic manner to the count of ten.

Abdomen stomach muscle exercise: Lie flat on your back with hands under hips and legs straight, with the toes pointed up. Then raise the feet and legs slowly to the count of ten until the legs are perpendicular to the ground. Slowly lower the legs until they are halfway to the ground. Holding that position, slowly spread the legs and then bring them back together, repeating this spreading motion for a total of eight times. Then lower legs until they are almost touching the ground and repeat the spreading motion another eight times. Then lower them to the ground. Do the complete exercise ten times.

Leg stretching. Stand erect with the hands at the sides, then bend forward slowly and touch the toes. Repeat 30 times. This will help stretch the hamstrings and back muscles.

The young athlete should always exercise with care. A ligament should never be stretched without muscle protection. The worst exercise is the deep knee bend. This can result in instability of the knee and loss of speed and agility. Stretched ligaments leave the joint vulnerable to injury. Also, exercises that are done against a fixed object such as a wall or a post will result in short, bulky muscles that have little value for athletics. For example, pushing against a post that is fixed in the ground is not going to develop ideal linemen for football; all it will do is build up muscle mass that has little of the explosive power that linemen need.

Warming up before exercising or participation in sports is very important and, if properly done, can reduce injuries and improve performance. It is like a rehearsal before a play. The warm-up fixes in the athlete's neuromuscular coordination system and gets him ready for the exact tasks that are to come when the event begins. The warm-up also tells him the movements that will be necessary in the event. It also helps raise the body temperature so that the biochemical reactions supplying energy for muscular contractions is begun and the body will be tuned up for the upcoming contest.

One of the most important periods—and one that is often ignored by coaches as well as players—is that time when the game is going on and the subs are sitting on the bench. If they do not get themselves ready to play by warming up on the sideline, when they do get into the game, they will be prime candidates for injuries. So when there is a time-out, the bench warmer should do some sort of stretching exercise; if he is on the sideline, running in place for a few minutes and stretching will help. Another good exercise, especially for baseball and basketball players, is to take a towel and roll it around in the hands. This will keep the hands loose and also help strengthen the fingers.

There is one special exercise that I like to recommend to all athletes. It has to do with the mind. The best mental training that you can give yourself is to visualize in your mind's eye a successful effort, a shot going through the hoop, a completed pass, a base hit with men in scoring position. This mental exercise is to prepare yourself for success; if you think like a winner, you'll play like one.

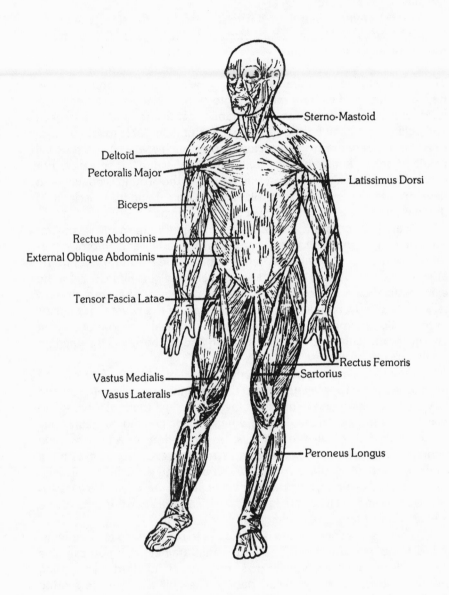

Muscles of the body (front view).

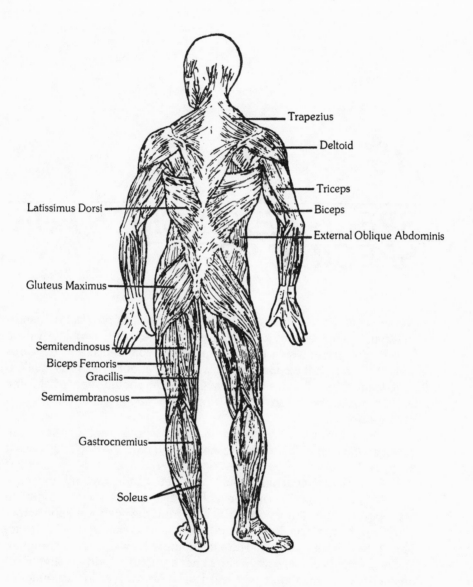

Muscles of the body (rear view).

4

SPECIAL EXERCISES FOR SPECIFIC SPORTS

Proper training requires mental discipline as well as physical demands. However, completion of a training program leaves the athlete with a feeling of success, which in turn breeds self-confidence and develops greater interest in the sport. Earlier we talked about Coach Bud Wilkinson's feeling that all of his players at Oklahoma should succeed at some task during the practice so they developed the "good" feeling from having been successful.

I have never known a superior athlete who did not feel he or she deserved the victory, because it came through hard training and "paying the price."

Parents and coaches should help set up the training and conditioning programs but should never force the young athlete to complete the program. The motivation must come from the youngster, and sometimes it will take one longer than another to complete the program. Threats and shouting will only turn the youngster away from the program and may even eventually drive him or her away from sports. A simple pat on the back and encouragement will go a lot further to help the youngster complete the training.

This training period is an excellent time to help the athlete develop motivation. And the more the athlete works, the more his or her pride will be developed and that is as important as muscular development.

68

HOW TO BEGIN A TRAINING PROGRAM_____

Before beginning a training program for a sport, it is important to understand the state of one's physical condition and proficiency in the sport. The best way to find this out is to sit down and write out in outline form one's strengths and weaknesses, the bad points and the good points, the handicaps and the physical advantages. Then the athlete should go over the outline with the coach or a person who is knowledgeable about the athlete's characteristics.

In setting up an individual training program, you must be aware of the time of year it is in relation to the particular sport. In other words, is it pre-season, in-season, or off-season?

In general, the rule is that in the off-season the athlete should work on gross physical improvements. As the pre-season training is entered into, work is aimed more at developing the finer points and the specifics of the particular sport. This chapter offers suggested training programs for various sports, based on these principles.

The Off-Season_____

A good guideline for the training program in the off-season is to practice the things that you *don't* do well. Work on overall strength. Participate in other sports, stay active, and remember that the body is constantly growing and developing and that exercise is vital for a healthy body that is always ready for sports. It is all right to train with friends, but you must have your own personal overall program and not just follow others.

Make a chart that lists the goals you want to accomplish in the off-season training program. This checklist may seem a form of regimentation but it will be a guideline to keep you on your plan. And when you have completed the list, you'll have that feeling of accomplishment that comes from having set a goal and achieving it.

Make sure you give yourself enough time to accomplish all your goals. Don't bite off more than you can chew. If injury or illness takes place during the program, adjust your goals realistically.

Pre-Season_____

As the season nears, you must concentrate on developing the skills needed for competition. The off-season exercise program was to improve weaknesses and develop areas of greater strength. Now the fine points will be stressed. Concentrate on your strengths, and work with others to be sure you are competing against players who will help you develop these strengths. In other words, do what you do best against good players.

For an individual sport such as golf or tennis, concentrate on the best aspects of your game, because in competition they will carry you further.

In-Season
Your training program now is dictated by the coach or manager. The most important thing now is proper rest. With practice and the actual games or events, you'll be in excellent condition, so rest now becomes your key ally. Professional athletes rest as much as possible in-season; while they are playing so many games, traveling great distances, and sleeping in strange rooms, rest is their single most important conditioning factor for competing at that level. Similarly, a sound rest program, coupled with concentration on school work, will keep the young athlete ready for the games and eligible to play. I've seen too many good young athletes so wrapped up in sports that they forget their school work. Without proper rest during the season, they tend to skip their homework for the sleep their body needs, and soon their grades do what the opposition can't—keep them off the team.

TRAINING PROGRAM TO DEVELOP PHYSICAL CAPABILITIES FOR SPECIFIC SPORTS

The following chart, giving a breakdown of exercises for specific sports, is designed to show what is important for developing one's capabilities in a desired sport. Degrees of importance are given for each category, with 1 being the least important and 5 being the maximum. Also, the letters O, P, and S are used to indicate, respectively, off-season exercises, pre-season exercises, and exercises during the season.

Remember, there is always a great deal of overlapping in the exercise programs, and many of the same exercises are used for different sports. You will note, in looking at the chart, the value of stretching. We spoke earlier of the importance of stretching in an exercise program; it probably constitutes the single biggest improvement in exercise since the days when I was a player.

TRAINING PROGRAM TO DEVELOP PHYSICAL CAPABILITIES FOR SPECIFIC SPORTS

Degrees of Importance: 5, Maximum; 4, Very Important; 3, Important; 2, Good; 1, Minimum
Time of Program: 0, Off-Season; P, Pre-Season; S, Season

Sport	A — Endurance (Heart and Lungs)	B — Speed and Quickness	C — Hand-Eye Coordination	D — Stretching	E — Strength: Upper Chest, Shoulders	Strength: Back, Neck	Strength: Arms, Hands	Strength: Legs
Baseball	O,P,3	O,P,4	O,P,S,5	P,S,5	O,P,2	O,1	O,P,S,4	O,2
Basketball	O,P,4	O,P,S,5	O,5	P,S,5	O,2	O,1	O,P,S,3	O,5
Football — Linemen	O,P,3	O,P,3	O,2	O,P,S,4	O,P,5	O,P,2	O,P,3	O,P,S,5
Football — Backs	P,3	O,P,S,5	O,P,S,5	O,P,S,5	O,4	O,P,2	O,3	O,P,4
Golf	O,P,S,1		O,P,2	O,P,S,3	O,P,S,3	O,P,2	O,P,S,5	O,P,4
Hockey	O,P,5	O,P,S,5	O,2	P,S,5	O,P,3	O,P,3	O,P,5	O,P,4
Skiing	O,P,4	P,S,2	O,2	P,S,5	O,P,3	O,P,S,4	O,P,4	O,P,S,5
Soccer	O,P,S,5	P,S,5		P,S,4	O,2	O,2	O,1	O,P,4
Swimming	O,P,S,5	O,2		O,P,S,5	P,P,5	O,3	O,3	O,P,S,3
Tennis	O,P,4	P,S,5	P,S,5	P,S,3	O,3	O,3	O,P,4	O,P,2
Track and Field — Track	O,P,5	P,S,5		O,P,S,4	O,1	O,2		O,3
Track and Field — Field	O,P,2	P,S,4	O,P,2	O,P,S,5	O,P,3	O,P,3		O,P,4
Volleyball	O,P,4	P,S,3	P,S,3	P,S,4	O,1	O,2	O,P,2	O,P,3

Column group headings: C and D fall under "Areas of Development." The final four columns (Upper Chest, Shoulders; Back, Neck; Arms, Hands; Legs) fall under "E — Strength."

BASEBALL

Off-Season

1. Run one mile three times a week. You can use any track, or even run around the block at home.
2. After running a mile, do short sprints full out, about 30 yards, preferably going up a short hill. Repeat about ten times.
3. Play catch, bouncing a tennis ball off the steps.
4. Develop strength of the wrist and forearms by using weights to do wrist curls (see weight-training section in this chapter). If weights are not available, use a broom handle: tie a rope in the middle of it, about three feet long, hang a heavy object from the rope, and then roll the weight up, rotating hands. Unwind and repeat ten times. Do the weight work every other day, alternating with the running.
5. Play other sports in the off-season—basketball, tennis, squash, handball, or any sport that will increase hand-eye coordination.

Pre-Season

1. Continue to run one mile every other day.
2. Run the bases. Practice running between bases as if caught in a rundown or going from first to third. Work on starts and stops from the batting box and from off the bases. Do this at least four times a week for a half hour each day.
3. Continue to play catch, now working out with a teammate. Make sure the throws are such that each of you has to move to make the catch and still be in position to make a quick return throw. In other words, practice your judgment of distance and speed.
4. Continue arm- and hand-strengthening exercises three times a week.
5. Each day, swing the bat 50 times as hard as you can. Line up an imaginary pitcher, take your stance, and swing at the imaginary pitch. Gradually increase the number of swings to 100. Make sure that you do not lose balance or sacrifice your form in swinging hard.

In-Season

1. Running will now be part of your daily warm-up before practice and games.
2. Have a game of pepper for ten minutes before practice or a game.
3. Whenever you have more than one day off between games, do your hand and arm exercises. Also, on days off, practice swinging

the bat at that imaginary pitcher. Do this also at home in front of a full-length mirror. The greatest hitter in baseball, in the opinion of many, was Ted Williams; he always had a bat with him, and when traveling, he'd stand in front of the mirror in his hotel and practice swinging by the hour. It paid off for him.

4. Limit your play in other sports except for relaxation and recreation.

A further tip for young batters. We have all heard commentators talk about how a good hitter "sees the ball all the way from the pitcher's hand to the catcher's mitt." Well, that's not true. Good hitters do *not* try to follow the ball from the time the pitcher starts his windup. The good hitter picks the ball up just after the pitcher releases it. So concentrate on picking the ball up after it leaves the pitcher's hand, and all that windup and body action by the pitcher will not confuse or break your concentration.

Remember, hitting a baseball requires great technique. The exercises you should concentrate on are those that will increase your hand-eye coordination and the quickness and strength of hands. Ping-pong, handball, basketball, and volleyball are games that will increase your hand-eye coordination. Exercises such as squeezing a rubber ball or doing finger push-ups are very good for developing hand strength. Finger push-ups are push-ups in which the torso is held up by the fingertips, and the palms do not touch the ground.

The exercise program outlined above includes a great deal of running. There is an old but very true saying about athletes, and especially baseball players, that "it's the legs that go first." Great pitchers and hitters agree that bad legs are the first thing that weakens their abilities. So, run all year round to make sure your legs are sound. Running is also the best thing for your cardiovascular system.

One other thought about "picking up the pitch." Watch the pitcher and develop a mental image of where he throws the ball each time. You can do this from the bench and from the on-deck circle. Good batters concentrate on the pitcher in this way as they wait their turn. Then, because of this mental picture, when they get in the batter's box, they are able to pick up the pitched ball faster.

BASKETBALL

Off-Season
During this time, work on developing strength, particularly in the legs. The best way to do that is to run.

1. Run at least one mile a day to keep in shape and develop endurance.
2. To develop speed, run up and down hills, ten times. When you run up, run as hard as you can; run down carefully.
3. Develop jumping ability. Throw a basketball up against a backboard; jump up and tip the ball up against the board, then come down and jump up again, tipping the ball again. Repeat this to a count of 25, keeping the ball tipped up. Repeat with either hand. If you are near a pool, lake, or ocean, stand in water up to the hips, squat, and explode out of water, jumping as high as you can. Do this as many times as possible. Try and jump as quickly as possible to explode out of water.

Pre-Season

Continue to work on speed, endurance, and leg power with the exercises above.

Also, begin working on basketball abilities by doing the following skill exercises:

1. Run up and down the court as fast as you can, dribbling the ball and driving to the basket, shooting at top speed. After each shot, grab the ball and dribble the length of the court the other way, repeating the shot. Repeat this maneuver up and down the court as many times as you can.
2. Practice shots you'll take in the game, concentrating on your best shots, working on form and delivery.

In-Season

During the season, just be sure you maintain good diet habits, and get plenty of rest.

One of the best techniques for improving ball-handling ability is to constantly have a basketball in your hands, whenever possible. If at home watching television, have the ball with you and just flip it from hand to hand. Or walking down the street or along the beach, carry the ball as often as practical. When Ernie DiGregario, the fine ball-handling, back court man of the Buffalo Braves, was in school, he even carried the basketball with him when he went on dates.

This constant handling of the basketball off the court greatly helps the player to develop the "feel" for the ball and will improve his passing ability, dribbling, and shooting.

Today there are a number of exercises that have been programmed through weight training and jumping machines to help improve the jumping ability of the athlete. However, few schools have these machines so we will limit this program to exercises that can be done by any player to improve jumping power.

We mentioned the method of exploding out of water. The reason for using water is that the water serves to decrease the weight of the body, allowing the smaller muscles and muscle fibers to get to maximum contraction at the same time because they do not first have to overcome the normal weight of the body. After a few weeks of this exercise, these muscles are now "programmed" or educated to contract more rapidly and in concert with the other muscles. With the muscles all exploding at once, the height that the athlete can reach is increased, and so are the speed and quickness of the athlete in jumping. A simple example will explain the desired effect. A string of penny firecrackers when placed under a can explodes in succession and the can jumps about. However, if all the firecrackers were set off at the same time the can would be shot in the air like a rocket. This exercise trains your muscles to react simultaneously.

Great shooters are not born; shooting, like any skill, is developed through practice. The natural shooter has an advantage in that his ability and coordination make shooting easier for him. But that naturalness will take him only so far; he still has to develop his skill.

There are some exercises that will help the player's shooting techniques. First and foremost, the player must develop the proper delivery of the basketball to the basket. Any coach or father can teach this. Once this technique is achieved, it is important to find the spot on the court where the shot can be consistently repeated to the point where the player is completely comfortable shooting from that spot and is confident of success. For centers, the spot might be around the key; for forwards, along the baseline or just off the foul circle; for guards, just in back of the free-throw circle. I'd recommend that a tape be placed on that spot—or an X if it is on the playground—so the player can find the spot easily when playing.

Remember, the spot selected should always be within the capabilities of the player and where there is no strain to shooting the ball. But I strongly recommend that the player find that one spot on the court where he or she is confident of making the shot and keep practicing from that spot. Let that spot be your insurance—when you need to score, you'll be confident of success when shooting from that spot.

Earlier I spoke about a drill of dribbling down the court at top speed and shooting a lay-up. This exercise is important for those times when you'll get a breakaway and must make that lay-up, moving at top speed. This drill is also good for ball handling, shooting, and developing body control and endurance. Also, it is a lot of fun to race up and down the court.

In practice, especially on days between games, you should practice shooting at the end of practice when you are most tired. In shooting free throws, you'll really be simulating the game situation, because the key free throw in a game often comes at the end of the game when the player is most exhausted.

The most successful college coach in the history of the game is John Wooden of UCLA. He spelled out his thoughts on what it takes to be successful as a player and a person. Here are some of his ideas:

John Wooden

(*On conditioning*) Success is built on fine condition. Fundamentals and form leave you as you begin to lose condition. Never think of bruises or fatigue. If you are tired, think how "all in" the other guy is. It is the hard work in practice after you are all in that improves your condition. Make it your own personal objective to be in better condition than any player on the floor. Your mental and moral condition will determine your physical condition, if you are industrious.

(*Training suggestions*) Get at least eight hours' sleep each night and get to bed by 10:30 the night before a game. Eat balanced meals at regular hours and drink plenty of milk, fruit juices, and water. Take care of your health—mental and moral as well as physical. Practice moderation with good judgment in all ways, and earn the right to be proud and confident of your physical, mental, and moral condition.

(*Training demands*) Don't use alcoholic beverages of any kind. Don't smoke, don't use profanity, be on time, and always be a gentleman.

FOOTBALL

Football is a contact sport and a hitting sport, one that requires strength, agility, and a mental framework in which the athlete is willing to accept the bodily roughness that comes from the game. A lot of young athletes enjoy the rough and ready contact that is football. All young men growing up enjoy some form of "roughness" in their everyday playing, be it "catch-one-catch all" in the playground or just two-against-two touch football. There is a great deal of fun in running and throwing and catching a football; even kicking it is fun. But sometimes I'm worried that too much emphasis is placed on "butting heads" or one-on-one at the early levels of the game.

Off-Season_____

Here let us look at a couple of programs. I recommend role playing during the off-season. In other words, this is the time for the linebackers to play quarterback, and the backs to be receivers, and the linemen to be running backs, and the receivers to play the interior linemen in touch football games. It is a great way for the players to get a feel of what the others do and it is also a lot of fun.

The off-season should also be used to develop strength and agility, so a responsible weight-training program should be started at that time. In all weight programs, work out *every other day*.

As the season approaches, other exercises should augment the weight program and eventually, when the season begins, the weight training will probably cease except in special cases.

Pre-Season_____

The following pre-season training program comes to us from Bart Starr, the former all-time great quarterback of the Green Bay Packers. This was his pre-season warm-up program when he was playing; and now, as head coach of the Packers, he has installed this program for his players in the pre-season. It is readily adaptable to football players at all levels because its emphasis is on physical condition, not strength.

Bart Starr_____

There is only one way you can play football. This is to be physically and mentally prepared—not only prepared but peaked to the finest physical condition possible. Every workout should begin by merely loosening up. Never start any type of heavy exercising until you are thoroughly warmed up. Otherwise, you're asking for pulled and strained muscles.

1. The "side-straddle" hop is a favorite among athletes for a brisk, quick warm-up. Begin with an upright stance, hands at the side. On the count of one, hop to a spread position of the legs, with the hands touching atop the head. On two, return to the starting position. Repeat to 25 times.

2. Here is another good exercise for stretching muscles. Begin in an upright stance. Lean over and, with legs straight, touch your toes. Come up and slap your midsection. Next, reach your hands as high and as far back as you can, then return to the starting position. Repeat to 25 times as rapidly as you can.

3. The "windmill" is an excellent warm-up exercise that stretches

the upper body as well as the backs of the legs. Begin with an upright stance, feet spread shoulder width, with arms out to the sides. On the count of one, reach over with the right hand and touch the left toe, keeping the legs straight. On the count of two, return to the original position. On the counts of three and four, repeat the maneuver, this time touching the left hand to the right toe. Repeat this exercise 25 times with each hand.

4. Rotating the upper body helps loosen the upper trunk. Begin in an upright position, hands on hips. On the count of one, lean forward from the waist. On the second count lean to the left, on the third count lean to the rear, and on the fourth count lean to the right. After five of these, reverse the windmill and go in the opposite direction. Do 25 times in each direction.

5. The push-up has and always will be an excellent conditioning exercise. It does a wonderful job of developing the arm and shoulder muscles, which is particularly good for a passer. Push-ups on the fingertips are equally beneficial for developing strength in the hands. Holding the body slightly off the ground, supported by your toes and hands, placed just below the shoulders, raise the body up by extending the elbows until they are straight, hold for a count of one, lower the body until the chest almost but not quite touches the ground. Repeat to 25 times.

6. The "six-count burpee" is a good exercise for developing stamina and, since push-ups are involved, the arms as well. Begin by standing erect. Assume a half-squat position with hands on the floor and knees outside the elbows. Kick the legs back and keep them straight. Lower the body and raise it as in a normal push-up. Bring knees back to elbows, then stand erect. Repeat to 25 times.

Strength in the abdominal or stomach area is vital to all athletes, especially football players, who can suffer a blow there anytime during a game. Having those muscles in proper shape is essential to a passer because the stomach muscles contribute so much to the throwing of the ball; in addition, this area takes considerable pounding from those defensive linemen, because you're usually left with your passing arm forward after the release of the ball and the stomach is exposed. For the running back, for the offensive linemen who must pull, and for all other players, strong abdominal muscles are a must. If you think about it, you can't play football at any position without strong stomach muscles. Here are three exercises I consider vital for strengthening that area.

7. One of the basic exercises in all sports is the sit-up. Lie with legs flat on the ground, body also flat, with hands behind the head. On

the count of one, raise the body up, touching the left elbow to the right knee. On two, return to the prone position. On three, raise the body again, this time touching the right elbow to the left knee. Repeat to 25 times for each side.

8. Start in the supine position, heels touching the ground. Raise feet off the ground about six inches, pause. Spread feet slowly, to about shoulder width, then slowly bring them back together, still six inches off the ground. Return to starting position. Repeat to 25 times.

9. This is another good stretching and conditioning exercise. Begin by lying flat on your back, heels flat on the ground. On the count of one, keeping feet together, raise them straight up, then over your head, toes touching the ground on the other side. On the count of two, raise legs and begin to "bicycle" with the legs and feet, holding hips with both hands. On the count of three, bring the legs to a 45-degree angle with the ground and hold. On four, lower legs to six inches above the ground and hold. On five, open and close legs once, then return to starting position. Rest and repeat to ten times.

I cannot stress how important it is that the football player, or any athlete for that matter, always be aware of exercises that will stretch as well as strengthen those muscles that are most prone to injuries—the hamstrings, the groin, the ankles, and the knees. The following exercises are good for stretching and strengthening those vital areas.

10. The "wood-chopper" is a great exercise for stretching the back and hamstring muscles. Begin by standing, feet spread, hands on hips. On the count of one, lean over, keeping legs straight, and touch the ground. On the count of two, touch the ground behind the legs. On the count of three, reach even farther back, trying to touch the ground. Return to original position. Repeat to ten times.

11. It is imperative to keep the hamstring muscles loose and properly stretched before beginning strenuous running. One of the best exercises is the "hurdle stretch." Sit down with one leg stretched in front and the other bent behind you. Reach as far out in front of you as possible over the toe of the front leg. Repeat to five times, then reverse the legs and repeat with the other leg five times.

12. This simple exercise is very good for the groin muscles. Stand erect, feet slightly spread. Step or stride forward, bending the knee of the front leg until the knee of the rear leg is touching the ground. Return to the starting position and repeat with the opposite leg. Keep alternating until you have done this 25 times.

Those are some of the pre-season exercises we used in getting ready for the regular season. We also used those exercises in a more limited fashion during the regular season. In pre-season, Coach Lombardi made us go through all those plus a lot more. The biggest thing these exercises did for us was to develop endurance as well as protect us against injuries to the hamstring muscles, groin, and back muscles. We seldom had those types of injuries during the season. Of course, there were the usual number of broken bones, but we played with them, unless it was a major injury. But pulled muscles can be the death of a team and a player because he never really gets into that midseason form when he's in the whirlpool trying to recover from a pulled muscle. So do these stretching and strengthening exercises before the season begins. It takes determination but it's worth it. I know.

With proper weight training and attention to the exercise program as outlined by Bart Starr, the football player can go into the regular season knowing that his body is ready to perform to its maximum. Don't ever think that you can "play your way into shape." All that will get you is a place in the doctor's office. Take the advice of the people who have been there—football is too rough a game not to be ready. A strenuous exercise and weight program as outlined by Bart Starr will put you way ahead of the game.

In-Season
Once the actual season begins, the regular workouts prescribed by the coaching staff are more than adequate to keep the player in shape. As I stated earlier, rest becomes the biggest physical fitness program during the season.

Weight training has recently become a great part of the off-season and pre-season training program for a lot of football players. This is fine if done under the proper supervision. But recently, I've noticed a good number of young athletes spending too much time building up muscles for football at the sacrifice of quickness and agility. In addition, this buildup of heavy muscle, while possibly adding some strength, is actually slowing the player down. This is not fat that can be sweated off, but solid muscle. The player tires more quickly because he is carrying around far too much weight. Even at the professional level, where men can weigh 280 to 300 pounds, that is too much weight to carry. Most coaches I know would prefer a quick, agile 240-pounder over the giant, no matter how strong. The agile player can do more things, lasts longer, and is less prone to injury that the over-muscled athlete, especially in a violent, hard contact sport like football

In the off-season, I like to recommend to football players, especially the big linemen, that they take up sports like paddleball, handball, and even basketball. These help them develop legs, power, quickness, and agility. Playing these sports in the off-season will loosen up those muscles tightened by the rigors of football, and will help their footwork and their hand-eye coordination.

One of the greatest football players of all time is O. J. Simpson. Twice All-America at USC, Heisman Trophy winner, and now the premier runner in the National Football League, O. J. had this to say about training for football.

O. J. Simpson_____

I really do not have any special instructions for the young football player as far as training and exercises are concerned. All I recommend is that they concentrate on the basic exercises, and in my opinion running is the best conditioning program that the young player can find. Get a lot of good hard running in, work on sprints for 30 yards, full out, then jog a little, then repeat.

Also, the diet is very important, especially to the youngster who can live off hamburgers and hot dogs and pop. He should have a balanced diet, pay attention to the vitamins. I know that if I skip breakfast, I feel bad the rest of the day. I think that breakfast is the most important meal of the day, especially for the young athlete who is going to school and eating in the cafeteria or "brown-bagging" it to school. He usually has practice after school, and without a good foundation at breakfast, and lunch, he's not going to have the energy necessary. He needs milk and vegetables and protein.

During the season, I find that I need a lot of sleep. I get to bed early, and when I get up I eat a good, big breakfast.

So, to sum up, to me the most important things for the young athlete are: one, have a good balanced diet, especially a full breakfast; two, get plenty of rest; and three, run to get in shape, run to keep in shape, and run to develop that leg power to be a good football player.

GOLF_____

Off-Season_____

There are a number of isometric exercises that are designed to improve the player's strength in the hands, wrists, fingers, arms, and even the legs. Any golfer, particularly the younger golfer, can use these exercises to improve strength. Make sure to begin the exercises gradually.

Always warm up before beginning an isometric workout. This can be done with a simple touching of the toes and with the side-straddle hop. For this, stand with hands at the sides, then hop and spread the legs, touching hands over the head; return to starting position, and repeat to 25 times.

1. Sitting, interlock hands in front of chest; pull for a count of six seconds. In the same position, push hands against each other for six seconds. Repeat pushing and pulling two more times each. Later increase time to count of eight seconds.

2. Sitting, clasp hands under knees. Pull up with arms, resisting with knee, for a count of six. Do three times, later increasing count to eight.

3. Sitting, place hands on top of knees. Push down with arms and hands for a count of six. Do three times. Later increase to eight count.

One of the best exercises for the golfer is the fingertip push-up. Lie down on your stomach, then put your hands on the ground next to shoulders, with the fingertips holding the upper torso up. Then do your push-ups, not allowing the palms of the hands to touch the ground. Do as many as you can each exercise period.

Another good exercise is called the "grippers." Just squeeze a rubber ball as many times as you can, in each hand. Later, concentrate on squeezing the ball with only the three fingers of the left hand.

Another exercise to strengthen the forearms is to take a five-pound dumbbell and do wrist curls. Rest and repeat to three times.

Jogging helps build up the legs so the golfer will not be tired by long matches, like a 36-hole match in one day. Strong legs are as important to the golfer as they are to other athletes, and jogging each day builds up that leg strength.

In-Season

The exercise program is lessened in the isometric area but the running should continue.

One thing that is definitely not recommended for the golfer, at any time, is weight training. Working on the legs might be okay to rebuild a torn leg or ankle muscle. But weight training for the upper torso and the arms is bad except for wrist curls. You do not want to get big across the chest because that will inhibit your body turns.

Of course, the best exercise in-season is long hours on the practice tee and putting green. That's the best way to improve your scores.

HOCKEY

Hockey is not a major national sport as are football, basketball, and baseball. In much of the country, the winters are too mild for the outdoor rinks necessary to develop youngsters' interest in the sport. In the northern parts of the country and certainly in Canada, where outdoor facilities are available in winter, hockey has become an important sport. There has been a large increase in hockey at the grammar school and high school levels.

Hockey requires many of the same athletic skills that mark all sports: hand-eye coordination, strength, agility, endurance, and speed.

Off-Season

Because the young hockey player needs good hand strength to control the stick and the puck, he should work on exercises that will strengthen the hands. Squeezing a rubber ball in each hand is one of the best and easiest of exercises.

To strengthen the muscles in the shoulders and arms, a series of light weight exercises are recommended. We don't want to develop bulk in the shoulders, so using weights at a level that can be handled easily, you should do ten presses in sets of three (see section on weight lifting in this chapter).

But the single most important exercise program for the hockey player deals with the developing and strengthening of the leg muscles. The demands of hockey require excellent leg strength and the best exercise program here is, just as it is for other sports, running. The off-season running program should have two elements: first, running long distances to develop endurance; and second, running uphill to develop strength. Another good exercise is bicycle riding, which also helps the cardiovascular system.

To develop hand-eye coordination, I'd recommend taking up such sports as tennis, handball, volleyball, and basketball. Handball helps the hockey player to play a ball coming off a wall or out of a corner, much as he might take a puck off the boards as it ricochets.

In-Season

During the season, you should continue a stretching program, especially before practice and before a game to protect the hamstring muscles and the ankle muscles. The stretching program should involve the heel cord, the hip flexors (see p. 58), and some fingertip push-ups (push-ups in which the fingertips hold up the torso, and the palms do not touch the ground).

A good exercise to strengthen the fingers is to take a towel and twist it in the hands before the game. This will be beneficial to the hands and the wrists for handling the stick.

Youngsters have a habit of tying the laces of the skates too tight around the ankle. The laces should be snug, but tying them too tight can reduce circulation, so the feet soon become cold and the skater loses effectiveness.

SKIING

If there is one sport that demands extensive off-season exercise and conditioning, it is skiing. The sport is most demanding in terms of agility, endurance, strength, and overall good condition. There is also the factor of injuries that can happen in skiing. The skier who jumps off onto the slopes without being in condition is asking for a broken leg or worse.

The training program recommended in this section is for the general skier, not someone who will be racing in competition or ski jumping. Skiers at that high a competitive level should be under the full-time direction of a coach and their training program would be a year round program.

Off-Season

In the off-season, the skier should work to develop the cardio-vascular system through a running program. The kind of running program would really depend on the age of the skier but here we'll concern ourselves with the young skier. A running program that takes place at altitude will be more advantageous than one at lower levels because of the extra strain running at altitude puts on the system. Consequently, those running at altitude get their cardiovascular system in shape sooner than the others.

The running program should be similar to that taught to cross-country athletes in high school. In fact, the skier in the off-season should probably go out for the cross-country team; their season ends before skiing season begins in most parts of the country.

If not part of a cross-country team, the individual skier should develop his own guidelines in training. He or she should establish goals such as running two miles every other day for the first couple of weeks. Then as the endurance and stamina grow, the mileage should be increased to perhaps four miles every other day. Also, if there are hills around, the skier should run up and down those. Overall, running is the most important factor in the off-season training for the skier.

The skier can get a great deal of benefit from weight training. You are not interested in developing mass muscles, but rather working with the major muscles of the legs, strengthening the back muscles. The weight program should be one that develops calf muscles, the quadriceps, and the large leg or thigh muscles. The anterior muscles or opposing muscles should also be developed, so any program should involve both flexion and extension strengthening.

If your school has a Universal gym setup, you should use that system to work on the legs. However, most schools do not have such a system, so the regular barbells must be used.

Sit-ups and push-ups are ideal to develop the middle trunk area. Ten of each, repeated three times each day, are of great value.

Upper body strength can be developed with pull-ups or chin-ups as well as push-ups. If weights are available, a series of curls and presses can be used.

Gymnastics is a fine program for the skier, especially in the off-season.

This off-season program is vital to the protection of the skier. Otherwise, the skier is inviting injury when the season begins. Parents of children who are interested in skiing should insist that they run and do the necessary exercise during the off-season.

In-Season

Before going out to the lift, you should engage in a series of stretching exercises, sufficiently intense to almost break a sweat. This goes for all skiers. The Achilles tendons, the quadriceps, and the hamstrings should all be stretched before going on the lift. When you get to the top of the hill, before coming down, a quick series touching the toes, rolling the hips, and more stretching should be done before starting down.

Most often, skiing injuries come on the first run because you have not taken the time to loosen up. Or they happen at the end of the day when you want one more run before going to the lodge. Then the fatigue catches up and injuries come because you have not gotten into condition in the off-season.

Injuries also come when skiers are fooling around or "hot-dogging" on the slopes. Beware of this, unless you are in great physical shape, especially if you have no gymnastic ability. Too many serious injuries result from fooling around or from trying to imitate someone who is doing flips or other trick moves.

SOCCER

Soccer is a sport that requires great endurance, so physical condition at the highest level is required when the season begins. Therefore, the training in the off-season and the pre-season is very important. It usually requires about six weeks pre-season training to reach a state of fitness for playing soccer, maybe even eight weeks. The program outlined below is designed to bring the soccer player from the pre-season practice and training into a level of fitness for regular competition.

Pre-Season

Do the following each day for eight weeks. Make a chart to check off each day's accomplishments.

For ball control:

1 minute, jog while dribbling the ball, changing speed and direction in a confined area, simulating a game situation where many changes would be required.

1 minute, head juggling.

1 minute, repeat dribbling.

1 minute, thigh juggling.

1 minute, repeat dribbling.

1 minute, foot juggling.

1 minute, rest by walking.

5 minutes, three-touch juggling; on the third touch either kick, bounce, or head the ball away into a space from five to ten yards away. Run to control the ball as quickly as possible, dribble a few steps, and begin juggling again. Repeat until 5 minutes are up.

1 minute, rest by walking.

For strength and flexibility:

30 sit-ups with ball behind head.

30 standing bounces: bouncing on toes, throw the ball up, leap and catch; repeat, throwing the ball up every third bounce.

30 push-ups.

30 jackknife jumps—touch the ball held in outstretched arms to feet.

30 leg-raisers from a sitting position, with ball between feet: lift up legs about twelve inches, back down without touching ground.

30 steps running in place; lean back and bring knees high to chest.

30 times lying on stomach, arch back; bring ball, held in outstretched arms, and feet off the ground, relax.

10 forward rolls: toss the ball high in the air, do a forward roll, and come up and catch the ball before it hits the ground.

30 hops over the ball from side to side.
30 hops over the ball from front to back.
1 minute, rest by walking.

For endurance and speed:

Set up an area with a starting line and five one-yard markers. From the starting line, sprint-dribble to first mark and return. Sprint-dribble to second marker and return. Repeat until you have sprint-dribbled to all five markers and returned.
30 seconds, rest by walking.
Stand at starting line, throw ball to fifth marker, sprint after the ball, control it, and sprint back to starting line.
15 seconds, rest by walking.
Repeat the above four steps, five times.

This entire fitness program should take about 30 minutes a day. It is very important to go through the entire program without rest except where called for.

In-Season
Continue the pre-season program on off days. Use Sundays as your rest day, unless that is a game day. Then pick another that suits you.

Remember that it is important to train at the same time each day. Regularity will give the body continuity and also will increase the benefits of the program. This program requires dedication, but it will help you become a better player.

SWIMMING

I talked with George Haines, swimming coach at UCLA and a former coach of the United States Olympic swimming team, about the exercise program he would recommend for the young swimmer in the pre-season or off-season period as well as during the competitive season.

Coach Haines
Off-Season
The main objective of any off-season training program is to maintain your weight and keep the body in good condition and to keep up your strength and flexibility.

Another important part of the off-season training program is the mental aspect that gets the swimmer away from actual competitive swimming. Swimmers need a break from the discipline and drudgery of swimming training, and the off-season can be a good time to recharge the batteries. By getting away from swimming training, the swimmer can relax and pick up other interests. It also is a break-time for the parents.

Thus the running and flexibility exercises and keeping the weight down should be done in a relaxed way through other sports.

Pre-Season

There are a number of programs that will help the swimmer in the pre-season training area, all of them designed to build up the cardio-vascular strength of the swimmer. I also recommend exercises that help the flexibility of the swimmer. Also there should be a good running program—not just jogging, but a planned running effort. At the University of Tennessee, the swimmers do repeat 220's, 440's, and 100-yard sprints just as they would in the water. This running does a lot to develop the cardiovascular system, so that when the swimmers do go back in the water after the layoff from competition, they won't be hurting so much.

In-Season

I think it is very important that your young athlete be brought along slowly so that his or her interest can be maintained. I've seen too many young children, girls and boys just in their teens, who have trained so intensely and so hard that by the time they reach high school they have lost their interest in swimming. And I know this happens in other sports.

Haines continued: Coaches should be very careful with young swimmers in the area of weight training. Youngsters should not be put on a concentrated weight-training program until about age 15 for girls, and maybe a little older for boys. Flexibility programs, mini-gyms, isokinetic machines, and that sort of thing are okay, but I never started my boys on heavy weights for strength building until they were in their junior or senior year of high school. And since I'm not an expert in weight training, I go to those who are for advice on the use of weights for my swimmers. I recommend you do the same.

I never knew a great swimmer who did not have the support and encouragement of the parents. Now, when I was a young coach I thought I knew it all and I did not encourage the parents to come to practice. As I grew older, I recognized how important they were to the success of my swimming program. I remember one coach whose team had a great season. He told everyone that he did not have great swimmers, he had great parents, and that's why his program was a winner. Of course, some parents can be too pushy, but by and large, the coach can handle that. It is parental indifference that causes problems, so the parent is most important to a swimmer, and to a coach.

I coached the great Don Schollander at the Santa Clara Swim Club and his mother was absolutely responsible for his success. I've had other athletes who had the potential to be just as good as Schollander, but when they got to be old enough to drive to the meets or to the practices, their parents stopped coming and soon the swimmer was not doing as well or not developing to the full extent of his or her potential. When we went back to find out why the athlete was slipping, we often found it was because the parents had lost interest or were no longer needed as a means of getting to practice and the meets. Someone has to care, has to be there, has to encourage the swimmer, because swimming can be dull, demanding, and lonely. So the parents must make sure that they don't allow the athlete unintentionally to cut them off from continued interest in the swimmer.

TENNIS

I spoke to one of the all time-great tennis players, Tony Trabert, to get his thoughts about an exercise program for the young tennis player. Tony had just completed coaching our Davis Cup team, and his thoughts about the off-season and pre-season training are very valuable.

Tony Trabert
Off-Season

In the off-season I find that one of the most important things the youngsters can do is to be aware of proper diet and get plenty of rest. This is very easy to forget when you are not playing regularly. But it is important to eat properly, avoid junk food, just as you would in-season, and get plenty of rest.

As for off-season exercises, the best ones are those that build up endurance and strengthen the stomach muscles. I was a little larger than the average player when I was playing. I stood about 6 foot, 1 and weighed about 190. Now that is still big for a tennis player, so I had to work on endurance and quickness.

To develop endurance, run up and down the steps of a stadium or up and down a hill, pushing yourself to run as hard and fast as you can. Do this for half an hour. Then run one mile. Repeat daily.

I consider the strengthening of the stomach muscles very important, because all of your power in hitting a tennis ball and in moving the body comes from the stomach area. If those muscles are weak, then your serve, volley, and other strokes will break down in a long match. The following exercises are for developing stomach muscles.

Do 50 sit-ups at a time; rest and repeat.

Lie on back, hands behind head, knees flexed. Curl to sitting position, touching right elbow to left knee; return to flat position, curl to sitting position, touching left elbow to right knee. Repeat, alternating elbow touching, 25 times for each elbow. Rest and repeat another 50 times.

Next, stand with feet apart, arms sideways at shoulder level. Bend forward, touch left toe with right hand, return and repeat to opposite side. Repeat 25 times.

After these stomach-strengthening exercises, I worked on developing greater quickness. Not only the stomach, but the thighs also are a very important area for the tennis player. Running will help develop the thighs, as will jumping rope. I find also that skipping rope, in addition to developing leg power, is very helpful in creating better coordination and quick feet.

I strongly recommend that tennis players play basketball in the off-season. Basketball requires the quick stops and starts that tennis does. The constant need for acceleration (stop and start) develops the lungs and the heart, as well as the legs. Furthermore, basketball develops great hand-eye coordination so necessary for the tennis player.

I don't recommend a weight-training program at any time for the tennis player, except those exercises that strengthen the hands. You can do that just squeezing an old tennis ball or a rubber ball, or use dumbbells and do wrist exercises. But weight exercises to develop the biceps and the shoulder muscles are not for the tennis player. They will cause loss of suppleness in the shoulders, which is so vital in serving and stroking the ball. Tennis is not a game of power for most players. You do not have to hit the ball far or hard. So pure muscle strength in the upper torso is of no value to the tennis player. The exercise the player gets in hitting a tennis ball is enough to develop strength in the upper body.

In-Season

During the season I always try to go on the court already perspiring. I warm up in the locker room by running in place, skipping rope, or doing some sit-ups. I do all of these exercises with my sweater on so that when I go on the court I'm loose and sweating. Remember, in the season, you have only a brief warm-up; unless you have already broken into a sweat, there is a chance that you will pull a muscle. That's why you should warm up before your match.

Pre-Season_____

Too many players never practice on their weaknesses. Some players will tell me that they played four sets or worked out for two hours, and when I ask them what they practiced, they tell me that they were working on those strokes that are already their best ones. Now it is human nature, even in a practice session, to try to win. And in doing so, we play with our best strokes. But the practice time is when you should work on your weaknesses. Sure, work on your strengths too, but make sure you spend more time on those strokes that are your poorest, even if you look bad. Otherwise, you cannot correct or reduce them.

Here is a little tip. Each week, make a list of what you think are the strong points in your game and what you think are your weak points. Show the list to your coach or a teammate and get his or her opinion. Then each day of practice make a note of how much time you spent working on the strengths and how much time working on the weaknesses. Be honest with yourself. You'll probably find that you're spending more time on the good points. If so, discipline yourself so that the next week you'll spend more time correcting the weak areas. And if you do, in no time you'll see your all-around game improving and you'll feel much more confident as a tennis player.

TRACK AND FIELD_____

Off-Season_____

No matter what the sport—basketball, football, tennis, soccer, or track and field—in the off-season the best exercise program is running. The only way to keep the body in shape is through running. Don Sutton, the fine pitcher of the Los Angeles Dodgers, began a program of running five miles a day, both in the off-season and during the regular baseball season. He has been doing this for five years and considers it to be the single most valuable thing that has kept him a big winner in the majors. He says that it has paid off in his legs and he feels better after running, so when the day comes that he is scheduled to pitch, he feels completely relaxed and confident of his physical power.

All athletes get their power from their legs. That goes for the sprinter, the broad jumper, the hurdler, and the weight man. If the basketball player's legs are weak, he has no jump shot, can't rebound, play defense, press, fake, and drive. He has nothing if his legs are weak. Neither does the football player, tennis player, golfer, soccer player, or any athlete. Running is the basis of all conditioning.

The young athlete, with his youth and vitality, may think his speed and stamina will be with him forever. However, he must at an early age recognize the importance of running in order to maintain that vitality. Without running and other proper exercise, one day that young man is going to reach down for that unlimited well of power and speed and come up short.

VOLLEYBALL

Most of the exercises that we discussed in basketball, apply equally well for volleyball, especially those that emphasize jumping ability, hand-eye coordination, and running. Here are some exercises that will be most helpful for volleyball specifically.

Off-Season

1. Start with jumping jacks; do three sets of 50 with a rest period between each set. Try to get a little extra "jump" into the jumping jack. Also, when extending the arms above the head, don't slap the hands together but touch the tips of your fingers together. This helps develop "feel." Also, keep the knees slightly flexed and always land on the balls of your feet.

2. I feel that good shoulder strength is necessary to some extent in volleyball, especially when spiking the ball. Do three sets of ten push-ups each, and later increase the number to 20, in sets of three. Do the first set of the three sets on the fingertips.

3. The running program should emphasize short sprints. If there is a hill nearby, run up and down that as fast and as hard as you can. On a flat surface, sprint as fast as you can for twenty yards, jog ten yards, and repeat as often as you like.

4. To improve jumping ability, hop up steps, first on one leg all the way up, then repeating with the other leg. As you gain more control of your body jumping up steps, you can increase to jumping up two steps at a time.

Pre-Season

As with basketball, the handling of a volleyball when you are not actually playing will improve your control of the ball, help with your timing, and increase your confidence. Dribble it, bounce it in the air about four to five feet, bouncing the ball on your arms. Next, try ten feet. Then try to bounce the ball five feet one time, then ten feet, alternating on each bounce, over and over. This will improve your feel for the ball and help develop hand-eye coordination.

Working on a basketball court or with a basket in the back yard, throw the volleyball into the air and try to hit it just over the rim of the basket. The basket height is about the same as that of a volleyball net, so this exercise will increase your ability to feel the proper height for clearing the net. When the ball comes off the backboard, bounce it in the air with your arms, and when it comes down, hit it back against the backboard. This will help greatly to develop the control and coordination that are so important in volleyball.

Another good exercise for developing hand-eye coordination—and for learning how to control the body and pick up overhead shots—is to take the volleyball and first bounce it off your arms, over your head in back of you; turn, run after the ball, bounce it again with the underside of your arms, back over your head; turn and repeat as many times as you can. Don't just spin in a circle, but hit the ball high and far enough away so you'll have to run to get it.

As you progress in volleyball, exercises that increase your quickness and foot speed, as well as your ability to tumble, will be important. Surprisingly, dancing is a good exercise to increase foot speed and overall coordination. So is skipping rope. Skip rope for five minutes, alternating the speeds of your skipping, and you'll notice a definite increase in foot speed and coordination. Skipping rope is also good for the development of endurance; boxers always skip rope as part of their training program to increase foot quickness and endurance.

WATER SKIING

Although water skiing is very popular, skiers do almost no preparation for the sport, and consequently there is a high degree of injuries resulting from water skiing. If your youngsters plan on doing any water skiing, they should exercise *at least two weeks* beforehand. Here are some suggestions:

To develop strength in the shoulder muscles, start a program of push-ups and chin-ups. Do them in sets of ten, each set three times.

To develop back muscles, have a program of sit-ups similar to the above, but do about 50 each set.

To develop the legs, running and stretching exercises are very important.

This exercise program will help prevent soreness and aching muscles after the first day of water skiing. It could also prevent serious injury, and maybe even drowning. Remember, too, that you are on the water and the sun can be very harmful to the skin if there is no protection. I recommend that the skier wear a light T-shirt under the life preserver to protect against the sun while on the water.

WEIGHT TRAINING PROGRAM FOR GENERAL DEVELOPMENT AND MAJOR SPORTS

Years ago it was thought that weight lifting would cause an athlete to become muscle-bound and to lose agility and speed. Weight lifting was for those who wanted to be a Charles Atlas and not for real athletes. But over the past two decades, as weight training for sports has grown out of weight lifting, it has proven very beneficial to the athlete and has disproved the old wives' tales.

Weight training can be as helpful to girls and women as it can be to boys and men. The fears of women becoming muscle-bound, incurring a hernia, or hurting their spine because of weight training are not substantiated by research; rather, it can result in better posture, firmness of the body, strengthening of weak areas, and improved general body condition.

There is much to be gained through a controlled program of weight training, and the closer the movements in the weight-training program simulate those of the sport one is training for, the more the benefits.

Weight Training Systems

There are a number of training systems. Which one is used, depends on the athlete's level of physical ability, his age, what he or she wants to accomplish, the athlete's experience in weight lifting, and the length of time available for taking on a weight-training program. Of the four systems described below, I recommend the 3 × 10 basic system for the beginner or young athlete.

The 3 × 10 System

The individual goes through a series of various lifts, repeating each exercise ten times, starting over after completing each exercise until he has done three sets of ten repetitions. This is excellent for all-around development. The 3 × 10 basic system is best for beginners and young athletes, and the results will be seen in increased strength and endurance.

Here is a typical 3 × 10 program:

1. Two-arm curls
2. Lateral raises
3. Military presses
4. Straight-arm pullovers

5. Upright rowing motions
6. Heel raises
7. Flying exercises
8. Sit-ups with weight behind head
9. Half squats

Each of the above exercises will be described later in the chapter.

The Working-Up System

The lifter does a series of exercises ten to twelve times, then adds weight to the barbell or dumbbells and repeats the exercise, this time maybe five to six times. He adds more weights, with decreased repetitions, until he reaches the point where there is only one lift. After resting, he starts on the next exercise with the same method of adding weight until only one movement can be made. This exercise system is for older athletes because the program is very fatiguing.

The Working-Down System

Here the lifter takes a certain weight and does, say, ten curls or presses. Then he decreases the weight by ten pounds and does as many of the same exercise as he can at the lighter weight. He rests, then reduces the weight by ten pounds and again does as many as he can until tired. This program should be done only once a day and, again, by an older athlete.

The Heavy-Light System

Here the lifter does an exercise first with a heavy load of weights; after three to five movements he stops and picks up a lighter weight and repeats the exercise, maybe twice as many times as with the heavy weight. The lifter should try to go through the program three times each session.

Never begin an exercise program without warming up. The warm-up can be a simple one, like running in place for 30 seconds or doing 25 toe touches and 25 side straddles. Make sure you allow time for warming up before each exercise session.

When doing the exercises, always breathe in deeply when lifting the weights, and exhale while lowering them. Also, make sure that you do each movement slowly.

The exercises that follow are designed to develop specific muscle groups and to improve the athlete's endurance and increase strength. It is important that you know what the exercise recommended actually does (note charts at end of chapter).

1. *Leg Raise:* Primarily develops the muscles of the lower abdomen (rectus abdominis) and lower back.
2. *Two-Arm Curl:* Develops the biceps and, to a lesser degree, the forearms (biceps, deltoids, and brachioradialis).
3. *Two-Arm Press:* Develops the back of the upper arms and the front of the shoulders (biceps and deltoids).
4. *Two-Arm Bench Press:* Develops the chest, the back of the upper arms, and the shoulders (pectoralis major, triceps, deltoids).
5. *Two-Arm Bent-Over Rowing Motion:* Primarily develops the muscles of the upper back (latissimus dorsi).
6. *Hack or Half Squat:* Develops the front muscles of the thighs (quadriceps).
7. *Toe Raise:* Primarily develops calf muscles (soleus and gastrocnemius).
8. *Two-Hand Dead Lift:* Develops muscles of the back, legs, and hips (gluteus maximus and quadriceps).
9. *Sit-Ups with Weight:* Develops abdominal muscles and firms the waist (external oblique and rectus abdominis).
10. *Shoulder Shrug:* Develops muscles of the upper back (trapezius).
11. *French Curl:* Develops the back of the upper arms (triceps).
12. *Forward Raise:* Develops shoulder muscles (deltoids and trapezius).
13. *Lateral Raise:* Develops the upper chest and the front section of the shoulders (pectoralis major and deltoids).
14. *Straight-Arm Pullover:* Develops chest muscles and increases their size (latissimus dorsi, deltoids, and pectoralis).

Here is how to do the different exercises.

1. *Leg Raise:* Lie on back on floor or bench. Keeping legs together, raise legs slowly until they are at right angles to the torso. Then lower legs to the floor. Repeat ten times, and do three sets of ten each.
2. *Two-Arm Curl:* With feet shoulder-width apart, grasp barbell or dumbbells with palms up, bar at thighs. Bring bar upward until forearms meet biceps. Lower and repeat.
3. *Reverse Curl:* Grip bar with an overhand grip and do as above.
4. *Two-Arm Press:* Place feet about shoulder-width apart and under the bar. Place hands over bar with knuckles facing out. Squat, then inhale and lift as you raise up to standing position, bringing barbell to shoulders. Then pause and raise bar overhead. Repeat press position. Do not bring barbell down to floor until you have pressed ten times.

5. *Two-Arm Bench Press:* Lie on bench or floor. Place barbell on chest, with hands little more than shoulder-width apart. Inhale while pressing barbell overhead, completely extending arms. Return to chest and repeat.

6. *Two-Arm Bent-Over Rowing Motion:* Spread feet to shoulder-width, bend over barbell, legs straight and back parallel to floor. Grasp barbell and raise it straight up to the chest. Return and repeat.

7. *Hack or Half Squat:* Stand in front of barbell, feet spread to shoulder-width. Squat, grasp barbell behind you with knuckles facing out, rise to standing position, then squat slowly. Repeat to ten times.

8. *Toe Raise:* Spread feet shoulder-width, lift barbell overhead, and place behind head on neck and shoulders. Rise up on your toes as high as you can, count to two, return heels to floor and repeat to ten times.

9. *Two-Hand Dead Lift:* Grasp barbell as in two-arm press, and rise up to standing position, with arms fully extended in front of you. Lower and repeat.

10. *Sit-Ups with Weight:* Lie on floor with small weight in hands, and hands behind head. Sit up as far as possible, keeping weight behind head. Lower body and repeat.

11. *Shoulder Shrug:* Spread feet, grasp barbell with the overhand grip, raise it to thighs. Shrug shoulders upward, inhaling as you do. Lower shoulders and repeat.

12. *French Curl:* Spread feet, grasp barbell with overhand grip, hands about ten inches apart at center of barbell. Clear bar to the shoulders, then inhale while pressing overhead. Exhale while lowering barbell behind head to neck. Come back to overhead position and repeat to ten times.

13. *Forward Raise:* Grasp barbell in the overhand position, spread feet, and raise bar to thighs. Inhaling through the movement, raise the barbell outward from chest with arms extended and stiff. Lower slowly to starting position while inhaling.

14. *Lateral Raise:* This is done with dumbbells. Lying on bench, raise dumbbells over the chest with arms extended. Keeping arms extended, lower them to each side of body until they are parallel to floor. Raise arms to starting position and repeat to ten times.

15. *Straight-Arm Pullover:* Lie on floor or bench with barbell or dumbbells behind head, arms fully extended. Keeping arms straight at all times, bring the weight slowly over the head to the thighs and then return to the starting position. Repeat to ten times.

16. *Good Morning Exercise:* With barbell resting behind the head

on the neck, bend forward slowly, keeping head erect, until back is almost parallel to floor. Rise to starting position and repeat to ten times.

17. *Wrist Curl:* Sit on bench with forearms on thighs, wrists extended over knees, barbell or dumbbells in hands in an underhand grip. Raise and lower with just wrist action. Repeat. Reverse to overhand grip and repeat.

Here are some suggested weight-training programs for specific sports. There are a number of good programs for each sport; the following are just some of the ones that can be helpful. The athlete can speak to the coach or trainer about other programs he might recommend.

Baseball (use dumbbells and barbell):
    Lateral raises, 3 × 10
    Straight-arm pullovers, 3 × 10
    Reverse curls, 3 × 10
    Two-arm curls, 3 × 10
    Forward raises, 3 × 10
    Posterior raises, 3 × 10
    Wrist curls, 3 × 10

Basketball:
    Forward raises
    Two-arm bench presses, 3 × 10
    Wrist curls, 3 × 10
    Lateral raises, 3 × 10
    Half squats, 3 × 10
    Straight-arm pullovers, 3 × 10
    Reverse curls, 3 × 10

Football (use dumbbells and barbell):
    Wide-arm bench presses, 3 × 10
    Heel raises
    Curls, 3 × 10
    Shoulder shrugs
    Straight-arm pullovers
    Two-arm bent-over rowing motions
    Good morning exercises
    Sit-ups with weight

Hockey:
    Two-arm curls, 3 × 10
    Straight-arm pullovers
    Sit-ups
    Wrist curls

Two-arm bench presses
French presses
Two-arm bent-over rowing motions
Upright rowing

Swimming:
Two-arm bent-over rowing motions
Upright rowing
Straight-arm pullovers
Half squats
Leg lifts with iron shoes
Wide-arm bench presses

Tennis:
Wrist curls
Wrist rollers (palms down)
Sit-ups with weight
Lateral raises

Track and Field (all exercises 3 X 10):
Jumpers:
Lateral raises
Heel raises
Half squats (using heavy weights)
Good morning exercises
Sprinters:
Leg curls with iron boot
Two-arm bench presses
Reverse curls
Half squats
Heel raises
Shot Putters and other weight events:
Two-arm bench presses
Half squats
French curls
Side bends
Wrist curls
Pole Vaulters:
Military presses
Upright rowing motion
Straight-arm pullovers
Sit-ups with weight
Two-arm curls
Distance Runners:
Two-arm curls (light weights)
Half squats

Military presses
Good morning exercises

Wrestling:

Two-arm curls
Two-arm bench presses
Two-arm bent-over rowing motions
Upright rowing
Straight-arm pullovers
Sit-ups with weight
French presses
Wrist curls

Another area that athletes often neglect in weight training is that of developing the opposing muscle groups. For instance, runners develop huge calf muscles from running and weight training, but do not develop the muscles in the front of the leg, the peroneus longus, and as a result of this failure they very often suffer shin splints and increase the exposure to stress fractures. Another example is an exercise such as the two-arm curl, which is designed to develop the biceps. The opposite muscles are the triceps, so a program of French curls should go along with the two-arm curls. Make sure that you don't neglect the opposing muscles from those you are trying to develop.

Speaking of shin splints, the best way to protect yourself from those is to do a simple exercise. Just sit on a chair, put your feet under a low couch, and try to raise the couch by lifting your toes, keeping the heels on the floor. That will strengthen the weak anterior leg muscles.

Today many schools have special weight "gyms" that have been developed in recent years. These gyms are huge lever and pulley apparatus that combine in one unit all the different movements and resistances necessary for a complete weight-training program. Usually they are supervised by the school trainer and used by the school athletes. Two of these systems are the Universal Gym and the Nautilus Gym. Both are excellent; if you are fortunate to have such equipment in the school and if it is available to individual students, the athlete should use it.

These special gyms are safe and easy to use. Their apparatus allows for the development of both sets of muscles (extensors and flexors). Several athletes can work out at the same time, thus relieving some of the drudgery of weight training. These new gyms, though expensive, are a great aid to athletic programs.

Of course, there is a right way and a wrong way to do everything. To get the most out of this sophisticated apparatus, the advice and supervision of a coach or trainer are necessary. Before using the machines, be certain you know how to use them correctly.

Colgate's Ernie Vandeweghe nets a hook shot in 74-68 win over Holy Cross in Boston Garden. Crusaders' Cousy looks on (2/8/49). (*Boston Garden Photo*)

Colgate freshman Ernie Vandeweghe starting for the East All-Stars in the annual East-West All-Star game in 1946. He's in the center (16) looking with complete concentration at the legendary coach Joe Lapchick. (*New York Herald Tribune*)

Here is the Vandeweghe family at home in 1969. Tauna (9) on the left, Bruk (5),
Kiki (11), Colleen, Heather (8), and Ernie.
(The family, today, appears on the back cover.)
(*Sports Illustrated*)

Kiki (11) listens intently as his mother comments on his performance in the pool that day.
(*Sports Illustrated*)

Father tries to help five-year-old Bruk with his golf grip as oldest son Kiki looks on.
(*Sports Illustrated*)

Tauna Vandeweghe after she qualified for the 1976 United States Swimming Team at a Long Beach pool in June 1976. (*Bill Walters Photography*)

Kiki Vandeweghe, a starter for the UCLA varsity, out rebounds two USC players in a 1977 game at Pauley Pavilion. (*Courtesy of University of California, Los Angeles*)

Kareem Abdul Jabbar, the great center of the Los Angeles Lakers, doing his stretching exercises before a game. The Lakers' warm-up consists of the team doing stretching drills rather than a lot of shooting. (*Barbara Moore*)

Bruce Jenner, 1976 Olympic decathlon champion, worked long and hard to build his strength and stamina in preparation for his grueling event.

Bart Starr, the great Green Bay quarterback, being tackled after throwing a pass. Being scissored by two charging linemen is a common experience for football quarterbacks. It is easy to see the possible injuries that can result from such action. (*Vernon J. Biever*)

Jerry West driving on Oscar Robertson, two of the greatest that ever played the game. Consider the size and build of West as a professional with the picture he draws of himself as a scrawny youngster.

Rick Barry driving around his man to the basket. Rick is one of the best all-around big men ever to have played the game.

Rick believes you're never too young to start.

The great Donna de Varona training under the watchful eye of her coach George Haines at the Santa Clara Swim Club in 1962. (*Sports Illustrated*)

Tony Trabert, tennis champion and United States Davis Cup captain and coach.

The "Juice" cuts and stretches for yardage against the New Orleans Saints. O.J.'s exceptional balance, agility, and quickness made him one of the all-time greats of football. (*Robert L. Smith*)

The legendary coach Vince Lombardi exemplified the qualities of all successful coaches and teachers—the ability to analyze, communicate, and lead.

Summary

In general, a weight-training program should be well planned and under as much supervision as possible. Also this program should complement the other exercises that the athlete is doing for the sport he or she is involved in. For girls, remember that muscles developed for sports soon atrophy when not used and rapidly decrease in size. For all, remember to watch your eating habits when you are not training, because the calories you burn up in training will turn to fat if you're not exercising. Remember, too, to use an alternate-day method of weight training, and balance your muscle development by developing the opposition muscles.

5

INJURIES: Their Cause and Rehabilitation

If you participate in sports, there is a chance that at some time you will be injured. This chapter is about injuries and how to treat them. For the parent, I want to stress one fact. Make sure, if your son or daughter is injured, that you get proper medical attention. Obviously, some injuries like a skinned knee or scraped elbow can be treated by the parent or the athlete. But any other injury, like some that we will discuss here, should be treated and observed by proper medical people.

The focus of this chapter is to explain what the different type of injuries are, what has happened to the body when the injury takes place, what the proper treatment is for each injury, and what recuperative measures are needed.

The strength and recovery powers of youngsters are amazing. But parents and coaches must, especially with young athletes, make sure that the athlete has completely recovered. Then, and only then, should he or she be allowed to participate in the sport. The child will want to play as soon as possible. Parents and coaches must be the final judge, along with the doctor or team physician, as to when the child can resume sports.

Injuries are part of sports, and of life, for that matter. Many a youngster has broken a bone or gotten cuts playing in the backyard. But in sports, especially contact sports, the possibility for injury is always

102

present. Most injuries are preventable. Proper conditioning of the athlete is the best safeguard against injury. Proper equipment and facilities is another important preventative of injuries. And good common sense on the part of the coach and the parents is the third best preventative.

Maybe common sense is the best of all. Too many times I have seen injuries that could have been prevented had someone been thinking and paying attention to what they were doing. In Little League baseball, Pop Warner football, basketball, soccer, or any of the sports that are town or community sponsored, there is often the parent who exhorts his child to "shake it off and get back in there." That parent should be booed out of the stands. That is the worst advice to give a child. Let the coach or trainer determine if the child can go back. If there is a head injury, the athlete should not play anymore that day. I know that the professional athlete can shake it off: but we are not talking about professionals. Parents should insist that their child be kept from further competition until a doctor has seen the athlete.

In this chapter we will give you some suggestions on treating the different injuries and some help on taping an injury. Throughout, however, I'll stress the need for caution and use of a doctor in dealing with injuries.

Contusions

A contusion is caused by a direct blow against the skin which bruises the outer skin and the underlying tissues. This results in capillary rupture or bleeding, followed by swelling and an inflammatory reaction in that area.

Proper treatment of a contusion in the early stage is to limit bleeding by applying cold compresses and a pressure bandage. After the swelling subsides, apply heat locally, and have the athlete rest until the bleeding has been completely controlled. The bruised area must be protected from further damage by another direct blow; cover it with a bandage, sponge, or plastic guard.

Rehabilitation should begin slowly within the limits of pain. A simple bruise will not require a long period of rehabilitation but a bruise that is deep into the muscles will require more time.

Hematomas

A hematoma, usually caused by a blow to the body, is a collection or pool of blood within a small area under the skin. In a hematoma, bleeding takes place in the tissues and accumulates in the tissues. The area and size of the hematoma will vary with the degree and the amount of bleeding. If the area is close to the skin, the area will have discoloration in the skin. Bleeding deeper inside the tissues may require treatment by a doctor.

Treatment for hematoma consists of the application of ice packs and pressure dressing to prevent further bleeding.

I strongly recommend *against* aspiration, the placing of a needle into the area of the hematoma. There is a possibility of secondary infection with aspiration, and serious complications can result. The pool of blood is a perfect place for bacteria to grow. Also, the pressure from the hematoma itself helps stop the bleeding, and removal of that pressure may start the bleeding all over again. I am also against the use of enzymes injected into the hematoma area; enzymes have the effect of breaking down the clot and allowing some secondary bleeding and may extend the area the hematoma occupies. The old phrase "work it out" has no place in the treatment of a hematoma, either; running and stretching and massaging the area should not be part of the treatment.

The application of ice packs to the area will help ease the pain and control the bleeding and swelling. These packs should be applied as soon as possible after the injury and should be kept on the area for up to an hour before a new pack is put on. After the swelling is controlled, usually the next day, heat can be applied to the area. The heat should be applied two or three times a day, no more than twenty minutes at a time. The amount of heat applied should be reasonable and comfortable.

Activity can be begun within the limits of pain with full range of motion and muscle strength. The activity will help increase the blood supply to the area that is injured and the contraction of the muscle will aid in the absorption of the blood in the hematoma.

Open Wounds

A *laceration* is a wound to the skin caused by a sharp object, where the skin is actually cut through its full thickness. In sports a laceration will usually result from a blow that causes a contusion as well. The skin will split because the pressure over the skin stretches it to the point where it rips. Lacerations are most common on the chin and over the eye. The bleeding will often be enough to clean the wound.

A *puncture* is a wound made by a blunt object which pierces through the layers of the skin. When the puncture wound is near a joint, medical attention should be sought. Also, if there is very little bleeding, it is advisable to seek medical attention as soon as possible, because the penetrating object may cause a secondary infection by implanting bacteria into the wound. It is very important to examine the penetrating object to see that no part of it has been left in the wound.

Puncture wounds may not require suturing, whereas lacerations often will. If the skin in the area of the wound does not come back together, it will require suturing or stitching. If the edges of the skin do come together, a bandage or some covering will be enough; the skin will form a scab and heal nicely.

When there is a laceration, there will be a resultant scar. Prompt medical attention and treatment to protect against infection will reduce the eventual size of the scar. Although lacerations need attention, such a wound can be adequately cared for and sutured anytime within the first six hours.

An *abrasion* is a scraping injury to the skin which removes the outer hard skin and exposes the underlying tissue. This tissue will have small bleeding points that ooze a thick serum. If promptly and properly taken care of, an abrasion is not a serious injury. Clean the entire area with soap and water. There is no need to paint the wound with iodine or other chemicals and probably no need of a pain killer. However, the application of a good antibiotic ointment to the wounded area is recommended to provide protection from further infection and other irritation. Infection is indicated by the following signs: red, tender, swollen area about the abrasion and the appearance of a red streak under the skin running toward the heart.

Strains_____

A strain may be defined as damage to a tendon or muscle due to overuse or overstress. It is therefore related to an injury to a muscle or the extension of the muscle that is attached to the bone or tendon.

In an ordinary strain, there is usually very little damage, and there will be a small degree of swelling and tenderness in the area. Resting the injured area for a few days and allowing only pain-free activity during that rest period will allow the recuperative functions of the body to work on the injury.

If there is a rupture or tear in the muscle or tendon, the strain is more serious. In this case there will be limitations in movement after the initial shock of the injury wears off. For this kind of strain, medical attention is needed. Immobilization will probably be necessary to allow the injury to heal.

Determining the time for the athlete to return to full activity after a serious strain can be difficult. The athlete thinks he's ready and the coach is not above prodding him; that combination often brings the athlete back before the strain is completely healed. Parents should make sure, especially where the strain has required medical attention, that the athlete does not begin competition without the doctor's okay. Complete healing will help prevent recurrence and an even longer period out of competition next time.

Sprains

A sprain can be defined as an injury to a ligament. A *ligament* functions as a "band" attached across a joint to prevent abnormal movement of the joint. Some ligaments bind the joints tightly together while others are looser. The knee ligaments are binding and restrict movement of the knee joint; the ligaments attached to the ankle are looser, allowing the ankle much more flexibility. Overstress of the ligament causes damage to the fibers at the point of attachment to the bone.

The extent of damage caused by a sprain depends on the degree of abnormal motion, the duration of the motion, and the force that caused the abnormal motion. A sprain can be very minor, a slight stretching of the ligament, or there can be complete separation of the ligament from the bone. The latter is a very serious injury.

Sprains are divided into three general categories. a *mild sprain* is one in which a few fibers of the ligament have been torn and there is slight internal bleeding but there is no loss of ability to function. This type of injury is most common. It requires only small protection, like an Ace bandage, and should not interfere with physical activity.

A *moderate sprain* is one in which a portion of the ligament is torn and there is some degree of functional loss. Protection here is important so that the repairing process can begin. Moderate sprains can sometimes be completely healed, but more often than not, "once a sprain, always a sprain" is all too true for the moderate sprain. If it is properly treated, and if there is an adequate amount of rest and the ligament is kept inactive, then there should be no weakness of the ligament or recurrence of the sprain.

In a *severe sprain* there is a complete loss of the ligament because it has been torn from where it is attached to the bone. The functional loss is complete and the ligament must be treated in much the same way as a fracture of a bone. This type of sprain may require surgical treatment to bring the torn part of the ligament back to its proper place on the bone. If the tear leaves the ligament close to its proper place, surgery may effect a complete repair. However, if it is torn too far from its proper place, scar tissue will build up and the ligament will probably never have its former strength.

Dislocations

A dislocation is defined as the actual displacement of the opposing continuous surfaces of bone making up a joint. There will also be displacement of the ligaments placed there to prevent a dislocation. A partial dislocation is referred to medically as "subluxation." In this case the ends of the bones merely slid slightly against each other without full dislocation.

A dislocation is the result of a severe sprain. Treatment involves more than just returning the bone parts to their normal place. There has been damage to the ligaments as well, and time must be allowed for their proper treatment and for their normal healing. I stress this because many people think that if a dislocated bone is put back into place, physical activity can continue. Most dislocations are greatly *undertreated,* and early return to activity without proper care for the damaged ligaments can cause further damage and repeating of the dislocation.

Frequently when fingers are dislocated, players are allowed to return to action as soon as the dislocation is repaired, without any protection or consideration for proper healing time. This may result in permanent disability of the involved joint.

Fractures

Fractures are common in youngsters who participate in sports. A fracture should be immediately X-rayed and medical treatment begun. Because of the suppleness of young bones, sometimes a minor fracture can escape initial X-ray diagnosis and will not be discovered until two weeks after the injury. If the athlete complains of pain, even after the first X rays, another set should be taken. The fracture then may be recognized and proper medical attention started.

Fractures may be divided into various types. In a *green-stick* fracture, the bone is cracked but not completely broken off; this is usually found in younger children and is similar to what happens to a green twig of a tree or shrub.

In a *simple* fracture, the bone is broken but not the skin. A *compound* fracture is one in which both the bone and the skin are broken, and the bone may protrude through the skin. In a *comminuted* fracture, there is a splintering of the bone or a crushed bone at the site of the fracture. An *impacted* fracture is one in which the ends of the bone are jammed together. A *spiral* fracture runs in a circular manner, up and around the shaft of the bone.

A fracture can be recognized by some of the following symptoms:

1. A "click" coming from some part of the body which the athlete may hear when injured.
2. Tenderness and swelling at the point of the injury.
3. "Cretitus" or grating of the bone.

4. Sudden, stabbing pain on movement.
5. Muscle spasms in the area, or hard contractions of the muscles.
6. Deformity of the area.
7. Signs to the body system that something is wrong, even though not obvious to the outside—only the athlete knows something is wrong.

The treatment of fractures will vary greatly, depending on the extent and type of injury. Immediate proper treatment will hasten the athlete's return to normal activity. A program of rehabilitation is necessary because the muscles surrounding the fractured area atrophy during the recovery period. Also, the remainder of the body should be exercised during the recovery period, as best as one can. Obviously, if the fracture is of the leg or ankle, running is out, but the athlete can do exercises to keep the upper body in shape. If the fracture is of the upper body, running can help keep the lower body and the respiratory system in good shape. This exercising will enable the athlete to return to competition more quickly.

Muscle Spasms and Cramping

A muscle spasm or cramping occurs when there is a hard blow to the muscle or when the muscle is stretched beyond the normal length. A change in the amount of blood that is fed to the muscle can cause spasms or cramping, as can lack of salt in the system. Changes in the temperature, sudden cold, or even overheating can cause spasms or cramping. Whenever adequate blood supply fails to get to the muscles, spasms or cramping can occur. Tight elastic bandages, collars, and other materials that cut off circulation will cause spasms.

While muscle cramping can occur in any area of the body, it is particularly prevalent on the lower parts of the body: the legs, the back, and the feet.

The best immediate treatment for a muscle cramp is to rub the area, applying pressure to the spastic muscle, and then to try to force it through a normal range of activity. I stress normal range because excessive stretching may further damage the muscle. There should be no beating or pounding on the muscle, nor should there be a hard rubbing of the area— only a firm, continuing stretching of the muscle, rubbing easily at the same time.

The pain from a muscle spasm can be very intense. Warm but not hot compresses will improve circulation. Cramps have a tendency to recur, but with warmth and stretching, there is no reason not to allow the athlete to continue play.

Nerve Injuries_____

The nervous system is not too commonly involved in injuries to young athletes because of their excellent condition and the strong muscles that protect the nerves from direct injury or stress. However, near the joints, the nerves are close to the surface of the skin and not protected by muscles. This is especially true of the elbow, where a blow to the so called "crazy bone" can be very painful. This is discussed more fully in the section on elbow injuries.

Pinched nerves are discussed in the section on neck injuries.

Head Injuries_____

It is very important that the parents and the coaches understand that head injuries are complex and should always have immediate medical attention. Possible damage to the internal structure of the brain is more important than any external injuries, even a fracture of the skull.

The most important point about head injuries is that everything must be done beforehand to prevent the injury. And the best preventative to a head injury is proper equipment, supervision, and experience. This is evident when we look at the relatively small number of serious head injuries there are in professional sports, especially the contact sports of football, baseball, soccer, and basketball.

The beginning athlete must be taught by his coach and his supervisor how to avoid injuries to the head. Proper equipment is a must. It is also essential that the coach and supervisor teach the athlete how to use that equipment properly.

One thing that must *not* be taught is the technique, in football, of "spearing." This technique, which was gaining some popularity a few years ago, is simply to tackle a runner by throwing the body at him with the head lowered and aimed at the runner's midsection so that upon impact, the tackler's helmet would hit the runner, thus hurting the runner and possibly causing a fumble.

First of all, any coach that espouses that technique should be fired. The name of the game is to score more points than the opponents in the time allowed, not to see how many of the opposition can be hurt. Furthermore, spearing almost never hurts the ball carrier; most often the boy doing the spearing is hurt, and usually quite seriously. That injury can be anything from a sprained neck to a broken neck or serious brain damage, and sometimes even total paralysis or death. Fortunately, this technique is not practiced by the majority of players, coaches, and supervisors.

In addition to proper equipment, supervision, and experience, all possible safety precautions should be taken on the field to prevent head injuries, as well as any other kind of injury. Any player who has been ill or who has suffered some prior head injury should not participate without approval from the doctor. And any athlete who has been taking medication or drugs should not participate, because these are certain to slow up the athlete's ability to react and could expose him or her to injury.

If a player falls to the field as a result of a blow to the head, the immediate responsibility of treatment rests with the officials, the coach, the trainer, and the teammates for his care. The nature and force of the injury should be noted to help serve as a guide for diagnosis and treatment.

1. If the athlete is unconscious, see if he is breathing. If not, immediately begin artificial respiration. Do not delay, except to make sure that there is no unnecessary movement of the head and neck.

2. In most cases, breathing will begin immediately and return of consciousness will be prompt. As soon as breathing is resumed, consideration for movement begins.

If the athlete regains consciousness promptly, he has suffered a concussion. This does not indicate any actual damage to the brain but is simply a momentary lapse of consciousness. If the athlete can answer questions, has strength in his grip, knows where he is, and has normal eye reaction to light, he may be allowed to return to action, *if he is a professional athlete or a college athlete.*

But if the athlete is younger, I strongly recommend that there be no further participation. If any young athlete is unconscious at any time from an injury on the field, he or she should be removed from the field and taken to the nearest medical facility for further observation. We all know the stories of athletes who have been knocked out and then return to lead the team to victory. That's fine for movies and books only. If a youngster has been knocked out for even a second, that person should be removed from the game and taken for observation. The fact that the athlete was unconscious for a brief time indicated a shock to the brain and the nervous system.

It is possible to suffer severe head injury without loss of consciousness. If there is bleeding from the nose, ear, or throat, this also indicates need for medical observation.

Our youngsters tolerate head injuries very well, and it should be pointed out that in the great majority of cases the recovery time is short, the results are excellent, and seldom are there any complications. But never allow a child to continue playing after he or she has been knocked out.

If the player remains unconscious, the most important immediate treatment is to make sure that he is breathing and to open his mouth so that the continual accumulations of saliva and possibly blood in the nasal pharynx can escape. The head should be lower than the body so that these secretions can drain from the mouth.

Very infrequently, there will be symptoms of shock. These symptoms are a marked pallor of the skin, rapid respiration, and a weak, fast pulse. If these symptoms are present, immediate emergency medical aid is needed.

The nature of the accident or injury should be noted to be sure that other parts of the body have not been injured. Remember, whatever measures are necessary to maintain respiration are more important than regaining consciousness. If the unconscious athlete is to be transported, make sure that someone calls ahead to the emergency room of the hospital so they have time to get a neurosurgeon. And it is more advisable to go right to emergency than to a doctor's office.

It is important to watch for abnormal signs after a head injury. Abnormal sleepiness, changes in behavior, disorientation, or inappropriate answers to questions should not be taken lightly, even if there had been no loss of consciousness. Vomiting immediately after a head injury is not significant. Vomiting an hour or two after the injury is. Vomiting indicates some degree of swelling or irritation within the brain and calls for further medical attention.

The status of the pupils of the eye is important for telling if there is damage to the brain. The parent can do this test himself. Take a flashlight and shine it into the pupil of the child's eye. The pupils should be equal in size. Shining the light into the pupil should cause the pupil to constrict or shrink down. The reaction should be very rapid and should take place in the other pupil at the same time. If the reaction is slow or if there is any abnormality in the reaction of one pupil versus the other, then there is an indication for medical attention.

When your athlete comes home after being observed by the doctor, you will frequently be asked to observe the youngster. The doctor will tell you what to look for, and the above symptoms are likely to be included. Any additional points are to be followed.

When an athlete can return to competition will vary greatly with the type of head injury and the kind of competition he or she is participating in. A simple rule of thumb, assuming that all symptoms have cleared up, is that the athlete should be allowed to practice without contact two days after the symptoms have cleared up. Also, he or she must have received medical clearance for contact sports.

Think of a head injury or a brain injury as you would a sprain; as long as there is any pain or tenderness, then there is still some degree of damage, and contact should not be allowed. If there is any lightheadedness or pain in the head when workout begins, then the youngster should stop and rest until there are no symptoms. Any jarring motion or hard exertion that produces that reaction indicates that the athlete is not ready to resume participation in sports, especially contact sports.

Face Injuries

The old cliché about leading with the chin certainly applies to sports, because nowhere is the body more prone to injury than the face. Cuts and bruises are part of playing sports, and the list of injuries to the face can be endless. But usually the injury is minor, and with a little attention, players seldom miss much of the action from injuries to the face.

Because the skin is so tight over the bony area of the face, lacerations almost always result from a hard blow. The treatment for a facial laceration is the same as for any laceration. Thoroughly clean the wound, cover it to protect the area, and, unless the laceration is extremely deep, the player can return to competition. Upon completion of the game, the wound should be seen and treated by the doctor or trainer. If bleeding is not a problem, any stitching that is required can be done anytime within the first six hours.

A blow to the face will sometimes be followed by immediate swelling. This is a contusion, caused by a rupture of the small blood vessels. The swelling can be easily controlled by the application of cold compresses to the area. The lump or swelling is blood and will often cause a discoloration below the area as the body begins its own healing and draining. There will be pain, swelling, and discoloration, but with applications of heat to the area, it should clear up in a few days. The area above the eye is the place where contusions most often take place.

Fractures of the face most commonly are in the cheekbone. They are usually caused by an extremely hard blow or by falling or running into an object. Sometimes a fracture here is hard to detect without X rays because of the contusion to the same area. The treatment is to apply cold compresses to the area to clear up the contusion. There will be pain, discoloration, and swelling. After the swelling goes down, the fracture can be found by gently feeling the area with your fingers to detect the break. But the break should be detected by X rays and a doctor should treat this injury.

Eye Injuries

A direct, forceful blow to the eye may cause the eye to close within a short period of time. If possible, the player should move the eye from side to side to determine if there is any bleeding or any injury to the muscles of the eye. If there is no evident damage to the eyeball itself, then local treatment with crushed ice and a cloth put over the eye may be all the treatment necessary. The cloth used should be very fine, not coarse like a towel.

Very severe or persistent pain in the eye, especially in shutting the lid, or the feeling of roughness or irregularity under the lid, is an indication that there is an injury to the cornea either by the presence of a foreign body or a direct abrasion. In either case, the eye should be padded in a closed position and medical help should be obtained. Should there be any degree of irritation about the eye, any disturbance of vision, excess watering, double vision, loss of focus causing blurring, or any other abnormal feelings about the eye, then an ophthalmologist should be consulted.

Nose Injuries

Any blow to the nose can be very painful. Immediately after the injury there is a short period of time before the swelling begins and this time is very important to the proper treatment. Careful examination of the face by someone who is familiar with the features of the player can determine if there is any change in the appearance of the nose. During this time before the swelling, it is possible to feel along the edges of the nose to determine any underlying tenderness or irregularity. Obviously, any deformity implies the possibility of a fracture. In a short time from the striking of the blow, swelling may begin and the chance for a simple diagnosis may be lost.

Most injuries to the nose are followed immediately by extensive bleeding. If the following steps are taken, the bleeding can quickly be brought under control:

1. The player should stand or sit upright. Do not have him lie down.
2. Put a cold cloth or ice pack over the nose. This may be all that is necessary to control the bleeding.
3. If the bleeding is profuse, take the thumb and forefinger and align them along the edges of the nose, applying steady and continuous pressure for three to five minutes. This should stop the bleeding.

It is rarely necessary to pack anything inside the nose. Should the bleeding continue despite the pressure, then a large piece of cotton coated with ½ percent Neo-Synephrine nasal jelly will make an excellent packing. Never use a small piece of cotton or anything that can be pushed up into the nose totally.

Remember, approximately an equal amount of blood will be swallowed into the back of the throat as will come out of the nose. If the player does not spit out that blood, he may become nauseated and vomit. This is not a serious problem, but it's certainly preferable to get rid of the blood by spitting it out.

If your athlete is subject to frequent nosebleeds, just before bedtime he might try ½ percent Neo-Synephrine; apply with the little finger, putting the jelly inside the nose, massaging slightly. This will provide a lubricant and prevent the drying out and cracking of the nasal mucosa, which is the primary cause of recurrent bleeding.

Mouth Injuries

One of the most common injuries in sports is that caused by a blow around the mouth, tearing the skin inside the mouth and around the outside surface. Wounds inside the mouth rarely need suturing; they will heal very quickly if left alone. For two or three days following an injury to the inside of the mouth, the athlete should take semisolid to liquid food. Then he should rinse his mouth out after eating with a mixture of half water and half hydrogen peroxide solution. This will prevent the accumulation of food particles between the edges of the wound as it heals.

The gums will frequently turn white as they heal, but this does not indicate any infection. Infection is indicated by swelling, redness, and tenderness around the edges of the wound, and in this case medical attention is required.

The Teeth

Any blow or laceration of the lip demands close examination of the teeth. Direct pressure over each tooth, with a clean finger or wooden applicator, will determine if there has been any damage to the teeth. Most injuries to the teeth do not require immediate medical attention. If a tooth should remain loose after two or three days then a dental X ray may be necessary.

If a tooth is knocked out, the area should be cleaned and kept as sterile as possible and the athlete should be taken to the dentist. Most often, a tooth is chipped or broken off and the piece lost. If the tooth is tender or painful, it can be protected by a small piece of wax until a dentist can be reached.

Dislocated Jaw

Any blow to the jaw can dislocate the jaw. Even opening the mouth too wide yawning can dislocate the jaw. It is very painful. However, at times the dislocated jaw can be fixed easily. Here is what to do: Place the thumbs on top of the lower back teeth, with the other fingers outside of the jaw. With the thumbs, slowly and gradually apply pressure on the lower teeth in the back of the mouth. At the same time, slowly and gently use the fingers on the outside to roll the jaw forward. This will unlock the jaw and allow it to slide closed. If this simple procedure does not work, then medical attention should be sought.

After the jaw is back in place, eating and chewing should be done with some caution. Also, yelling, yawning, and even speaking should be done with care.

Persistent pain or tenderness about the jaw may indicate a fracture of the lower jaw. Also, the athlete may notice that his bite is off and X rays may be needed to determine if there is a fracture.

Ear Injuries

The ear usually does not suffer serious injury in sports competition. Of course, we know about the cauliflower ear that boxers and wrestlers suffer from, but other than that, only the rubbing of the football headgear could cause the infection that would develop into cauliflower ear.

What happens is that the ear swells and there is an accumulation of solidified blood or fluid between the skin of the ear and the cartilage. This can be painful and should be treated by applying a cold compress to the ear for thirty minutes. If a blood clot appears in the form of a bulge on the ear, a physician should be consulted.

Cauliflower ear can be prevented by applying a skin lubricant such as Vaseline to the football player's ear and making sure that the headgear fits properly. If the headgear is causing discomfort, remove it and have the gear fixed or get new headgear.

Most frequently, the ear is cut in competition. This usually happens in the area between the ear and the head, and the injury is called a tear. Treat with cold compresses to control the bleeding, then clean the area and put a large bandage over the ear. If bleeding continues, stitching may be required, so a doctor should be consulted.

Neck Injuries

The neck and back region of the body comprises the spinal column. The spinal column is divided into seven cervical vertebrae, twelve dorsal or thoracic vertebrae, and five lumbar vertebrae. These vertebrae are separated and cushioned by cartilage (discs) and joined by ligaments. These unions provide flexibility at each vertebra so that movement is possible. Because of the spinal column's structure and because it contains all the nerves that run from the brain to the rest of the body, an injury to the spinal column or neck is very serious. So, handle with great caution.

Contusion of the neck usually involves the nerves associated with the operation of the arm and hand. It is most often called a "pinched nerve," and it is very painful. There will sometimes be a loss of movement accompanied by a tingling sensation in the arm. The numbing sensation is similar to that felt when the "crazy bone" in the elbow is hit. A blow to the neck or a violent twist of the neck is the usual cause of a contusion to the neck nerve. The treatment is to gently pull, shake, and rotate the arm. Follow by a light massage to the arm, neck, and upper shoulder. It is extremely important to recognize this as a simple "pinching of the nerve" and not serious injury to the cervical spine.

Dislocation of the neck vertebrae, on the other hand, is a very serious injury. This can cause muscle spasms, severe pain, a degree of paralysis, and deformity of the back and neck. This should be treated as a fracture of the neck. The athlete should not be moved until proper medical treatment is on hand. If he must be moved, it should be done as follows:

1. Keep movement of the athlete to a minimum.
2. Have enough people around to lift him or her onto the stretcher.
3. To prevent motion between head and neck, one person should hold the head steady and two others hold the shoulders steady with the neck.
4. The stretcher should be carried slowly and evenly.
5. The athlete should not be allowed to sit up.
6. There should be no forced manipulation of the head.
7. During transportation, a rolled-up towel should be placed under the curve of the neck, and someone should hold the athlete's head during the trip.

If the athlete is unconscious, he should be treated as if he had a broken neck until he regains consciousness. Medical attention should be immediate.

If the athlete begins to vomit, his body should be turned to the side and the head be held so that it does not rotate.

Even if the athlete is not lying down or unconscious, if he complains about the neck, he should be removed from the event and be examined immediately. He should not return until he has been checked by a physician. This may mean that he will miss a game or practice, but examination by a doctor is more important than the time missed.

Contusion of the Throat

This usually involves the Adam's apple. There will be severe pain, coughing, and at time blood may be coughed up. There will be pain to the throat when talking or coughing and the area will be tender.

To treat the contusion, cold packs should be immediately applied to the throat area to stop the bleeding. The athlete should refrain from talking, because the area of the contusion should be as relaxed as possible. He should be able to resume talking after a short time, however. In most cases, the injured athlete should not be given anything to drink because swallowing causes pain and can start the bleeding again.

If there is spitting of blood after the injury, and if it keeps up for a period of time, medical attention should be sought. If there is inability to talk right (called "aphonia") after the injury, the athlete will naturally feel great concern; parents and coaches should assure him that this loss of voice is just temporary and will soon pass.

Breathing should be short and through the nose. Deep breaths will cause pain, whereas short, easy breaths will fill the lungs enough without causing any pain. This breathing through the nose will also help relieve the anxiety that is so common in the athlete from a blow to the throat.

Chest Injuries

Injuries to the chest area are fairly common in sports and there are several that we will discuss here. The most common injury is having the "wind knocked out" of the lungs. This happens when there is a heavy blow to the chest area or to the stomach. The treatment is to let the athlete rest, have him take short breaths, and lift on his belt to start relieving the pressure around the stomach. This injury is seldom serious but always painful. The pain should subside within minutes, even though there will be a sore spot where the blow landed.

Muscle strains about the chest area are also common, because of the great number of muscles that we have in that area and because of the many positions the muscles must take during exercise. Treatment depends entirely upon the muscles involved but the usual treatment of rest, heat, and gradual working of the strained area is the best course. Stay within the limits of pain when beginning.

Rib Fractures

This is a relatively common injury in athletics. A hard blow struck to the chest area will cause skin contusions, and there is a possibility that a rib may be fractured. The way to tell is to move the skin around the impact area in a gentle manner, up and down. If the pain moves with the skin, you have a surface contusion of the skin and the layers underneath. Treat this as a simple bruise: apply cold compresses to the area, cover it to protect the skin, and allow the athlete to continue participation.

To test for a fractured rib, place one hand on the back and the other on the front, and gently press in on the area of the blow. The pain will tell you if the rib is broken. Another signal is that the athlete cannot take a deep breath without pain. X rays should be taken of the area and the athlete should be taken from the field without further delay. There should be no further participation in sports until the doctor says that the rib is healed.

If the athlete comes home and complains of pain around the injured area, take him for X rays. If his shortness of breath becomes severe and there is a slight discoloration or blueness around the lips or fingernails, this is a good indication that there are internal injuries and emergency treatment is necessary.

Breast Injuries

Both boys and girls can suffer injuries in the breasts. These are usually bruises to the breast area or inflammation of the nipple area. For a bruise, the treatment is the same for both: cold compresses to take down the swelling, and then after the swelling is under control, heat to loosen the muscle contractions. If there is an inflammation, the area should be protected with a bandage. If the inflammation lasts for an unreasonable period, then medical advice should be sought.

For girls, should there be a nodule in the breast area after the injury and should this persist after treatment of the bruised or inflamed area, medical attention should be sought. This symptom could be quite significant.

With more female participation in sports, there is greater possibility of injury to the breast area. In the physically immature girl there is little likelihood of serious injury to the breasts or nipples. But in the more developed girls, any athletic competition should be stopped if there is an injury to the breast area or while there is inflammation.

Girls are reluctant to tell about injuries to the breast area. Parents and coaches must emphasize how important it is that the girls advise them when they think that there is an injury or inflammation. If there is a persistent nodule in the breast area, as I have said, it must be looked at immediately by proper medical people.

Abdominal Injuries

Injuries to the abdomen usually do not involve much bruising to the abdominal wall itself. The overriding concern from a blow or contusion is injury to the contents of the abdomen. Strain to the muscles of the abdominal wall is very difficult to distinguish from injury to the abdominal contents and diagnosis requires close observation. Early examination by a physician is important, and much safer than "waiting to see how he feels tomorrow."

With a strain of the muscle wall of the abdomen there is usually tenderness and rigidity along the muscle mass and there can be pain. If the muscle mass is stretched or aggravated, the pain can be intense. In the majority of cases, a strain of the muscle wall does not involve a great deal of damage. However, there is a tendency among athletes to return to action too soon and reinjure the muscles. Often a player will sit out a whole season because of his impatience. The only adequate treatment for a muscle strain of the abdomen is rest.

A painful muscle spasm on the right side suggests appendicitis. Vomiting is frequently a symptom of appendicitis and if that is accompanied with muscles spasms, then the child should see a physician right away.

The Solar Plexus

The athlete who receives a blow in the stomach or the so-called "solar plexus" will have immediate pain and cramping, along with severe air-hunger. This could lead to involuntary bowel movement and urination. There may even be some early symptoms of shock. Usually, the pallor and rapid heartbeat that are associated with shock clear up quite quickly. Even if they do, there can still be serious injury to the contents of the abdomen. Surviving the acute phases of the blow to the stomach does not rule out other manifestations later.

If the athlete who has collapsed does not respond rapidly with or without treatment, he has a severe injury that demands emergency care. Because a hard blow to the the stomach can cause injury to the solid structures in the abdominal cavity, there can be bleeding into the abdomen. Any tenderness or rigidity of the stomach with signs of blood loss, such as rapid pulse, dizziness, fainting, and other signs of shock, all represent severe emergency conditions and require immediate hospitalization. Take him right to the emergency room: do not take him to a doctor's office unless that office has equipment for emergency treatment. When taking the athlete to the hospital, keep his feet somewhat elevated, with his head lower than the feet and turned to his side so he can vomit if necessary. Keep him warm but do not apply heat directly to the abdomen.

If there seems to be no emergency situation, the athlete should be observed on the sideline or off the field for pallor and for cold, clammy skin. His respiration should be observed carefully and medical attention should be obtained. Nausea and vomiting may occur with any abdominal injury and not necessarily indicate a severe injury.

Kidney and Bladder Injuries

The kidneys are very subject to injuries in contact sports. This can be seen by the frequency of blood in the urine after violent contact and exertion. If this is accompanied by pain in the lateral flanks, there should be immediate examination.

The presence of blood in the urine does require medication but will usually clear up following a short period of rest in bed. The most common cause of blood in the urine is a blow to the kidney area resulting in contusion, or bruise, of the kidney. Once the blood has cleared from the urine, there should be no residual effects and the athlete can resume normal competition.

The bladder, which holds the urine, is rarely injured during athletic competition. Most athletes have "butterflies in the stomach" before an event and this makes them go to the bathroom before competition and keeps the bladder empty. This is good because it is a good idea to compete with the bladder empty.

Testes Injuries

The male genitalia are much more exposed and naturally more prone to injury in sports than those of the female. Therefore it is necessary that they wear the proper support or jock strap. For sports with some degree of contact, such as football, boxing, wrestling, soccer, and baseball, the jock should have a protective cup with it. Sports such as basketball, tennis, swimming, track and field, and the individual sports, with little or no contact, do require a jock but no cup.

A blow to the testes will cause immediate, severe pain, with swelling, and sometimes discoloration. There may be constitutional symptoms—abdominal pain and faintness. The injury is treated as follows: the athlete should lie on his back, then his knees should be gently bent back to the chest a number of times until the pain subsides. If available and practical, the application of cold packs to the area will reduce swelling.

If the athlete complains of pain after the treatment with the knees, then his testes should be examined by a doctor for any undue bleeding or swelling or the possible testicular displacement into the groin area. When the symptoms subside, there is no reason the athlete cannot continue in competition.

Spine and Back Injuries

The spine and the back are particularly susceptible to contusions, sprains, and strains because of the massive number of muscles. Any injury to these muscles will usually cause severe pain and interference with the athlete's ability to perform. The muscles that we are concerned with are in two major areas of the back; one is the dorsal spine or upper back area, and the other is the lumbar spine or lower back area.

Dorsal Spine: Contusions in the upper back area are common. Usually the result of a blow, both muscle and bone can be affected. It can also result when an athlete falls and the upper back muscles are pressed downward on the spine. There can be swelling, pain, and in some severe cases, muscle spasms. But usually a contusion to the upper back muscles is not a serious injury. The treatment is simple: Immediately apply cold packs to cut down the internal bleeding and swelling. The next day apply heat, massage, and exercise, and continue until the contusion is completely healed.

A sprain of the dorsal spine area sometimes involves the ligaments as well as the muscles. There is swelling and tenderness and sometimes dislocation because of internal bleeding. The injury usually comes about because the back was twisted very hard or "hyperextended." A pile-up on a football field is often the place where the sprain is incurred. Cold packs should be applied to the area immediately, and the athlete should be checked by a physician as soon as possible. In the meantime the athlete should be kept immobilized, if possible. If the physician finds no serious complications, the treatment will consist of heat and exercise during rehabilitation.

A strain of the dorsal area is caused by the back muscles being twisted or jerked past their normal range. It can be very painful. There will be immediate tenderness, swelling, some spasms, and any movement will be painful. The treatment is the same: immediate application of cold packs to the area, and then the next day the application of heat and massaging. Also, there are exercises that will be important in the rehabilitation program. The team physician or trainer will set up an exercise program.

The Lumbar Spine: This area, between the chest cavity and the pelvic girdle, is very movable and the muscles are much more stable. A contusion to the lower back is usually caused by a blow and is treated with cold packs as with the upper area; after the swelling is under control, usually the next day, heat treatments can begin. This is usually not a serious injury and should not prevent the athlete from participation.

A sprain to this area sometimes involves the ligaments as well as the muscles and can be serious and painful. It happens, as with other sprains, when the muscles are stretched or twisted beyond their proper or normal range. It can happen in any sport. Here again, the treatment is cold pack immediately, and heat and exercises after the swelling has gone down.

Because the ligaments might be involved here, there will be pain on movement, swelling, stiffness, and loss of movement. The rehabilitation program requires constant heat, and exercise for the injured area.

A strain to the lumbar spine is usually caused by violent contraction of the spinal muscles in fixed resistance to the back or by over-stretching the muscles. This will produce immediate tenderness over the involved muscles and pain on any motion. There might be some spasms. Immediately apply cold packs to the area and the next day begin heat treatments. The rehabilitation program requires the application of heat and massaging the area.

"When can the athlete return to action?" is the question often asked of the doctor by coaches and parents. Constant application of the heat packs, say about twenty minutes a day, will help speed the healing process, but the athlete can return to some activity as soon as the pain subsides. The activity should be carried out within the limits of pain; in other words, movement and activity are allowed up to the point where there is pain, then stop, continue again until pain, and then stop. Unfortunately, most athletes want to get back into action too soon and many coaches are not afraid to put pressure on a boy to "get in there" before the athlete is ready. This only extends the injury period and can cause other damage.

I strongly recommend against the young athlete wearing a corset or being taped so that he or she can return to active competition. That is okay for professionals who have the strength and pain-threshold to play while hurt. It is not for youngsters, no matter how much playing means to the individual or the team. The athlete's health and proper healing are much more important than one contest. Furthermore, the use of a corset, taping, or other method to get the athlete back into the game sooner is of no help to the child's young body.

Any injury to the back that does not respond to the simple treatments that are discussed above requires medical attention. There is always the possibility of a fracture in any back injury, and if the young athlete has continued pain after the application of the cold packs, heat treatments, exercises, and rest, then medical attention is advised.

Upper Arm Injuries

Because of its exposed position and constant use, the arm has a greater chance for injury than any other part of the anatomy. Anything from a contusion to a fracture can happen. It is important to determine whether the injury is a contusion, a muscle strain, a rupture, or a bone fracture. This can be done by studying the injury. If there is pain on pressure and less pain on movement, then there is probably a bruise or contusion. If there is less pain on pressure and more on motion, then there probably is a strained muscle. If you feel along the arm and there is some deformity or structural change or bulging, this would indicate the possibility of muscle rupture or a fracture of the bone with muscle rupture.

Here are some steps to follow in trying to determine the type and extent of injury to the arm:

1. First look at the arm to see if there is any bleeding, swelling, or discoloration or anything out of the ordinary.

2. Then feel the arm. Run your hand along the arm and apply pressure, gently, to see where the tenderness is and to feel any possible breaks in the bone.

3. Next, have the athlete do the following:

   a. To see if the biceps are injured, place the palm up and bring the arm up so the elbow and forearm are parallel to the ground. Then put the other hand on the palm and press down gently. If there is pain, the biceps are probably injured.

   b. Reverse the process to check on an injury to the triceps. Turn the hand over, put the other hand under the palm, and exert pressure upward. If there is pain, there is possible injury to the triceps.

The treatment depends on the injury. A contusion of the upper arm is treated with the immediate application of cold packs. If there is excessive swelling then you have a fracture. If there is no swelling, then the treatment calls for protection of the injured area with a sling and for heat, massage, and exercise.

If the injury is a strain, it is important that the muscle be rested completely. This can be done with a sling. The athlete must be careful not to use the muscle until the pain is gone. The rehabilitation period should be carried out within the limits of pain around the strained area.

If the injury is a fracture, there will be pain, tenderness in the injured area, and limitation of movement. In extreme cases, the bone may pierce the skin and there will be bleeding. The immediate treatment of a fracture is to immobilize the upper arm by applying splints and wrapping them to the arm with a cloth or tape. If there are no splints available, a rolled-up magazine or newspaper will do. The outside splint should reach from the top of the arm down to the tip of the elbow. The inside splint should be from the top of the arm down to the crook of the elbow. The lower part of the arm should be placed across the body at the waist before the splints are put on. This should be done without causing undue pain, as it will further stabilize the arm during transportation. After the splints are in place and firmly held, a sling should be used to hold the arm. The next step is to get the athlete to the doctor.

Shoulder Injuries_____

Dislocation of the Shoulder: The most common type of shoulder injury to youngsters is dislocation of the shoulder, unaccompanied by any fracture. The injury is very easy to recognize. The athlete will have his arm away from his body and he'll be leaning toward the side. Under no circumstances should the arm be moved toward the body. The arm can be moved away from the body but never toward it. There will be severe pain and possible tissue damage.

What has happened is that there has been a complete separation of the upper arm bone from where it joins the shoulder. It can result from a blow to the shoulder, a fall, or a twisting of the arm.

When there is a dislocation, cold can be applied to the shoulder to reduce the swelling, but the athlete should be taken to a doctor right away. There should be no manipulation of the shoulder because of the potential for further damage.

Broken Collarbone: The clavicle is the bone that sits above the chest. It is the major supporting structure for the shoulder and is frequently broken in sports. Because of the angular position, it is particularly prone to fracture in young athletes. Also, there is little protection for the clavicle because there is only a small layer of skin over the area and there is no fat or muscle to help protect it.

Sometimes there is little indication that there has been a fracture. A "green-stick fracture," an incomplete break of the bone, may not cause a great deal of discomfort and so may go unnoticed. But pain can be detected by tapping on the bone. If there is pain, an X ray is necessary.

Shoulder Strains: Strains about the shoulder are quite common. The best treatment is rest and heat applications. A direct blow to the shoulder will sometimes produce a severe numbing pain into the arm that will make the arm feel useless. But this simple bruise will clear up quickly and the use of the arm and the feeling in it will return quickly. There is no permanent damage. What has happened is that the blow hit the nerve that passes through the shoulder to the arm, and the bruising of that nerve has caused the numbness.

Rest, with the use of a sling for 24 to 28 hours, may be all the treatment necessary. The sling should always support the arm at just a little more than 90 degrees so that the weight of the arm is taken off the shoulder cup.

Elbow Injuries_____

As might be expected, a bruise or contusion is a common injury to the elbow. Falling on the flexed elbow crushes the skin against the hard underlying bone and results in contusion, abrasion, or at times laceration. This area is relatively insensible to pain, and therefore the injury is at times overlooked; however, one should be mindful of the injury and treat it appropriately. The wound should be kept clean and an antibiotic dressing applied to any open areas. The best treatment for this type of injury is prevention.

Because of the frequent exposure of the elbow to this type of injury, it is advisable that an elastic elbow pad be worn whenever there's a possibility of injury. It is important that the elbow pad be comfortable, fit snugly, yet not be too tight to interfere with motion and/or circulation. It should not be constrictive, but should be well-positioned to allow the athlete freedom to compete without the worry of injury to the elbow.

The "Crazy Bone": A direct blow over the inner aspect of the elbow may produce a sudden severe pain with a shocking sensation extending down the hand to the fourth and fifth fingers. There may even be some persistent numbness and weakness and inability to move these fingers. This injury to the so-called "crazy bone" should really be called an injury to the crazy nerve: the ulnar nerve has been compressed between the blow and the underlying bone. The symptoms are usually very transient and will disappear within a few moments. Although it frequently feels better to rub or massage the area, this is not advisable, particularly at the point of injury. If there is some bleeding or bruising, then the application of cold packs for fifteen or twenty minutes will limit the swelling, but for the most part, if the hand and elbow are kept at rest, the symptoms will clear and the athlete can resume participation. Should the pain persist along the route of the nerve, a more serious injury may be indicated. If, after the early symptoms of numbness and pain wear off, there is still disability or loss of muscle function, there may be nerve damage. There may also be an increase in skin sensitivity or numbness along with the weakness. That would indicate the need for further medical examination.

Elbow Strains: Frequently, there are strains about the elbow because of the extremely powerful force that is required in most sports. The powerful muscles of the upper arm—the triceps and the biceps—exert their action through the flection and extension of the elbow joint. This powerful force is in turn exerted on the elbow tendons and ligaments, sometimes causing injury. The most common strains produced are epicondylitis or "tennis elbow," and "epiphyseal" or "Little League elbow."

Tennis Elbow: Tennis elbow results from a variety of inflammations in and around the elbow joint. It is caused by the frequent strenuous motion of the elbow while the wrist and hand are held in a firm, fixed position. In the tennis stroke and the golf swing, the player holds the wrist and hand firm while trying to generate a tremendous speed through the elbow and forearm area. The pain and discomfort often do not appear while participating but occur afterwards.

There are a great number of causes of this type of inflammation and it may be advisable to see an orthopedic surgeon who is involved in sports medicine to have proper treatment. One method of relief that I often recommend is to rest the hand, wrist, and elbow daily for a long period of time. This can be done by wrapping or strapping the forearm to the chest at night and leaving it in this position through the sleeping hours. The reason for limiting the use of the wrist is that rotation of the wrist also affects the elbow and can cause pain and further inflammation.

Sometimes local heat applied to the elbow area will provide relief. Allow hot water to run over the elbow for twenty minutes and then rest the arm.

Remember that activity will cause the symptoms to recur, and that is why rest of the arm and elbow is so important. With the treatment of hot water and the rest period at night, the symptoms can be controlled, and with proper management by the athlete, participation need not be interfered with.

Little League Elbow: The so-called "Little League elbow" or "pitcher's elbow" is a strain placed upon the immature epiphysis, that is, the growing end of the bone. This strain comes from the violent motion the elbow is subjected to when throwing. The strain can be accentuated when the motion requires a snapping action, such as that needed for a curve ball. Pain in and around the elbow is an indication for prompt medical attention, and further throwing should be stopped.

Unfortunately, after the athlete has stopped throwing, the symptoms sometimes disappear and the elbow will feel normal. Nevertheless, the pain is a signal that there is inflammation and it is an indication for observation by a doctor. X rays at times will show the early beginnings of a fracture or dislocation of the epiphyseal plate or growing end of the bone.

The Little League organization is aware of the damage done to the young throwing arms of boys and girls and has done a great deal to limit the innings one pitcher can pitch. But I feel that the throwing motions they must use in the game can be damaging to the immature player. It may seem drastic to have the youngster sit out a year while the bones mature, but the potential hazard of permanent injury to the elbow—and maybe of an injury severe enough to require surgical correction—calls for strict supervision of young baseball players. Care of the throwing arm and prevention by limited activity in this early age group is mandatory.

Because youngsters at the Little League age level vary so greatly in physiological development, it is impossible to have a fixed age limitation on when they can pitch. But, I recommend that boys and girls from ages 8 to 10 not pitch more than one inning and not be allowed to throw curves. I'm also against the older boys throwing curve balls because their bones are also still growing and the curve is too much of an unnatural motion and puts too great a strain on the pitching arm.

The elbow joint is very complex. Any strain or severe injury like a fracture should be treated by a doctor, and the athlete should not be allowed to return to competition until the elbow is completely healed. This means that the athlete should have a free range of motion with the elbow without any pain before he or she is allowed to participate in any kind of activity.

Wrist and Forearm Injuries

Because of their prominence and their continual use in competition, the wrist and forearm are subject to contusions, sprains, fractures, and dislocations.

A contusion of the wrist or forearm is treated with cold packs and then protected with proper padding so that the contusion will not be too painful if hit again in play. There should be no heat treatment for this injury.

A wrist sprain, caused by the stretching of the ligaments, tendons, and tissue surrounding the wrist joint, often results when the athlete puts his hand out in front to break a fall and the wrist bends back too violently. It can also be caused by hard twisting of the wrist. The treatment depends on the extent of the sprain. If the athlete cannot move his hand in an upward movement toward the body, bending it at the joint, then the sprain is very severe; it should be put in a splint and the athlete should be taken for X rays. A moderate sprain is treated by cold packs and a compression bandage to the area, and the next day, after the swelling goes down, heat treatments.

The bones of the wrist and forearm are subject to fracture and this often happens. In the young athlete, the "green-stick" fracture is very common; the growing bone or epiphysis needs only be slightly displaced. The so-called sprained wrist is actually a fracture or partial dislocation of the epiphyseal plate. If there is any gross deformity and/or angulation through the wrist and forearm area, it is highly possible that there is a fracture, and X rays and medical treatment are required

We have all seen the professional athlete on television who continues to compete even with a fiber glass or molded cast on the wrist and forearm. For youngsters, this is out. There is still growth potential in that arm, and allowing the youngster to participate with a cast when there has not been a complete healing of the fracture exposes him or her to potential damage such as shortening of the arm or permanent angulation of the wrist or forearm. A complete recovery of the wrist and forearm is necessary before any youngster is allowed to participate.

The intelligent athlete will not let a fracture of the wrist or forearm keep him from taking advantage of the injury. When I broke my right wrist, I learned to use my left hand better, and that gave me more than one shot. As a right-hander, I had taken all my basketball shots with the right hand. Practicing with my left hand, I developed it to the extent that later in professional basketball my left-handed hook shot was better than my right-handed shot. Bob Cousy as a young man hurt his right wrist and had to practice his dribbling with his left hand. He became the greatest ball handler the game of basketball has ever known.

The wrist can also suffer a dislocation. Usually one of the arm bones will be displaced from its position at the wrist bone. The symptoms are swelling, pain, loss of movement, and probably muscle spasms. The treatment is the immediate application of a splint. Then take the youngster to the doctor. There probably is a fracture associated with the dislocation.

Sometimes persistent stress to the wrist can cause a wrist ganglion to form. This is a condition in which the tendon sheath herniates and the area becomes filled with a fluid that causes a bulge on the wrist. To remove the ganglion, surgery is required, but sometimes a doctor can drain off the fluid with a needle.

Hand Injuries_____

Injuries to the hand can be quite common in sports. The hand can suffer abrasions, contusions, cuts, ruptured blood vessels, fractures, and "stone bruises."

Contusions of the hand are particularly common because of the exposure of the hand. There will be rapid swelling in the hand and pain. A contusion is treated immediately either with cold packs or by placing the hand in a bucket of ice. After the swelling goes down, apply heat. Any contusion of the hand requires full examination. If there is an underlying fracture of one of the bones in the hand, this can usually be detected by feeling along the top of the hand for local points of tenderness and deformity in the area. If there are any signs of a fracture, then an X ray and medical attention are needed.

If there is any break of the skin resulting from an injury, then the early treatment consists of a thorough cleansing of the wound. Use soap and plenty of water, and after the wound is cleaned, apply a good antibiotic ointment. Next, a bandage should be put over the area, snug but bulky enough to protect the cut from further injury. The hand may remain swollen for a little while, but if there is any sign of redness or warmth around the cut area, a secondary infection might be taking place and medical attention is necessary.

The palm of the hand is subject to contusions and cuts. A contusion here is known as a "stone bruise" and can be very painful. It is not a serious injury, but it will limit the athlete because he will have a hard time gripping a bat or racket. However, the area can be protected with a foam sponge over the contusion and the athlete may continue to play.

A fracture of the bones of the hand (there are five bones) will cause swelling, loss of movement, and deformity. The most common fracture is just behind the knuckle resulting from a punch. This injury requires the splinting of the hand. Place some object like a roll of tape in the athlete's palm, have him hold it with his fingers, and then wrap the entire hand, starting at the wrist. Then take him to be X-rayed; the doctor will take over from there.

Finger and Thumb Injuries

Because of their exposed position, the fingers and thumb are often subject to contusions, fractures, cuts, dislocations, and sprains. The immediate observation of the symptoms of the injury and the limits of motion will indicate the severity of the injury.

The thumb, because of its position and the type of joints it has, is particularly prone to sprain, dislocation, and even fracture. A mild sprain of the large joint is very common.

With a sprain, there will be pain about the joint and tenderness to pressure in the area, and the pain will continue as long as there is continued motion of the joint. Within a few hours after the injury, there will be swelling and pain. The sprain can be treated by having the athlete immerse his finger or thumb into ice water and keep it there for about thirty minutes. After the ice treatment, a splint should be applied for one or two days. After that, apply heat around the sprained area. When the athlete returns to play, tape the sprained finger to an uninjured one. If it is the thumb, wrap it with an adhesive support to prevent further overstretching.

The fingers and the thumb also can be dislocated very easily in sports. The dislocation can involve any of the joints of the fingers or thumb. There will be pain, swelling, loss of movement or function, and deformity. It is usually caused when the end of the finger or thumb is hit or is jammed against an object, such as a baseball that the player is trying to catch.

You must *never* try to fix a dislocation by pulling the end of the dislocated finger or thumb. A sudden yanking motion may actually chip or fracture the edges of the bones and cause more damage. It should be treated by a trained individual. Usually, it will be about ten days after a dislocation before the young athlete can begin participation—but only with the doctor's approval.

Taping the thumb: The thumb may be taped at least two ways depending on the severity of the injury.

Figure 1 shows how to tape the thumb for restriction of its movement in all directions. Apply one-inch tape around the wrist, under the thumb, and back over the wrist. Continue this procedure until you have immobilized the thumb.

Figure 2 shows how to tape the thumb to keep it from being hyperextended. Take one-inch tape and form a closed loop that rests on the first joint of the thumb and the base of the forefinger. Then tape the loop in its center so that it will fit snugly against the forefinger and thumb. This will hold the thumb close to the hand.

Fig. 1   Fig. 2

A fracture of the finger or thumb can vary from a hairline fracture to a complete break. To find out if there is a fracture, gently pull (don't yank) the thumb or finger and move it from side to side as you feel along the finger for some deformity. Gently tap along the bone or the tip and feel for the break or splinter. If there is a fracture, splint the finger or thumb, just as you would a sprain, and take the athlete to the doctor. The doctor will tell you what the rehabilitation program will be and how long it will be before the player can return to action.

Baseball players are particularly prone to what is called a "mallet finger." Often their fingers are hit on the end by a batted or thrown ball. Catchers are very prone to this injury. It usually is in the first joint of the finger and the tendon is pulled away from the bone. The treatment here is to see the doctor because this is a dislocation. Youngsters get these injuries because they do not keep their bare fingers away from the glove until the ball hits the glove. There is no easy treatment or cure except prevention, and that comes with experience. However, do not neglect the injury. Mallet fingers are the result of permanent damage to the extension of the distal joint and should be cared for immediately.

Hip Injuries

The hip area is subjected to great stress, and consequently there can be injuries to this area. The hip is a joint that is made up of the long bone of the leg, the femur, that fits like a ball bearing into the socket of the pelvis or hip bone. The area is heavily muscled and protected. There are strong ligaments and muscles that hold the hip together, and even though the area may suffer from bruises or contusions, it is seldom seriously hurt by fractures or dislocations.

One of the most painful injuries in sports results when there is a heavy blow to the top of the hip bone. When you hear sportscasters mention that someone is suffering from a "hip-pointer," this is the area that they are referring to. This is a common injury, especially in sports that entail aggressive attitudes and hard contact, such as football. There is little that can be done to treat an injury to the top of the hip. Ice packs should be applied to the bruised area to keep down the internal bleeding and the swelling. The next day, heat can be applied. The injured area should be protected by a pad or rubber doughnut placed over it and taped to the body. Contact with the area will usually cause severe pain, and therefore I recommend that contact be avoided until the pointer heals.

Very seldom will the hip dislocate. If the athlete falls very hard or is hit in such a way that the ball joint of the femur leaves the socket of the pelvis, immediate medical attention is called for. The athlete should not be allowed to move. A stretcher should be brought out to the field and the athlete put on it and taken to the hospital. No one should try to relocate the hip.

Because there are so many muscles and ligaments in the hip area, even though they are quite strong, there is the possibility that a muscle can be strained. The treatment is similar to that of any other strain: apply cold packs to the injured area, then begin heat treatments the next day. Continue the heat and moderate exercise until the sprain heals. Sometimes, for a severe strain, bed rest is needed; usually this is not necessary.

Hip sprains are usually the result of hard twisting of the hip area with the legs implanted on the ground; they can also be caused by slipping on a wet floor or in a shower. Treatment consists of cold packs to strained area, then heat treatments the next day; heat and moderate exercise daily until healed.

Groin Injuries

Injury to the groin area is quite common. It can happen in most sports and is the result of the thigh's being pulled too far away from the body. Track and field athletes often suffer this injury. The treatment is similar to that of any other muscle injury, but because of its location and the functions of the groin area, complete rest and treatment are necessary before the athlete can return to action. This is another area where the early return to action only causes the injury to linger longer.

When there is an injury in the groin, cold compresses should be applied to the area for fifteen to twenty minutes. Then the area should be wrapped with a figure-eight type of wrapping. To do this start the elastic wrap at the groin area, wrap around the waist, then come back to the groin area and repeat. The next day, begin heat and massage and keep the area wrapped. Also begin passive exercises up to the beginning of pain. Do not try to go past the pain. It does no good and further injures the groin muscles.

The best prevention for groin injuries is proper warm-up and stretching exercises.

Thigh Injuries
The thigh area contains powerful muscles and the longest bone in the body, the femur. The thigh also suffers from contusions at a better than average pace because in contact sports the thigh often bears the brunt of the contact. The symptoms of a contusion in the thigh area are often much less local than in other areas. Usually the athlete will not be disabled by the injury and can continue to play. But after the contest, he will complain of soreness and aching and, later, stiffness in the thigh. Sometimes there will be muscle spasm in the area.

The treatment is similar for this area as for any large contusion. Application of cold compresses and a compression bandage should be kept on for twenty-four hours. Also, motion, including walking, should be limited during this period because there is internal bleeding and walking will only increase the bleeding. After the ice, the heat treatments begin along with exercise. There is no place for massage here and there should be no forceable stretching of the muscle. The so-called "working it out" or rubbing it out simply increases the damage to the muscle.

Sometimes the thigh bone will fracture. This is usually the result of a kick, a fall from a great height, or a pile-up in football. When it happens, the shaft of the femur will cause injury internally—there will be bleeding, deformity, great pain, and loss of motion, and the foot on the injured leg will turn in. As with any fracture, immediately apply a splint and get the athlete to the hospital. The doctor will take over from there. If there is no material to make a splint, tie the broken leg to the good leg and put the athlete on the stretcher. Shock is possible here, so make the injured player as comfortable and warm as possible.

of direction in basketball; a quick movement made when the athlete has not warmed up properly; even lack of salt in the diet can cause muscle strains in this area. But the treatment to the area is the same: cold compresses on the injured area, wrapping, and then the next day, heat treatments and exercises. Prevention of the strain can come from proper conditioning, adequate warm-up time, good diet that includes salt, and making sure that stretching exercises are done before active participation.

Knee Injuries

From the standpoint of injury, the knee is probably the most vulnerable point of the body. It is the area that holds the body weight, and it is where the power of the body's movement is transferred to the muscles of the upper leg and locomotion begins. Yet the knee does not look like it was designed for sports, especially contact sports.

The knee, like the hip, is a hinge joint—the femur from the upper leg joins with the tibia, the largest bone in the lower leg. Unlike the hip, the knee does not have powerful muscles and tendons to protect it. However, the knee does have very strong ligaments to stabilize it. Those ligaments are: front (patellar), back (popliteal), the outside (lateral), and the inside (medial). The place where the femur meets the tibia is cushioned by cartilage. The tendons from the upper leg muscles also help stabilize the knee and give it strength. The tendons from the thigh muscles are the quadriceps (front) and the hamstrings (back); from the calf muscles in the lower leg come the gastrocnemius and soleus.

There is fluid in the knee joint which helps lubricate the joint. It is contained in the knee capsules. Any injury to the knee may involve any of the tendons, ligaments, and bones in that area.

A contusion to the knee should be treated like a contusion to any other part of the body. However, you must *first* rule out any internal damage. The contusion will cause local swelling and some tenderness, and there may be some bleeding of the outside skin area or some discoloration. The treatment is to apply cold packs and then wrap the knee. Then the next day, heat can be applied. Make sure that there are no other findings that might indicate a more serious injury.

A knee sprain is caused by an abnormal motion of the knee. The motion can be in any direction: adduction or abduction (which are side-to-side), overextension, internal or external rotation, and/or forward or backward displacement can cause the ligaments to strain. The classical type of knee injury occurs in football when the foot is fixed into the ground by the player's cleats, the thigh rotates inward and the leg outward. The knee is forced inward toward the opposite leg, the stress is on the inside (medial) ligaments, and they tear. In football, this injury is often caused by an illegal block, like a clipping block or a crack-back block. Many a fine player has had his career cut short by this kind of injury.

In a mild ligament sprain, there will be tenderness, pain on active use, local swelling, and possibly some pain when the knee is moved in the direction of the injury. In a mild sprain, there will be no external bleeding, and little internal bleeding. For the first twenty-four hours, the knee should be packed with ice with a pressure bandage to minimize the degree of swelling. Frequently with a mild sprain, wrapping the knee will allow the athlete to resume activity. In a young athlete, there is no need for a knee brace. An elastic knee wrap may give the feeling of warmth and security but it will not increase the stability of the knee.

With a severe sprain, the symptoms will be the same as with the mild, but the degree of pain and swelling will be greater. There will be extreme tenderness at the point of the injury and marked swelling of the joint. Movement will produce immediate pain. Any degree of locking of the knee indicates internal damage, most likely involving the cartilages, and in most cases this will require surgery. Therefore, with a severe sprain, the doctor must be brought in immediately. To relieve some of the discomfort while taking the player to the doctor, wrap the knee in ice packs and use an elastic bandage. Keep the leg straight and raised above the head.

It is very important to give the doctor factual information on how the injury took place. This will greatly assist him in the examination. Here are some points to remember:

1. Was the player immediately disabled or was he able to keep playing?
2. Did the player think he had a serious injury?
3. Did he leave the field on his own power or was he carried?
4. Was he in extreme pain or was it milder?
5. What was the position of the leg at the time of the impact and what was the direction of the force that hit the knee?

The earlier the knee can be examined by competent medical people who understand knee injuries, the easier the diagnosis will be.

When there is a severe sprain to the knee, the athlete will be laid up for some time. Before he begins any participation after the ligaments have been healed, a definitive rehabilitation program of exercise is necessary to return the quadriceps and hamstring muscles to their former strength. I cannot stress too strongly the importance of reestablishing the strength of these muscles. No competitive athletics are to be allowed until the muscles have returned to their normal size and strength and until the athlete has the full range of motion with the knee. A program of gradual exercises carried out on a regular basis with dedication by the youngster is absolutely necessary to reestablish the complete working function of the knee.

Dislocation of the kneecap or patella: In sports, the dislocation of the kneecap or patella is very rare. It can happen, however, with a very hard blow to the area. Ordinarily, the patella will simply snap off and snap right back into place. We describe this as "the knee gave way." In most cases, there is so little damage that the athlete can continue to play.

If there is a dislocation, it can be noted by putting the fingers around the patella to see if it is out of place. Also, attempting to move it from side to side will produce pain and that tells you the patella is dislocated. Take the athlete to the doctor right away. Pack the knee in ice and do not attempt to straighten out the leg or have the athlete walk on that leg. With the leg held still and immobile, there will be some relief from the pain. Surgery will be required and the rehabilitation program for strengthening the hamstring and quadriceps muscles should begin after surgery. The doctor will set up the program.

Water on the Knee: There is no such thing as water on the knee. The excess fluid is not water, but excessive joint fluid or blood within the knee capsule. It is caused by an inflammation of the membrane that covers the bones. Severe blows to the knee joint can cause this inflammation. Usually, all that is necessary to treat the condition is to apply cold packs to the knee, wrap it, and rest the leg, usually in a raised position. Rest and heat are the next part of the treatment and there are to be no athletics until the condition disappears. If it continues after a few days and there is pain in the area, a doctor should be consulted.

Osgood-Schlatter Disease: This is not a disease, nor directly related to athletics, but it does occur in young people. There is swelling and tenderness over the tibia or calf bone, just below the attachment of the kneecap. The cause is usually related to the frequent minor injuries youngsters receive from falling and bumping the knee repeatedly. The best treatment is rest and a reduction in the amount of physical activity. Sometimes crutches will be necessary if the pain is too severe. Again, treatment with cold packs helps, and then heat can be applied the next day.

The length of time physical activity has to be curtailed will depend upon the degree of involvement, which is in turn related to how soon the condition is recognized. Therefore, painful, persistent swelling requires attention. Because the degree of swelling in the Osgood-Schlatter disease is great, the youngster should be reassured that the lump is not a tumor and is a self-limiting condition. As the youngster gets older, the bone in the lower leg will fuse with the growing end so that complete healing will take place.

Lower Leg Injuries

The lower leg is extremely vulnerable to injuries in sports and everyday activity. In most cases, the injuries are not serious, and even a contusion that causes the leg to develop a bruise will usually not cause the athlete to stop playing.

The bones of the lower leg are the tibia, sometimes called the shinbone, and the fibula or small bone. The muscles in the lower leg are the calf muscle and the front leg muscles. The calf muscles are subject to muscle spasms whenever there is a contusion to the lower leg.

A contusion can be caused by a hard hit on the leg, either from a kick, a fall, a blow, or running into some object. The treatment for a contusion, again, is cold compresses, a compression or stretch bandage to the area, and, if it is a serious contusion, rest. The next day, the heat treatment can begin and the athlete should exercise the calf muscles.

It is interesting to note that most fractures to the lower leg affect the fibula, not the tibia. Sometimes the fracture to the fibula is difficult to detect because it is not a weight-bearing bone and the fracture will not be immediately noticed. The athlete will continue to play and only after the excitement of the event is over will he notice the pain. Of course, when there is a fracture to the tibia, he'll know right away because of the pain and the fact that he can't bear weight. Fractures to either bone will cause pain, swelling, and deformity, but these will be less noticeable in the fracture of the fibula than of the tibia.

A fracture, of course, is to be treated by a doctor. To help the athlete get to the doctor, first apply a splint to both sides of the leg, from the knee down to the ankle, wrap the splint with tape or a cloth, carry the athlete to the car, and take him to the emergency section of the hospital.

Normally, the calf muscle is affected by strain. Strain can result when the muscle is not properly warmed up and the athlete puts too much force on it. It can result when the muscle is pushed beyond its normal range of motion by a sudden movement or by a severe blow. The application of cold packs and compression bandages is required immediately. And most important, when there is a strain to the calf muscle, the athlete should never try to "walk it out" or go back into action. After the cold packs and bandage have been applied, have the athlete rest on the bench with his leg raised, or if lying down, with a pillow under the leg. The next day, begin heat and exercise. I do not feel that a massage is needed here; that might aggravate the problem.

A simple exercise to help rehabilitate the calf muscle is to have the athlete sit on a table with the foot of the injured leg extended about six inches over the edge of the table so that the heel is parallel to the floor and the foot at 90 degrees to the leg. Then grip the foot, with one hand at the heel and the other against the bottom of the foot at the toes, and have the athlete push against the hand with the ball of his foot. Do this as many times as he can manage. This allows for controlled exercise and can be carried out without pain and little chance of aggravating the injury.

Shin Splints: This is inflammation of the tibial and toe extensor muscles. It is one of the most painful injuries in sports. It is also one of the most difficult injuries to diagnose and to prevent. What happens is that the lower front of the leg will feel like it is on fire and will be very tender. When you run your hand down the outside of the leg, the shinbone will feel as though it has sandpaper on it. Shin splints are usually the result of an athlete's not being conditioned properly for strenuous exercise. They can also come from an athlete's running too long on his toes, especially on hard surfaces. Weak or fallen arches will aggravate shin splints.

The best treatment is rest and heat. If the athlete wants to play, apply hot towels to the leg for twenty minutes. He should never play if the pain is too intense. (See conditioning exercises.)

Ankle Injuries

Like the hip and the knee, the ankle is a hinge joint. It is held together by powerful ligaments and stabilized by those ligaments as well as being supported by the tendons of the calf muscles and the front leg muscles, which form a cup for the ankle. The medial (inner) ligament is extremely broad and strong. This medial ligament also supports the arch. The anterior (front) part of the lateral (outside) ligament is the one that is most often injured. The two leg bones, the tibia and fibula, are bound together by the anterior and posterior (back) tibiofibular ligaments.

An ankle can be dislocated, fractured, or sprained. To examine an ankle injury, remove the shoe and sock if that can be done without pain. Then check for obvious deformity, localized tenderness, or limitation of normal movement. First hold the foot at a 90-degree angle to the leg, heel parallel to the ground. The left hand holds the heel of the foot, the right fingers on the toes. Have the athlete push downward against the hand holding the foot and upward against the fingers holding the toes. This will test for any injuries to the top or bottom of the foot. Next, holding the foot the same way, have the athlete try to turn the foot inward and pull upward, in order to test for injuries to the outside of the foot. Then reverse the process: to test for any injuries to the inside of the ankle, have him turn his foot outward and pull upward.

If the athlete can do these motions without pain, then the wrapping of the ankle in a simple figure-eight wrap for support will often be enough to allow him to return to the action and play at full effort without pain.

The figure-eight ankle wrap can also be used to care for an injured ankle while it is healing. It gives support to the ankle and allows the healing athlete almost free movement in normal activities. It is not designed to protect an injured ankle during competition, however. Also the wrap should not be worn while sleeping. These are the steps:

1. The foot should be held in a perpendicular position. Have the athlete sit on a table or bed with the foot hanging off the end, heel toward the floor, toes pointed up.

2. If the injury is to the outside of the ankle, start on the inside of the ankle with the wrap, bring the wrap under the heel, up the other side and across the top of the ankle. Repeat about three times, making sure that the wrap is not too tight.

3. If the injury is to the inside of the ankle, start on the outside and repeat as above. The whole technique is a simple "rolling" of the wrap around the ankle.

4. After you have completed the wrap, hold it fast with tape or some type of small clamp. Also make sure the wrap is smooth so the skin will not be pinched.

If there is still some swelling after the wrap is taken off at night, elevate the foot by placing it on a pillow at the foot of the bed.

Usually a dislocation of the ankle is obvious. There is severe pain, loss of movement, and disability. Fortunately, it takes a great deal of force to dislocate an ankle. If it happens, it is usually the result of severe twisting, a very hard blow, overextension, falling and extending the foot to break the fall, or stepping in a hole. Treatment of a dislocation is similar to that of other serious injuries. Apply cold packs to the ankle, splint, and wrap with tape or some cloth, then take the athlete to the doctor. He'll handle the treatment and recommend the proper rehabilitation program.

When there are swelling, local tenderness, limitation of motion, and muscle spasms, the ankle should be examined for possible fracture. Any harsh, grating sensation or abnormal sounds when the ankle joint is put through the tests calls for immediate immobilization of the joint, medical attention, and X rays. A fracture to the ankle can be caused by a severe blow to the area, a hard twist, falling or tripping, or having the exposed ankle fallen on in a pile-up. This frequently happens in football. If a fracture is suspected then the treatment is to apply a splint to both sides of the ankle, wrap with tape or a bandage, and get the athlete to the hospital.

An ankle sprain is one of the most common injuries to the young athlete. There are a wide variety of sprains ranging from the mild or partial sprain that does not interfere with participation down to the complete tearing of one or more of the ligaments around the ankle. The most common injury is on the ouside of the ankle and usually is the result of a twisting or turning motion that caused the ankle to turn inward, straining the outside (lateral) ligament. The degree of injury will depend on how long and how far the ligaments were stretched. The degree of pain, swelling, tenderness, and lack of motion will indicate the severity of the injury.

An ankle sprain should be immediately treated with cold. Put the foot into an ice bucket or put ice packs or bags around the ankle. Then wrap the ankle in an elastic wrap and keep it elevated until proper medical people arrive. Make sure that there are no clothes or tape restricting circulation.

Following the ankle injury, the sprain must be allowed to heal completely. The athlete must keep his weight off the ankle until it is free of pain. Using crutches for several days might shorten the recovery period. However, walking with a limp to keep weight off the injured ankle should not be allowed. While the swelling persists, keep the ankle in a neutral

Basketweave wrap

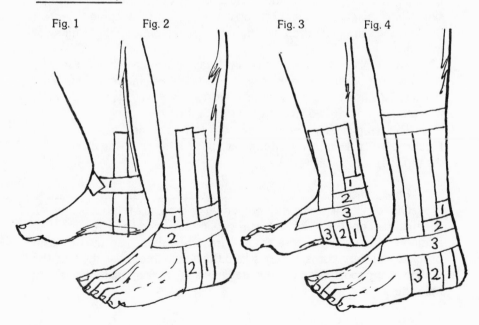

Fig. 1   Fig. 2   Fig. 3   Fig. 4

position. Treatment at home can be the simple use of the bathtub: allowing the ankle to soak in warm water. While it is soaking, test the ankle by putting it through a full range of motions. However, don't force the ankle against pain when moving it around. When the athlete feels the pain is gone and wants to begin exercising again, the ankle should be protected by taping and should remain that way throughout the rest of the season. It usually takes about six months before a sprained ankle is completely healed, so the taping is necessary when the athlete is exercising or running. We show two methods of taping the ankle. One is the basketweave and the other is the Louisiana wrap.

If there is a lateral sprain of the ankle, it should be taped with a basketweave type of wrap, as follows:

1. Have the athlete hold the foot perpendicular to the floor with a slight outward rotation if the injury is to the outside of the ankle. Reverse the procedure if the injury is to the inside.
2. Place tape, six to eight inches long, circled above the ankle as an anchor (see Figure 1).
3. Start the first piece of tape at anchor on the side opposite the injury, pull it around the heel and up the opposite side. Put the next strip of tape just at the ankle bone. (See Figure 2.)
4. Repeat moves 2 and 3 until the ankle is encased (Figures 3 and 4).

Before taping, shave the leg and apply a coating of benzoin called "toughskin." If it is available, use a pro-wrap at the ankle before taping to protect the hair and skin. Tape should be tight but not uncomfortable, binding, or irritating.

The application of the Louisiana wrap is over a sock illustrated by the drawings. Some trainers call it the heel-lock method. Figures 5 through 12 illustrate the application. Figures 7, 8, 9, 10, 11, and 12 can be repeated to provide two lifts on each side of the heel.

The wrap is then spiraled up over the ankle as illustrated in Figures 13–15. Two pieces of tape are used to secure, one around the top (14) and one across the heel (15).

Foot Injuries

Obviously, the foot gets a great deal of exposure to possible injury. It can be stepped on, kicked, cut, broken, scraped, and sprained. In addition to contusions, sprains, and fractures, there can also be skin problems, blisters, corns, bunions, and the like. Without healthy feet, the athlete in any sport is at a disadvantage; yet, the care of the foot gets very little attention.

Louisiana wrap

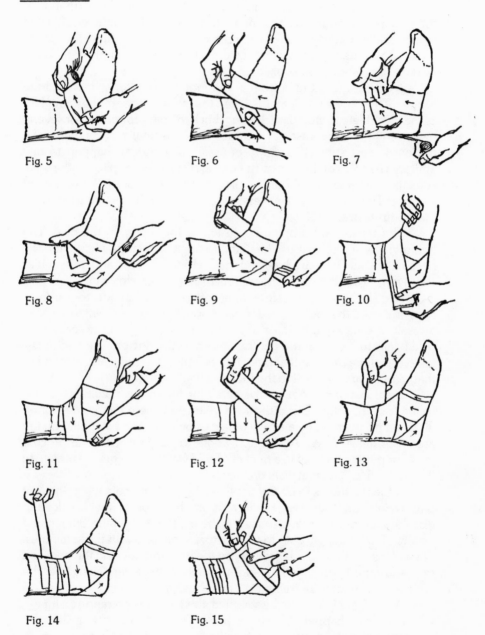

Fig. 5

Fig. 6

Fig. 7

Fig. 8

Fig. 9

Fig. 10

Fig. 11

Fig. 12

Fig. 13

Fig. 14

Fig. 15

Most contusions to the foot come to the top of the foot. Because of the thin skin covering and the lack of muscles, the tendons, blood vessels, and nerves on top of the foot are prone to injury. A hard blow to the top of the foot can cause pain, swelling, internal bleeding, irritation to the underlying tendons, and limitation of motion. Fortunately, after the pain subsides, participation usually can continue. When there is a severe contusion to the top of the foot, cold packs should be applied; then the next day heat should be applied.

A contusion to the bottom of the foot is characterized as a "stone bruise." This can be very painful. Often the injury is not serious enough to cause the athlete to stop participating, but if the pain continues for several days, treatment is necessary. Trackmen and basketball players seem to be the ones most subject to stone bruises, but they can happen to any athlete. The soles of the feet must be treated and heat applied to the area. A foam or sponge sole should be placed in the shoe or on the bottom of the foot. This foam sole is necessary to distribute the weight away from the contused area.

The most handicapping contusion to the foot is in the heel. The treatment here is also to use heat and to apply a foam pad fitted into the heel of the shoe. In fact, a heel pad should be worn in the athlete's regular shoes as well as his athletic shoes, until the condition clears up.

A dislocation to the foot most often occurs in the toe area. It happens when the toe is forced from its normal socket or joint, usually as a result of tripping, falling, or of someone's stepping on the toe. Apply cold packs to the area and get the athlete to the doctor. The doctor will take care of the treatment and the rehabilitation program, and most often that will simply mean rest to the foot and heat treatments.

Fractures of the foot involve either the toes or the metatarsal bones in the foot, directly behind the toes. A fracture here can come from a direct hit on the area by a heavy object or by someone's stepping on the area with heavy force. Again, apply cold to the foot, either using cold packs or putting the foot in a bucket of cold water. Then get the athlete to the doctor. Don't let him walk on the foot.

If the fracture is to one of the toes, there will be pain when the foot puts weight on the area, tenderness at the spot of the break, and discoloration of the area. Usually it is the big toe that is hurt, but it could be any of them. Apply cold to the fractured toe for about thirty minutes. Then place a pad or bandage between the fractured toe and the one next to it and tape them together—not too tightly, however. Then take the athlete to the doctor for treatment and rehabilitation.

Although the foot can be sprained, this is not too common an injury. When it does happen it usually takes place in an area called the "longitudinal arch," the main arch of the foot which runs from the back of the toes to the heel. A sprain here is caused by an overextension of the ligaments, usually the result of heavy stress or pressure on the area. When the arch is strained, apply cold packs and a compression bandage around it. Rehabilitation of the arch begins the second day with daily applications of heat and adequate support of the arch with tape.

When the toes are sprained, there will be pain, especially if it is the big toe. The athlete will probably be unable to rise up on his toes. This sprain can occur when the toe is stubbed or overstretched. Soak the toe, or toes, in cold water for at least a half hour and tape to the adjacent toes. Rehabilitate by soaking in warm water, and when the athlete is going to play, tape the toes together.

The traverse arch is the area under the ball of the foot. Sprains here are usually the result of constant play on hard surfaces. Treat with heat and use metatarsal pads, placing the pad just behind the middle toes and taping it to the arch.

The Achilles Tendon: The Achilles tendon is that tendon that holds the calf muscle to the heel bone. An injury to the Achilles tendon can be very serious. Many athletic careers have been cut short by an injury to this tendon. However, this type of injury is very rare in the young athlete. When the Achilles tendon is torn away from the bone, great pain and swelling take place and surgical repair is necessary. If there is a strain to the tendon, treat with cold packs and then put a pad in the heel of the shoe.

Summary

We have now covered the entire body, from head to toe. The most important points are that injuries do happen, that most of the time the injury will be minor, and that medical supervision should always be sought whenever there is doubt about the severity of an injury.

The coordination and cooperation among the parents, their youngsters, the coaches, and the schools or recreation organizations are vital to the protection of the young athlete. The parent has the responsibility and the right to demand that the children have the best in medical assistance and in responsible coaching. The parent can help by understanding to the best of his or her ability the type of injuries that can occur and by being ready to help at home or at the field if there is an injury. From reading this chapter, you should now have some understanding of what the possible injuries are and how they should be dealt with.

To repeat, injuries are always possible in sports or in any activity. Common sense and understanding about the injury are the best protection we can give our children when they do suffer an injury. Proper equipment, good adult supervision, and good physical conditioning of the young athlete are other means of protecting our children. And when in doubt, see your doctor.

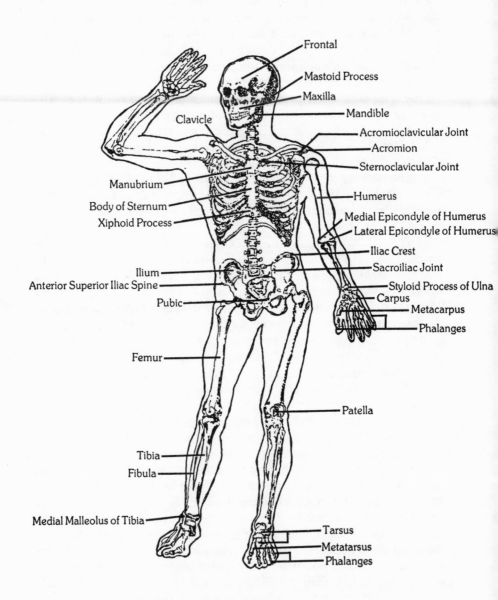

The Human Skeleton (front view).

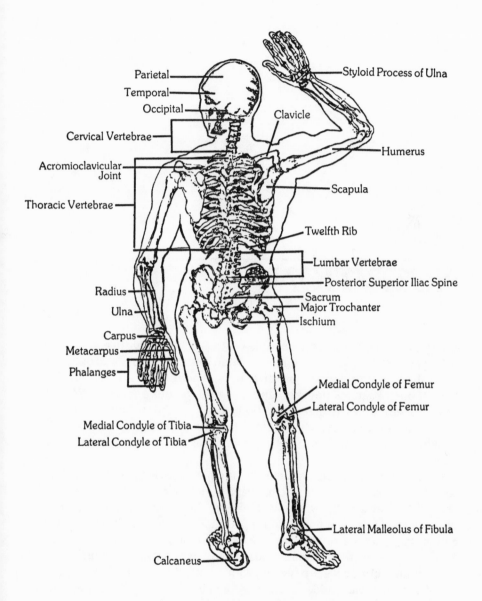

Parietal

Temporal

Occipital

Cervical Vertebrae

Acromioclavicular Joint

Thoracic Vertebrae

Clavicle

Styloid Process of Ulna

Humerus

Scapula

Twelfth Rib

Lumbar Vertebrae

Posterior Superior Iliac Spine

Sacrum

Major Trochanter

Ischium

Radius

Ulna

Carpus

Metacarpus

Phalanges

Medial Condyle of Femur

Lateral Condyle of Femur

Medial Condyle of Tibia

Lateral Condyle of Tibia

Lateral Malleolus of Fibula

Calcaneus

The Human Skeleton (rear view).

6

NUTRITION

There is an old saying, "Some people eat to live; others live to eat." There is a lot of truth to that statement. And when it comes to young people, we often think that the latter part of that statement is most true. But the human body requires nourishment, and through our appetite it tells us when to eat so as to keep our body healthy and strong. However, knowing what to eat and what not to eat is most important to a successful, healthy existence. And that is why the nutrition of our young athlete is so important.

Leaving our young athletes to their own devices diet-wise can sometimes mean the difference between their having enough stamina to finish the contest or tiring half-way through the event. It can also be the difference between winning and losing. Of course, skill, talent, and proper conditioning are the most important factors in athletic performance, but leaving proper nutrition unattended can lead to unnecessary handicaps.

In this country we are blessed with the most abundant food supply of any nation in the world. (In fact, our foodstuffs are so rich that they are causing serious problems in weight control and health.) Many investigators attribute our increased growth in stature, compared to other countries of the world, to the nutritious diet of our infants. Certainly, the continuing record-breaking performances of our athletes is also linked closely to our nutritional superiority over other nations.

146

The focus of this chapter will be to provide a general discussion of proper nutrition and to present a basic program that will produce sound nutritional habits without a complicated system of counting calories and calculating vitamin content of specific foods. Books, magazines, and newspapers in this country probably devote more space to diet and health fads than to any other topic with the exception of sports. Each day there is a "new diet" or a "sure-fire" answer to diet and health questions. But the reality of the situation is this: The amounts and kinds of food one eats affect one's ultimate size, strength, stamina, and general overall health.

From research has come a volume of knowledge on the nutritional needs of people at different ages and conditions. Unless there is a medical reason for a special diet, you can follow the guidelines set up by the Food and Nutritional Board, National Academy of Science, and National Research Council, regarding recommended daily allowances.

To simplify matters in planning a diet, Table 1 is the food group. These foods contain relatively similar amounts of calories, proteins, fats, and carbohydrates. In Table 2 you can see a daily food list which presents a menu that would include approximately 2,500 calories.

There are two general methods of calculating caloric requirements. One is to use the following formula: the *desirable weight* multiplied by the *calories per pound* equals the required calories per day. To determine the desirable weight, refer to a growth and development chart that includes the height and age of the individual. The calories per pound are shown in the following tables:

	Calories per Pound	
Age	Boys	Girls
10 to 12	32	29
12 to 14	24	23
14 to 18	23	21
18 to 22	19	19

It should be pointed out that the number of calories recommended above is what is required to maintain a desirable weight with moderate activity. With increase in activity, there will be a subsequent increase in caloric requirement. This leads us to the second method used to determine the total caloric requirements of an individual. This method is to: (1) control hunger, and (2) regularly examine one's weight and general body build and contour. It is very simple to remove one's clothing and stand in front of a full-length mirror to determine whether one is gaining or losing weight. If an athlete is overweight, he requires fewer calories per day. If he is underweight, he will require more calories per day. It is important to remember that a trained athlete may weigh more than his sedentary or less-active counterpart, and this is due to the fact that *muscle weighs more than fat.* This fact should be taken into consideration before starting a muscular athlete on a reducing diet.

Another method that can be used is to keep what amounts to a scoreboard. Over a seven-day period you keep one-day meal records to determine exactly where general imbalances are occurring and where there is a need to improve. It should be pointed out that the food scoreboards provide approximately 2 grams of protein per kilogram (one kilogram of body weight equals 2.2 pounds). This is well above the recommended daily dietary allowance of .09 grams of protein per kilogram of body weight for someone with moderate activity. Notice on the table that the increased protein is taken in the form of meat. This is necessary because the increased activity and increased muscle mass will raise the protein requirements of this age group.

While the total nutrition is the main consideration, it is important to consume a variety of foods. For example, iron is somewhat difficult to get in the average teenage diet. And remember that young girls particularly need a great deal of iron. The most common iron-rich foods are liver, oysters, prune juice, raisins, apricots, dried beans, and peas. As we know, these are not foods that athletes commonly eat, and they are not very popular with growing youngsters.

Don't overlook the calories consumed in between-meal snacks when calculating the daily totals. Snacking should be counted in determining the total scores for one-day meal records on the food scoreboard. Eating between meals is not necessarily bad if extra calories are needed. Snacks are often prohibited for young athletes. I think this is definitely a *mistake.* Snacks are, in fact, a teenage ritual, and they can be used for good if the proper foods are presented. Snacks can provide extra calories for the very active athlete, and they can be an important source of extra minerals and vitamins. Milk shakes, for instances, can be a very good substitute for milk. But carbonated beverages, soft drinks, coffee, or tea should never be substituted for milk. These are as bad as sugar in candy. The snack and dessert list on page 156 gives you a general idea of the caloric content of these foods.

Some fifty nutrient substances are known to be present in the various foods that are commonly eaten. In terms of nutritional needs for the young athlete, the most important elements in foods are carbohydrates, proteins, and fats.

TABLE 1

FOOD GROUPS_____
Foods within a group can be *substituted* or *exchanged* for each other.

MILK_____
(1 cup whole milk contains 12 grams carbohydrate, 8 grams protein, 10
    grams fat, and 170 calories; 1 cup of skim milk contains 80 calories; 1
    cup cocoa made with milk contains approximately 200 calories)
1 cup whole milk
1 cup skim milk
½ cup evaporated milk
¼ cup powdered milk
1 cup buttermilk
1 cup cocoa

MEAT GROUP_____
(1 ounce contains 7 grams protein, 5 grams fat, and 75 calories)
  1 ounce lean beef, lamb, pork, liver, chicken*
  1 ounce fish—cod, haddock, perch, etc.
  1 hot dog
  ¼ cup tuna, salmon, crab, lobster
  5 small oysters, shrimp, clams
  3 medium sardines
  1 slice cheese
  ¼ cup cottage cheese
  1 egg
  2 tablespoons peanut butter
*1 average serving of meat or fish (such as a pork chop or 2 meatballs) is about 3 ounces

---

CITRUS FRUITS OR SUBSTITUTE (½ cup is one serving)_____
The carbohydrate is averaged to approximately 10 grams per ½ cup and
40 calories

Orange	Grapefruit juice*	Tangerine
Orange juice	Cantaloupe*	Tomato juice*
Grapefruit*	Strawberries*	

*Represents low calorie fruits and vegetables

DARK GREEN OR DEEP YELLOW VEGETABLES (½ cup is one serving)
Greens and lettuce have very little carbohydrate content. The other vegetables contain approximately 7 grams carbohydrate and 2 grams protein and 35 calories

Broccoli*	Greens:*
Carrots	Beet greens
Chicory*	Chard
Escarole*	Collard
Pepper	Dandelion
Pumpkin	Kale
Tomatoes*	Mustard
Watercress*	Spinach
Winter squash	Turnip greens
	Lettuce*

OTHER FRUITS AND VEGETABLES

FRUITS (½ cup is approximately 10 grams carbohydrate and 40 calories)

Apple	Dates	Peach
Applesauce	Figs	Pear
Apricots	Grapes	Pineapple
Banana (½ small)	Grape juice (¼ cup)	Plums
Raspberries	Honeydew melon	Raisins (2 tablespoons)
Blueberries	Mango	Pineapple juice (⅓ cup)
Cherries	Papaya	Prunes (2 medium)
		Watermelon*

VEGETABLES (½ cup is one serving)
The vegetables without the asterisk contain approximately 7 grams carbohydrate, 2 grams protein, and 35 calories

Asparagus*	Cucumbers*	Radishes*
Beets	Eggplant*	Rutabagas
Brussels sprouts*	Mushrooms*	Sauerkraut*
Cabbage*	Okra*	String beans*
Cauliflower*	Onions	Summer squash*
Celery*	Peas, green	Turnips

---

*Represents low calorie fruits and vegetables.

BREAD GROUP

(1 slice of bread or 1 substitute contains 15 grams carbohydrate, 2 grams protein, and 70 calories)

½ hamburger bun	½ cup spaghetti,	⅔ cup parsnips
½ hot dog bun	noodles, macaroni,etc	1 small potato
1 cup popcorn	2 graham crackers	½ cup mashed potato
2½" wedge pizza	5 saltines	15 potato chips—1
1 slice enriched bread	6 round, thin crackers	ounce bag
1 biscuit or roll	½ cup beans or peas	6 pretzels, medium, or
1 small muffin	(dried or cooked)	20 thin sticks
1 small piece cornbread	(Lima or navy beans,	8 French fries
½ cup cooked cereal	split pea, cowpeas,	¼ cup sweet potato or
¾ cup ready-to-eat cereal	etc.)	yams
½ cup rice or grits	¼ cup baked beans	1½" cube sponge or
	⅓ cup corn	angel cake (no icing)
		½ cup ice cream (omit 2 fat servings)

FAT GROUP

(1 teaspoon fat contains 5 grams fat and 45 calories)

Bacon	1 slice	Cream cheese	1 T.
Butter or margarine or		French dressing	1 T.
fat spread	1 teaspoon	Mayonnaise	1 t.
Cream (light)	2 tablespoons	Oil or cooking fat	1 t.
Cream (heavy—40%)	1 tablespoon		

DESSERTS

(see Snacks & Desserts, page 156)

SUGARS

(1 teaspoon contains	Sugar	Syrup
5 grams carbohydrate	Jelly	Hard candy
and 20 calories)	Honey	Carbonated beverage (¼ cup)

Salt used in the home should be iodized.

MINIMUM DAILY FOOD LINEUP (Approximately 2,500 calories)

Food Group	Total Servings Per Day
MILK	4 cups
MEAT (fish, poultry, cheese or eggs)	5 ounces of edible meat without bone or fat
DARK GREEN OR DEEP YELLOW VEGETABLES	1 serving (½ cup)
CITRUS FRUITS	1 serving (½ cup)
OTHER FRUITS AND VEGETABLES	2 servings (1 cup)
BREAD (enriched or whole grain bread, cereal, or potatoes)	13 servings*
FATS (butter, margarine, or other fat spreads)	10 servings (10 teaspoons)

*If additional calories are needed by the active young person, servings of bread or substitutes may be increased. Extra calories will be obtained in desserts, sugar, snacks, and simple sweets.

e.g. 500 calories—Cookies—5 that are 3 inches in diameter
200 calories—Plain cake 3 by 2 by 1½ inches
300 calories—Malted milk—1 cup

FOOD SCOREBOARD Girls 10–12
(Approximately 2,250 calories)_____
To Score: Use the totals on your one-day meal record

RECOMMENDED FOODS	MINIMUM GOAL*	MY SCORE
Milk	4 cups	_____
Meat	5 ounces	_____
(fish, poultry, cheese, or eggs)		
Dark green or deep yellow vegetables	1 serving (½ cup)	_____
		_____
Citrus fruit or substitute	1 serving (½ cup)	
Other fruits and vegetables	2 servings (1 cup)	_____
Bread	10 servings	_____
(enriched or whole grain bread cereal, or potatoes)		_____
Fats	7 teaspoonsful	
(butter, margarine, or other fat spreads)		_____
Other foods, such as plain desserts, sugar, or jelly, carbonated beverages, ades, and snacks	1 small serving	

Take a look at your score. You may find that you have been leaving out important foods, and if so, you need to start including them. Or you may find that you have been taking too many "empty" calories such as carbonated beverages and candy.

Foods to Add   **Foods to Cut Down On**

_____   _____
_____   _____
_____   _____
_____   _____
_____   _____

*The amounts of each food, except milk, dark green or deep yellow vegetables, citrus fruit, and other fruits and vegetables, are guidelines. A person knowledgeable in nutrition and in food content can adapt these servings of food so as to obtain the same approximate calories and nutritive value.

FOOD SCOREBOARD Boys 12–14
(Approximately 2,700 calories)_____
To Score: Use the totals on your one-day meal record

RECOMMENDED FOODS	MINIMUM GOAL*	MY SCORE
Milk (2% fat content)	4 cups	_____
Meat (fish, poultry, cheese or eggs)	5 ounces	_____
Dark green or deep yellow vegetables	1 serving (½ cup)	_____
Citrus fruit	1 serving (½ cup)	
Other fruits and vegetables	3 servings (1½ cup)	_____
Bread (enriched or whole grain bread, cereal, or potatoes)	16 servings	_____
Fats (butter, margarine, or other fat spreads)	10 teaspoons	_____
Other foods, such as plain desserts, sugar, or jelly carbonated beverages, ades, and snacks	1 small serving	_____

   Take a look at your score. You may find that you have been leaving out important foods, and if so, you need to start including them. Or you may find that you have been taking too many "empty" calories such as carbonated beverages and candy.

Foods to Add   Foods to Cut Down On

_____   _____
_____   _____
_____   _____
_____   _____
_____   _____

FOOD SCOREBOARD Boys 14–18
(Approximately 3,000 calories)
To Score: Use the totals on your one-day meal record

Recommended Foods	Minimum Goal*	MY SCORE
Milk (2% fat content)	4 cups	_____
Meat (fish, poultry, cheese or eggs)	7 ounces	_____
Dark green or deep yellow vegetables	1 serving (½ cup)	_____
Citrus fruit	1 serving (½ cup)	
Other fruits and vegetables	3 servings (1½ cup)	_____
Bread (enriched or whole grain bread, cereal, or potatoes)	18 servings	_____
Fats (butter, margarine, or other fat spreads)	10 teaspoons	_____
Plain dessert, sugar, or jelly, snacks, carbonated beverages, ades, etc.	2 small servings	_____

Take a look at your score. You may find that you have been leaving out important foods, and if so, you need to start including them. Or you may find that you have been taking too many "empty" calories such as carbonated beverages and candy.

Foods to Add	Foods to Cut Down On
_____	_____
_____	_____
_____	_____
_____	_____

The amounts of each food, except milk, dark green or deep yellow vegetables, citrus fruit, and other fruits and vegetables, are guidelines. A person knowledgeable in nutrition and in food content can adapt these servings of food so as to obtain the same approximate calories and nutritive value.

SNACK AND DESSERT LIST*_____

	Approximate Calories
Milk shake (fountain size)_____	400
Malted milk shake (fountain size)_____	500
Sundaes_____	215–325
Sodas_____	260
Hamburger (including bun)_____	360
Hot dog (including bun)_____	210
Pizza (4"–5" section)_____	135
Popcorn, lightly buttered (½ cup)_____	75
Nuts (3 tbsp. chopped, or 30 peanuts)_____	150
Pound cake (⅜" slice)_____	140
Cup cake with frosting (2¾" diam.)_____	185
Layer cake with frosting (2" slice)_____	370–445
Pancake (4" diam.)_____	60
Waffle (medium, 4½" x 5½" x ½")_____	215

> Add 20 calories for each teaspoon syrup or sweetening
> Add 45 calories for each teaspoon butter or other fat spread

Brownies (2" x 2" x ¾")_____	140
Plain cookie (3" diam.)_____	120
Pie (⅛ of a 9" pie)_____	275–345
Fruit juice (1 cup)_____	110–165

*One slice of bread is approximately 70 calories. When these foods are used in place of bread they will not have the same nutritive value.

Carbohydrates

Athletes, like all of us, need energy in order to function. Most of our energy comes from the carbohydrates we consume in our food. The importance of carbohydrates has been stressed in recent studies of athletes' performance. They are particularly important for endurance events, such as running, swimming, and skin diving, and during pre-season workouts in various sports, when there are sometimes two sessions a day, and usually under rigorous weather conditions.

Carbohydrates, also known as starches and sugars, are found in potatoes, bread, sugar, cereal, and certain vegetables and fruits. These foods are the main sources of energy. A high-carbohydrate meal before a game or contest not only supplies the energy demanded for a highly competitive physical activity, but is also relatively easy to digest. Some sports may require as many as 4,000 to 5,000 calories per day, and it would be impossible to get that many calories without consuming foods high in carbohydrates.

The normal carbohydrate intake should amount to approximately 40 percent of the calories we consume. However, in a hard training or conditioning program of an athlete, this should be increased.

Training and conditioning are known to improve both the ability to perform and the ability to use body energy stores. Untrained persons in athletic ventures have been shown to use only a little more than half of their carbohydrate stores. Trained athletes, on the other hand, use almost all of their body carbohydrate reserves and are thus able to exercise longer. In the untrained individual who is exercising strenuously, exhaustion with its symptoms of chills, disturbances in vision, and severe muscular fatigue can occur in two hours or less. This is also a reason why breakfast is so important to youngsters, particularly the prospective athlete. Studies have shown that fatigue and laziness will hit later in the morning if breakfast is omitted. To be mentally and physically alert, one needs about one-third of the day's food intake at breakfast. The traditional breakfast of citrus fruit or juice, cereal, toast, and milk is the minimum breakfast, but is very important.

Proteins

The protein needs of the body are usually related to growth. In the developing athlete, where there is an increase of muscle mass, more protein will probably be required. Protein is provided by such foods as meat, poultry, fish, milk, cheese, and eggs. These are the best foods for tissue building.

Proteins are needed by everyone, especially during the periods of rapid growth that teenagers go through. As with carbohydrates, the amount of protein needed depends on the weight of a person. For example, a person weighing about 150 pounds needs approximately 65 grams, about 2½ to 3 ounces of protein a day.

When supplementing the diet with protein or any of the protein mixtures, one should check carefully to see that it contains all the essential amino acids. Steak is a good source of protein, but so are fish and poultry. Pork and lamb are just as good sources of protein as beef.

A cup of milk has 8 grams of protein; one ounce of meat substitute contains 7 grams. In general, bread, citrus fruits, and vegetables contain 2 grams of protein per serving. Eggs are an excellent form of protein, but there are several points that should be made concerning them. First, there is no advantage to eating raw eggs. That was a fad some time ago, and a lot of people still think that eating a raw egg is good for them. This is a mistake, because when eggs are eaten raw there is a greater chance of bacterial contamination, and raw eggs contain a substance that destroys one of the B-complex vitamins in the intestinal tract. Also, current research indicates a strong relationship between elevated serum cholesterol and heart disease, so it is recommended that no more than three eggs per week be eaten. Because of the increasing evidence linking early onset of coronary disease to egg consumption, youngsters might well begin very early to consider their arteries.

Years ago, when I was playing college and then professional basketball, the standard pregame meal for most athletes was steak. However, recent research shows that the protein gains of eating steak before the game are far less beneficial than the problems caused by such a high-protein pregame meal. The traditional pregame meal of steak or scrambled eggs, or other high-protein items, string beans, toast, honey and tea is widely used today because most coaches are not aware that, rather than giving you strength, a high-protein meal can cause physiological problems. Because proteins are so hard to digest, a meal like this can still be found in the stomach two or three hours after the game is over, and thus could have been of no value to the athlete. In essence, it is a detriment because of the additional weight.

Fats

Fats in the diet serve two very important functions. First, fats are the carriers of the fat-soluble Vitamins A, D, E, and K. Second, fats are an energy source. One gram of fat yields twice as much energy as the same amount of carbohydrates or proteins. (Remember that calories do not vary in value and that a calorie in protein is the same as a calorie in carbohydrates is the same as a calorie in fats.)

Fats also make meals more satisfying. Food is tastier and a person does not feel hungry as quickly if the meal contains some fats. On entering the intestinal tract, fats cause the release of a hormone, entrogastrone, which slows down the emptying time of the stomach. For this reason, fat is not recommended in pregame meals. However, as part of the regular diet, fat—whether in the form of butter, margarine, salad oil, or naturally fat foods—is completely digested and well utilized.

Vitamins

Vitamins do not themselves provide energy or serve as building units as other nutrients do, yet they are essential for maintaining life. They trigger and regulate many metabolic processes with such efficiency that only minute amounts of them are needed. All metabolic processes in our body are dependent directly or indirectly on vitamins. Nutritional studies in the past thirty years have given us information of the kinds and amounts of vitamins required for these processes.

The usual, and most reasonable, source of vitamins is food. If one eats a wide variety of foods in sufficient amounts, there is very little need for a vitamin supplement. However, vitamin supplementation is desirable in some cases, particularly for the young athlete, for often his or her diet leaves a lot to be desired. If we examine the basic foods that our bodies require each day, we see that frequently our diet, too, falls short of what is recommended. Vitamin supplement should not exceed the recommended dietary daily allowances. Vitamin preparations should be mixed with minerals, because minerals are just as necessary for proper growth and development. A recommendation is that extra vitamins should not be taken in therapeutic or higher dosages without medical supervision.

The U.S. Food and Drug Administration has established recommended daily allowances (USRDA) of available vitamins. Nutritionists point out that recommended daily allowances are dependent on the size, weight, and general activity of the individual. This argument opens the door to the possible use of high doses of extra vitamins, especially by athletes who are extremely active. To some extent it is true that athletes require more than the recommended daily amount, but, unfortunately, in many cases it has been carried to extremes.

Here is a list of the vitamins and some thoughts:

Vitamin A (USRDA, 5,000 IU). In general, Vitamin A contributes to healthy skin, the eyes, and the functioning of the reproductive system. There is no indication for increasing this dosage; in high doses it can retard growth in children and can cause insomnia, joint pains, liver damage, and severe headaches. Therefore, it is strongly recommended that high concentrations of supplemental Vitamin A not be used for young athletes. Vitamin A is found in carrots, lamb, liver, cantaloupe, butter, pumpkins, squash, bananas, yellow corn, tomatoes, oranges, as well as spinach and many other green vegetables.

Vitamin B-Complex: folic acid (USRDA, 4 mgs.); thiamin (USRDA, 1.5 mgs.); riboflavin (USRDA, 1.7 mgs.); niacin (USRDA, 15 mgs.); Vitamin B-6 (USRDA, 2 mgs.); Vitamin B-12 (USRDA 6 mgs.); biotin (USRDA, .03 mgs.); and pantothenic acid (USRDA, 10 mgs.).

The main use of these complex vitamins is to protect the body against a wide variety of muscular and neurological disorders. Vitamin B-Complex is soluble in water and therefore much of the vitamin value of the Vitamin B-Complex in cooked foods may be lost when the cooking water is poured off. The vitamins also tend to be lost when the foods are peeled or changed in any marked way. The Vitamin B groups work with the carbohydrate foods, and acting as a chemical agent help to bring about the oxidation of food, to produce carbon dioxide in water, and to release energy. Since none of the vitamins of this group can be stored in the body for very long, an adequate supply is needed each day. These complex vitamins are all found in whole wheat flour, kidney, liver, brewer's yeast and wheat germ.

Thiamin, a member of the B group known as Vitamin B-1, can be made synthetically. Thiamin helps promote growth, stimulates the appetite, and is essential to the normal function of the nervous tissue. In underdeveloped countries the disease called beriberi is caused by a lack of thiamin. Foods in which thiamin can be found are yeast, apples (eaten with the peel), vegetables, milk, eggs, liver, meat, and potatoes.

Riboflavin, sometimes called Vitamin B-2, has an important influence on the body's use of protein, and lack of it will retard growth and cause weakness, lack of vigor, sleepiness, and just a lethargic attitude. Riboflavin is made synthetically and can be bought in a drugstore. It is found in about the same foods that thiamin is.

Niacin helps promote normal health and growth and also will help maintain the functions of the skin and that of the mucous membrane in the gastrointestinal tract. Pellagra, a sometimes fatal disease seen around the world (but seldom in this country), can occur if there is not enough niacin in the diet. Like riboflavin and thiamin, niacin is found in foods already listed.

Vitamin B-6 is called pyridoxine. It is involved in the utilization of proteins and is believed to play a role in the synthesis of certain fatty acids in the body.

Biotin is involved in the functioning of several enzymes and works in combination with other B-Complex vitamins.

   Pantothenic acid is concerned with the metabolism of both fatty acids and carbohydrates.

   Vitamin B-12 and *folic acid* are known to be essential to the formation of red blood cells. Exactly how these two vitamins act is not fully understood, but each is involved in the enzymatic process and metabolism. Vitamin B-12 was chemically synthesized in the late 1940s and was an extremely important discovery by nutritionists.

   Vitamin C or ascorbic acid (USRDA, 60 mgs.; larger dosages may be recommended for individuals who smoke or who are taking birth control pills). Vitamin C contributes to the healthy growth of connective tissues or the general body cement, and thus helps the healing of wounds and resistance to infections. Some people claim that very high doses prevent and cure colds. The problem here is that Vitamin C is poorly stored in the body; one who takes very high doses can develop a dependency on Vitamin C, so when the high dosage is stopped a Vitamin C deficiency disease may occur.

   The point should be made that in an athletic contest of moderate severity approximately 400 milligrams of Vitamin C are consumed by the body. If this amount is not present and available in the system, the muscles are not capable of performing to their full capacity. Therefore, prior to athletic contests there is an indicated need for 200 to 400 milligrams of Vitamin C beyond the required daily allowance.

   The best source for Vitamin C in natural foods is the citrus fruits, melons, strawberries, tomatoes, and the essential greens. Scurvy, a disease which in the past afflicted explorers, soldiers, and sailors, who lacked vegetables and fruits in their diet, has been pretty well controlled by today's modern foods.

   Vitamin D (USRDA, 400 units). This vitamin is actually formed in our skin by a reaction from the sun's rays. It will prevent rickets and improve the calcium-phosphorus disposition in the bones. Rickets in former days often stunted growth and misshaped the skeletons of children. There is no benefit to consuming high doses of Vitamin D, and there are definite side effects: high stores of calcium can result in the hardening of the blood vessels and kidney disease. Any vitamin preparation should be closely evaluated for its Vitamin D content because of the number of Vitamin D fortified foods that we use. The most common sources of Vitamin D, other than the sun, are cod liver oil, liver, and fortified Vitamin D milk and dairy products.

   Vitamin E (USRDA, 30 units). It is reported that large doses of Vitamin E have the effect of increasing sexual potency and of preventing heart disease and scarring of tissues. In high doses, Vitamin E may cause a certain degree of fatigue and weakness. The medical literature is unclear as to what the benefits are of higher doses of Vitamin E, although there have been studies showing that whole wheat germ oil will improve the endurance and strength of an athlete who is in training or in a conditioning program. Vitamin E is found mainly in wheat germ and in other vegetable oils.

There are other vitamins not yet clearly understood that come to us through the foods we eat. The list undoubtedly will grow as medical and nutritional research continues. We are getting more information, for example, about Vitamin K. This is a vitamin that is necessary in the blood for normal coagulation and it is quite adequate in almost every American's diet. It is important that Vitamin K be considered as a possible supplement for people who suffer from excessive bleeding.

The best way to get all the necessary nutrients for your body is by well planned regular family meals. Unfortunately, most athletes eat by choice rather than by need and therefore food supplementation may be necessary to be sure that an active body is completely nourished. Over-the-counter vitamins are helpful and the natural food supplements can guarantee complete vitamin and mineral intake. Since athletes want to function at maximum performance it is unreasonable to take only minimum daily requirements. Therefore, a well rounded diet with basic food supplementation is important to growing athletes.

The Basic Food Groups

1. *The Milk Group.* Included here are milk, cheese, cottage cheese, butter, ice cream, and anything that comes from milk. Children should have three or more glasses of milk per day and teenagers should have at least four. For adults, the recommended amount is two or more glasses. Also, milk should be used in many recipes in combination with cereals, fruits, and other foods. The milk foods contribute great quantities of protein and vitamins to the system.

2. *The Vegetable and Fruit Group.* Everyone should have four or more servings daily from this group. It is recommended that every day some kind of citrus fruits or tomatoes be eaten, since they are a primary source of Vitamin C. To make sure that Vitamin A is in our system, at least three or four servings of dark green leafy or deep yellow vegetable are recommended.

3. *The Bread and Cereal Group.* Products chosen from this group should always be made from either enriched or whole grain flour. Four or more daily servings are recommended for all ages. In this group, of course, are breads, cereals, crackers, spaghetti, noodles, muffins, and so on.

4. *The Meat Group.* Two or more daily servings are recommended for all age groups. The amount taken every day should provide at least as much protein as is contained in four ounces of cooked lean meat. Balanced combinations of food in this group are provided by an average of three to five eggs weekly, plus four to five weekly servings of meat, fish, poultry, or cheese, and one weekly serving of liver, heart, kidney, or sweetbreads.

Liquids

Milk. Milk is one of the most nearly perfect of foods. It provides high-quality protein, as well as calcium, phosphorus, and other B vitamins. There is never any reason to eliminate milk from an athlete's diet.

There have been suggestions that milk may cause cotton mouth, which is dryness and discomfort due to decreased activity of the salivary glands. Studies have shown, though, that the condition of saliva is more directly related to perspiration and to reduction of water content in the body, and is not affected by the kinds of food eaten before the athletic event. Saliva flow may also be influenced by one's emotional state.

Some people say that milk curdles in the stomach. This is true, but curdling is a natural process of digestion. When milk is mixed with the acids in the stomach, there is a curdling effect which is not related in any way to stomach upsets. In fact, milk is an excellent buffer for the excess acids in the stomach and sometimes it will relieve discomfort.

There is also an old wives' tale that milk will decrease the speed of movement and cut wind. Studies have shown that there is no difference in the training response or in the all-out performance with or without milk.

It is much easier to plan an adequate diet for an athlete or any person if milk is included. Milk products are also among the best snacks when energy is needed for the young athlete—this includes milk shakes, malteds, cheese, and so on. If I were to try to choose the most perfect food, I would recommend milk, with some of the fat removed. Low-fat or non-fat milk is an excellent food that may be taken at all times before athletic participation.

Tea and coffee. Tea is a popular beverage with some coaches and is often thought to be preferable to coffee. They both contain caffeine, a temporary stimulant. A cup of strong coffee has one-tenth of a grain of caffeine, a cup of strong tea contains about the same. Tea and coffee should therefore always be taken in moderation. Taken in excess, they act only as a temporary stimulant and do not alleviate fatigue for any length of time. In the general diet, there is little to recommend tea or coffee. However, when the gastrointestinal tract is upset, tea with its caffeine content and its added salt is a simple and effective way to provide fluids for the body. Therefore, sweetened tea can be useful in cases of vomiting or diarrhea where other foods might not be as well tolerated.

Carbonated beverages. These types of beverages are mainly calories and fluids. Because of their pleasing taste, they are sometimes used as an easy way to replace a fluid loss. They also do contain moderate amounts of the salts that are lost by perspiration, and therefore can be of real value in a post-game situation. Coca-Cola was originally invented as a pharmaceutical preparation for use in upset stomach. It does have some value as a simple treatment for nausea or vomiting, and small sips of Coca-Cola may very well soothe the upset stomach. Like all things, it should be taken in moderation, certainly not to replace any part of a balanced diet.

Alcoholic drinks. Alcohol is a depressant of the central nervous system, and even a small quantity will definitely affect the finer movements of the body's coordination. There is no place for alcohol in the diet of teenagers. Recently there has been a great increase in the use of alcohol. It is often taken as a release or escape mechanism. Its effect, however, as a depressant, only further compounds the problems in the individual. Its use increases the need for alcohol itself, and rapidly leads to a vicious cycle. There is no question that at times we all need to relax and to get away from it all, but I would certainly not recommend alcohol for this purpose. It can have a disastrous effect on one's life. Extensive research on performance following the ingestion of alcohol proves conclusively that alcohol in almost any form will interfere with the performance of an athlete at any age. Therefore, there is no indication at any time for alcohol in an athlete's diet.

Water needs of the body. Every operation or motion of the body requires water. The digestion and proper utilization of foods cannot be accomplished without water. Nutrients are carried to the tissues and waste products are carried away by water. Water is also necessary to control the body temperature through perspiration. Water is more necessary even than food.

To prepare for sweat losses, particularly in hot weather, the prepractice meal should always include an adequate supply of liquid. Usually one to three cups of water or other beverage will ensure adequate hydration. It is not harmful to drink during meals, but it is a bad habit to use excessive amounts of a beverage to wash down food without chewing. Chewing is a very important part of the digestive process. Remember also that iced beverages should be drunk more slowly; if cold drinks are taken in excess, normal bowel movements are interfered with and cramping can result.

When pre-season conditioning and practice take place in warm weather, the problem of heat stress or exhaustion is likely to occur during the first several weeks of training. It takes a period of time for the body to acclimate itself to the hot weather. It is very important for anyone practicing or training where the weather is hot to take special pre-cautions for the problem of heat until the body adjusts to the stress and strain of heat and can better tolerate the activities. Anyone who plans to take part in an athletic event that occurs in hot or humid climates should be sure to have several weeks of preparation prior to the competition.

Heat stress is manifested by the individual's becoming easily fatigued. His pulse rate will increase and the general body temperature will rise. He will not be able to perform at a good level. There is always some associated weight loss, which is due mostly to the loss in fluids that have not been adequately replaced. Therefore, when training in hot and humid climates it is important to watch the weight of all the athletes. Any excessive loss should be considered a potential danger and medical advice should be sought. Certainly, during the practice period a regular program of water replacement should be instituted. The weight is an excellent guideline of how much water needs to be replaced: a loss of two pounds represents the loss of one quart of perspiration. Experience has shown that individuals seldom drink as much water as they lose in sweat. Therefore, frequent drinks must be emphasized during practice, and extra water should be considered an important part of the general diet throughout the day during hot and humid conditions.

Salt or sodium chloride is important to the general diet. It becomes increasingly important when the training athlete does a great deal of sweating, since the body loses salt along with the water. However, in most cases, the salting of food at each meal will take care of the necessary salt requirements. In addition, beef bouillon or broth will also supply a fair quantity of salt. In my opinion, this is much better tolerated than the use of salt tablets and much more nourishing to the athlete.

A word to the parents regarding the training of their young athlete in hot, humid weather. It is incumbent upon you to make sure that the coach has provided an adequate supply of water on the field or nearby, where the youngsters can go and get a drink during practice. Years ago coaches thought that water taken during practice would somehow slow the athletes down or make them ill, and many a boy suffered from heat prostration because of that archaic attitude. In modern coaching techniques there is an understanding that the replacement of water in the young athlete's body is vitally important for his or her well-being.

If your young athlete is going to be playing tennis or golf or doing any long-distance running in hot weather, he or she should bring along an adequate supply of water in a thermos jug or other container to ensure that there will be water easily available.

One of the most effective guides to fluid replacement was published by the Gatorade (Stokely-Van Camp, Inc.) of Indianapolis. It is reproduced here with their permission. Read the chart and you will find excellent tips to pass on to your young athlete.

1. ACCLIMATIZATION—Getting Your Men in Condition

Get your athlete in condition by getting him used to working in heat. Start with light exercise in gym shorts and gradually increase workout time and clothing to full uniform over a 5-day period. Workout sessions starting with 1 hour and working up to 2 hours in 5 days are recommended. Consider 10 minute breaks every 20 minutes of workout.

Day	1	2	3	4	5
Time in Minutes	60	80	100	110	120
Gear	Shorts	Shorts	Pants	Pants & Helmet	Full Gear
Workout	Calisthenics & Jogging	Calis. & Sprints	Sprints & Drills	Sprints & Drills	Practice

2. Weight Charts—Key to Good Training Practice

The weight charts are prepared to help you in your work. Set up a procedure of lining up your men for weigh-in and weigh-out before and after practice or workout. The difference in weight is the athlete's loss of sweat. Replacement of fluid loss is important. Replacement is necessary for performance. At least 80% replacement must be achieved before next practice session.

3. Weight Loss Check—Focus on Rehydration Need

The weight loss check is a convenient, reliable way of keeping tabs on the athlete's rehydration needs. If an athlete is given adequate access to fluids (Gatorade thirst quencher, water) by providing water breaks and encouraged to drink, he may be able to diminish his dehydration and replenish his fluid requirements. Such athletes will not show large losses in weight. If an athlete's weight loss is high, then his rehydration needs are great and should be satisfied. It is better to drink frequently, replace the fluid needed gradually, and maintain maximum rehydration throughout practice workout and game performance.

4. Water Replacement—Major Ingredient of Sweat_____

What goes out as sweat must be put back in the form of a fluid replacement. Since sweating helps to keep our body temperature from becoming excessive, it is in line to sweat, to minimize body temperature rise. Rehydrating the body of fluid lost is one of the best ways of insuring a continued cycle of performance. Rehydration must be encouraged—fluid replacement made available to make up for the fluid lost in sweat.

5. Salt Replacement—The Other Ingredients of Sweat_____

Along with water, when one sweats one loses electrolytes and body salts, primarily sodium chloride. In rehydrating the athlete with the water lost, we must replenish the lost salts as well. Gatorade has been formulated to supply those body salts in their proper ratios with respect to water and rehydration. If you drink water, however, make certain you use the proper ratio of water to salt tablets in order to keep the concentrations in balance. It is easier to stick to Gatorade and have the properly prepared, physiologically sound fluid replacement for your needs. No salt tablets should be used if one is drinking Gatorade.

6. Work-Heat Relationship—Elementary but Basic Facts_____

Work produces heat and increases body temperature. If we were not able to lose the heat produced, our body temperature could go from 98.6°F (normal body temperature) to as high as 114°F (fatal to humans) in one hour. Fortunately, our body has a built-in temperature regulator and control. Our body sweats, loses water and salts and cools the skin while evaporation is taking place. Under normal conditions this cycle and regulation is adequate. In periods of heavy work and/or heavy uniform and insulation, the regulation system needs a helping hand to be able to maintain reasonable temperature control. The properly hydrated athlete in top shape is able to perform to his capacity. Remember that even a 3% weight loss is sufficient to show up significant performance loss. The percent weight loss can easily be calculated.

$$\frac{\text{Wt. loss of athlete}}{\text{Wt. before workout}} \times 100 = \text{Percent wt. loss.}$$

If you want the athlete's best performance, keep a sharp lookout on his heat-work relationship. Give him fluid replacement to help keep that temperature in control. Rehydrate him continually.

7. Weather Effects—The Overlooked Factor_____

Hot and humid days can materially contribute to taking the zing out of your athlete's performance. On such days, the dehydration of the athlete is greater. His chances of heat illness are greater and his needs for rehydration are more acute. The use of the wet bulb thermometer is a means of quickly determining what the conditions are on the field during practice or a game. The sling psychrometer (about $15.00) may be purchased at any industrial supply company and assigned to a student manager, trainer or assistant coach. Careful observations of the wet bulb temperature and following the recommendations on the chart, can minimize dehydration. Frequent drinking breaks, fluid drinking encouragement, as well as allowing the body to dissipate heat, will be needed. The higher the temperature, the greater the humidity of the day, the greater is the degree or dehydration. Rehydrate your athletes.

8. Danger Symptoms—Keep a Sharp Lookout_____

They say an ounce of prevention is worth a pound of cure. A coach or trainer who is on the lookout for the danger signs will not only catch a situation before it becomes dangerous, but will also recognize that something must be corrected if it is producing such dangerous conditions. He then takes steps to correct the situation. Watch out for Muscle Cramps, Heat Exhaustion, Heat Stroke, Heat Fatigue and Sloppy Coordination. They all spell danger.

9. Proper Dress—Every Little Bit Helps_____

Particularly in football, the athlete is forced to wear heavy clothing which retards heat dissipation and acts as an insulator. Whenever and wherever it is possible, the body should be given a chance to throw off heat and become cooler. Clothing which can breathe and ventilate rather than insulate, can be helpful. Loosening the garments when not in action will help to cool. Keep using every means to bring your athlete close to normal body condition.

10. Emergency Measures_____

If you practice good performance habits you will cut down on dangerous incidents. When an emergency occurs, however, be prepared to handle it with professional efficiency. Have a telephone handy. Give quick, effective treatment on the spot by cooling the body, removing clothing and applying cold applications such as a sponge, towel or bath in cold water or ice. Transport to the hospital immediately while applying the cold applications. Give the doctor the background information so that he can quickly anticipate what must be done. Even with all this, you must orient and teach all your personnel to carry out such a program when the necessity arises.

Pregame Meals

Some researchers advised using fructose as the sugar in the pre-game meal. Like glucose, fructose provides four calories of food energy per gram. Fructose is essentially similar to glucose, except for the following differences: (1) Fructose does not stimulate the production of insulin. (2) Fructose does not require insulin for its metabolism or burning. (3) Fructose is slowly absorbed from the intestinal tract, whereas glucose is actively transported out of the gastrointestinal tract, a process requiring some energy. (4) There is some belief that fructose in the circulation can be utilized more rapidly than glucose.

The results of these differences can be important to the athlete. First, if the insulin level is not raised, there will not be typical insulin-induced decrease in the blood sugar. Second, because of its slow transport from the gastrointestinal tract, fructose is more readily available and provides some reserve of blood sugar which can be called upon to raise the blood sugar level during competition. (The carbohydrate stores are decreased as rapidly or as completely, however.) Therefore, in planning a pre-competition meal, the liberal use of fructose in place of glucose can certainly be recommended.

Fructose is obtained mainly from fresh fruits and fruit juices, although there are several products available on the market in the form of fructose tablets.

Pregame Supplements

There are a great many liquid products available as a pregame liquid meal. Two that have received a great deal of acclaim among the athletes are Ensure and Ensure Plus.

Nutritional Supplements During the Game

Sugar supplements seem to relieve fatigue and to increase the ability to continue performing during an endurance event, but apparently they do not enhance the performance during shorter events. Glucose is absorbed rapidly by the body, going to the liver and passing into the blood. The blood glucose level reaches a peak one-half hour after glucose has been taken, and then falls very rapidly. It is thus a source of immediate energy. Pure glucose is the most readily available source of energy, but table sugar and honey are both digested rapidly and are utilized almost as quickly as pure glucose.

The complex carbohydrates, such as starches, also break down to give glucose, but at a much slower rate. One school of thought believes that the sugar supplement during a game might better be fructose, which is another simple sugar. That was discussed earlier.

Since honey contains a combination of glucose and fructose, many individuals use honey as a sugar supplement. Tests have not been able to demonstrate any true beneficial effects from the use of honey, but it nonetheless represents a way of taking a sugar supplement. Since water is necessary for the absorption of glucose, it is sometimes better to combine the two and give a sweetened liquid as a gametime drink. Frozen fruit juices will fill this need very nicely. They already contain all the sugars: glucose, fructose, sucrose, and other forms of carbohydrates. Canned and fresh fruit juices, as well as ades, are also sources of quick energy.

The natural sources of glucose are grape sugar and corn sugar; of fructose, fruits and honey; of sucrose, cane sugars; and of lactose, milk sugar.

It is important always to test any planned sugar supplement in a practice situation to be sure that it will be tolerated. A concentrated sugar solution may cause extra distention of the stomach, and evacuation of the stomach's contents may be slowed. The reaction may take the form of cramps, nausea, and sometimes even vomiting. Therefore, rather than consuming a large quantity early, it would seem more advisable to take very small amounts, perhaps one cup each hour, to provide the body with a continual good supply of energy.

Post-Game Eating

After a game or practice session no athlete is hungry. Most professional athletes wait one and a half to three hours before they sit down to a solid meal. There is a feeling of exhaustion that frequently comes after athletic endeavors. The body has not reverted to normal, and it is certainly not ready for food. Complete relaxation does much to prepare the stomach for a meal. It takes time for an appetite to develop after strenuous exercise. For this reason, the only nourishment which may be advisable following competition is liquid, such as fruit juices. Surprisingly, plain water will not work as well as a liquid containing some salt, or even a carbonated beverage, in satisfying the body's thirst; there is need for salt along with the liquid because much salt has been lost with the perspiration. Also, the stomach will more readily accept a liquid that has some salt in it. Later, when the athlete feels like eating, any good-sized, balanced meal may be selected.

Many people take a break after the game and get together for a short period of time to have some liquid refreshment. This is an excellent time to promote good team spirits and will also serve to slow down the activity of the system.

When the athlete finally gets around to eating, he can consume very large quantities of food. A late evening snack, sandwiches, fruit, and milk are of great value. If the parents realize that the athlete will not want to eat right after participating in an event or even practice, the meal pattern and the preparation of food will be much easier. I have seen many competitors refuse a beautifully prepared meal after competition because they are not ready to eat. Then, several hours later they will end up eating a great deal of junk. Planning the meal pattern for the athlete is very important, even though sometimes it will disrupt the regular family routine. Seeing to it that a good pregame meal is offered prior to practice or competition, and that adequate time after the game is allowed before offering a bigger meal to the athlete, will be very beneficial and also save the family a great deal of expense in uneaten food.

Diets

Here are some diets that have been used and recommended by some of our leading coaches and teachers in this country:

Tennis: These are the comments of Dr. Norman E. Ruddy of Los Angeles, medical adviser to America's Davis Cup team. "The first point I would like to stress," Dr. Ruddy says, "is to avoid the innumerable food fads. They are generally useless and can be dangerous. The basic healthy foods are the ones we use. Don't go in for excessive consumption of any single food.

"We use a relatively high carbohydrate diet starting a few days before a match. Carbohydrates are the major fuel for muscle exercise; they spare the body the work of making its own fuel. If you consume a lot of carbohydrates before violent exercise, your body works more efficiently on the basis of calories expended per unit of oxygen intake. This action is protein-sparing.

"Fats also provide an important source of energy. Carbohydrate is converted into fat for storage. [Thiamin and other B-Complex vitamins are necessary for this conversion.] Excess protein is converted into carbohydrates and may then be converted into fat.

"We have the players eat a solid meal about three to three and a half hours before the matches, emphasizing carbohydrates and minimizing fats. Recently we have stressed fluid calories for more efficient digestion.

"Water and salt balances are vital. Most of the time, in an average temperature and moderate play, your body will tell you how much extra salt and fluid you need. If you sweat a lot during the day, dinner will not taste quite as good and you will just salt your food a little bit more. In very warm and humid climates and when long and vigorous match play lies ahead, it is often necessary to supplement salt, potassium, and fluid intake. This can be done with coated salt tablets and adequate liquids. Some of the liquid ades are also very good. I would recommend and warn against popping salt pills without first checking with your doctor.

"In summary, in the meal before a match the particular emphasis should be on calories, whatever is easily digestible and comfortably palatable to the individual athlete."

Breakfast
8 ounces fresh orange juice or ½ cantaloupe or 1 small banana
1 poached or soft-boiled egg
2 slices toast with 1 teaspoon butter
¾ cup puffed or flaked cereal
1 cup mik (with banana or cereal)
tea

Lunch
3 ounces cold cuts (such as turkey, roast beef, ham, or chicken), or seafood or fish or two frankfurters or 8 ounces cottage cheese
2 slices bread or 1 cup potatoes or corn.
1 teaspoon butter
½ cup green vegetables or 1 cup mushrooms or 1 tomato
tossed green salad with lemon, a moderately large portion if you like
2 apricots or 1 pear or 2 plums or 10 cherries or 1 medium apple
tea

Dinner
4 ounces beef, lamb, veal, chicken, halibut, salmon, or shrimp
½ cup green vegetable or a tossed green salad with lemon
½ cup carrots, beets, onion, or peas
2 slices bread or 2 small potatoes
1 cup noodles or macaroni
1 teaspoon butter
1 peach or 1 cup blueberries, strawberries, applesauce, or pineapple

Bedtime
1 cup milk or tea with honey or sugar
1 piece sponge cake

For extra carbohydrates, a cup of fruit juice will give you 100 to 130 calories, enough to fuel twenty to thirty minutes of brisk tennis. Drink it at odd moments during the day. Try unsweetened apple, grapefruit, grape, or pineapple or the sweetened apricot, peach, or pear nectars. Another pleasant source of carbohydrates are the fruits themselves. One big apple, or 1 cup of applesauce, ½ cantaloupe or grapefruit, 30 grapes, 2 medium oranges, 5 medium plums, or 5 teaspoons of raisins will give you 100 calories each.

Swimming: One of this country's outstanding coaches, and one of the most successful swimming coaches in the world, is Dr. James Counsilman of the University of Indiana. Here's what Dr. Counsilman has to say about the diet for his swimmers: "One of the biggest mistakes many of the swimmers make is that they think they get energy from protein. That's why they all eat those steaks. But straight protein diet messes up your respiratory quotient—you will need more oxygen to swim a given distance than if you are on a carbohydrate diet. So we try to keep a normal amount of protein but we also try to teach the boys that you can't swim faster or increase endurance just by eating proteins.

"The last few days before a competition I tell my boys to go high on carbohydrates—the breads, cakes, spaghetti—anything that is high in carbohydrates. Research has shown that carbohydrate-loading is beneficial to performance. We are actually calling it glycogen-loading because glycogen is carbohydrate that has been broken down and is ready to use in the body.

"I prefer my boys to have low-grain breads rather than the soft breads that tear your body down twelve ways. I prefer whole wheat, and not too much butter. But if they completely eliminate the fat they will get hungry too soon.

"We also recommend things like mashed potatoes and baked potatoes, and boiled rice is very good. Spaghetti is very good too as long as it is not highly seasoned."

A note here: Dr. Counsilman says that their swimmers have tried the vegetarian diet and absolutely nobody on the team went for it. It didn't make them feel satisfied. He says it's like eating Chinese food without the meat; you are hungry just a little while after eating. Lean meat is good, so is poultry, fish and eggs.

Before a meet Dr. Counsilman tries to get his boys to eat a moderate-sized meal. "We try to have them ready for the meet so that they do not have too much in their stomachs but so their stomachs are not completely empty." During long workouts Dr. Counsilman will give some candy to the boys in the middle of practice. And, he says, almost every night his kids go out for a pizza and split it, and he doesn't mind this. "Pizza is pretty good for a balanced diet, especially the kind with peppers and onions." So if your youngsters want to have a pizza at night, remember that the most successful swimming coach in the world says it's okay.

Here is the diet:

Breakfast
1 orange or apple or ½ grapefruit or 12 cherries
1 or 2 eggs, scrambled, boiled, or poached
2 slices bacon, very crisp and well drained
2 pieces whole wheat toast with a little butter and jam or honey
tea with skim milk

Lunch
4 ounces lean hamburger, or cold boiled ham, turkey, or roast beef, or 2 ounces of cheese
1 cup peas, carrots, beets, or lima beans
mixed green salad with tomatoes
2 slices whole-grain bread
yogurt with fresh fruit, such as pineapple
tea with skim milk

Dinner
4 ounces lean meat, poultry, or fish
1 cup asparagus, spinach, broccoli, or green beans
mixed green salad with tomatoes
2 slices whole wheat or whole rye bread
strawberries, blueberries, peaches, or bananas with milk and sugar
tea with skim milk

Bedtime
yogurt or milk with graham crackers

Tennis is a sport that requires quick acceleration, coordination, and stamina, and swimming requires a great deal of energy, stamina, and strength. Thus the two diets above for tennis and swimming could really apply to almost any kind of sport.

Obesity

Excess fat on the body is a problem for all ages. In today's society, fat reduction is usually undertaken for esthetic reasons. However, there are many vital reasons for doing so. Complications associated with obesity are far-reaching. There are serious organic impairments that can shorten life, many psychological maladjustments, unfortunate peer relationships—especially for children—inefficiency of physical movement, and ineffectiveness in motor and athletic activity. Obesity is consistently encountered as a cause of physical unfitness in boys and girls. These children always score low on physical and motor tests. Excessive weight places an additional burden upon the circulatory, respiratory, and urinary systems. Naturally, then, fat people tend to develop disorders of these systems. Overweight people have less tolerance to disease, greater difficulty in normal breathing, and high frequency of respiratory infections. Most seriously, obese people are subject to high blood pressure and hardening of the arteries. This has been shown to occur even at an extremely young age. This high blood pressure is frequently related to high blood cholesterol, resulting from the ingestion of fats.

Fat boys and girls have been subjected to ridicule by their unthinking peers. Such names as Tubby, Fatty, or Fats are common and unkind nicknames that stick with them throughout their school years. The entertainment media is constantly ridiculing overweight individuals, and this endless series of comments cannot result in anything but hurt feelings, inferiority complexes, and social withdrawal. A study done on admissions to colleges shows that obese boys and girls were strongly discriminated against, despite satisfactory grades, intelligence, entrance examinations, and teacher recommendations. Overweight girls had one third the chance of getting into college as normal girls; with boys there was less problem, but there was still a significant difference. Prejudice, discrimination, heavy burdens of inferiority, and blame imposed by society on the obese person is cause enough for all of us to take positive steps in correcting the situation.

Fat or excess weight or obesity or whatever you want to call it occurs very simply. When the individual diet produces more fuel than is needed to maintain bodily functions and meet the daily requirements of activities, the excess energy is stored in the fatty tissues throughout the body, gradually increasing the undesirable fat state. It would seem, therefore, that controlling the diet by balancing caloric intake with calorie requirements, or by reducing the intake so that there is reduction of existing fat, will correct the situation.

However, the cause of obesity is not limited to improper diets alone. There are many interacting factors which must be dealt with. For instance, obesity has been shown to run in families. This is due to both genetic and environmental factors. Even the lack of exercise in a family could be a vital contributary influence to the battle of the bulge, which seems to be a lifetime effort for those who are fat-prone.

The determination of obesity can be made by many methods. The simplest method, in my opinion, is to stand in front of a mirror completely undressed to determine the state of one's figure. Of course, there are tables that give averages, but these are not always adequate in determining the individual needs. Certain boys and girls will be considered obese according to a chart of comparison, whereas in actuality they are well-muscled and well-developed and do not have any excess fat. Their weight is higher because muscle weighs more than fat. There are more sophisticated measures, such as determining the amount of fat in the body by measuring specifically the triceps (back of the arm skin fold), but this should be done in a laboratory since most people don't have the proper instruments at home.

It should be emphasized that balanced nutrition is most important in the regulation of our own body size as well as that of our children. The best control for the problem of obesity is the establishment of proper nutrition and good eating habits, and this is a lifelong work that all of us must address ourselves to.

Physical activity is also extremely important for controlling weight. Many investigators believe that the lack of exercise is the most common cause of overweight and that a prescription for exercise is more important than medical treatment or any prescribed diet. In an evaluation of two groups of high school girls, one overweight and the other of normal weight, the obese girls were determined to have eaten less than the normal-weight girls, yet they also exercised considerably less. The overweight girls engaged in sitting activities much more than in walking activities. Watching television consumed four times as many hours for the obese than the non-obese children.

Motion picture studies of playground activities of obese children revealed that these children were physically less active during the time they were participating in sports. The degree of difference was extremely interesting, particularly in such sports as tennis, where they were 65 percent less active; volley ball, 80 percent less active; and swimming, almost 90 percent less active.

Exercise can affect the body composition of young growing humans by keeping down the amount of body fat and by increasing muscle tissue. Exercise has favorable effects on body composition even without actual change in body weight. An interesting study on the effects of participating in physical education compared eighth-grade pupils who participated daily against similar students who participated only two or three times a week. Both groups engaged in the exact same physical education activities for the same number of weeks. After two years a motor fitness test of six items for boys and four for girls was carried out with these children, and measurement of the triceps was also done to determine the amount of fat tissue. The results indicated that the five-day subjects were significantly superior in motor fitness and activity skills and had significantly less fat than did the students who had physical activity only two days a week. Interestingly enough, there did not seem to be a significant difference in the growth of the two groups.

The major problem in high school athletics, according to the National Federation of State High School Athletic Associations, is the indiscriminate and extreme practice of keeping a boy's weight unduly low during an important period of growth and development in order to make a lower weight division. Certain athletic groups such as bantam football leagues set weight limits, and junior high school boys who are big for their age may not make the team unless they diet. Wrestlers are concerned with making the weight for their next bout. These boys may use dangerous means to reduce their weights to below normal.

If there is a need for weight reduction, it should be carried out under the guidance of a physician. There is no place in sports for crash diets and for weight reduction by means of eliminating fluid intake. A lopsided diet may cause some weight reduction, but it also takes away some of the protective foods and energy that help maintain good health and performance. An added danger which the parent must look out for is the temptation to continue such a diet over a period of time, with possible harmful effects.

There is also no place for sweat baths in weight reduction. The dangers of excessive water loss in the body may very well be life-threatening. The individual who restricts water intake to lower his weight will suffer from poor performance and the added risk of collapse during the athletic performance. The physiological effect of quick dehydration by sweat baths or similar means seems to be much more drastic than the effect of semi-starvation. Studies show that weight losses up to 5 percent of body weight accomplished in less than 24 hours are apt to decrease ability to perform and cause stress on the cardiovascular system.

These ill effects do not occur when weight is lost gradually by properly planned diets. Wrestlers at one university proved this by losing weight equivalent to no more than 10 percent of their body weight over a period of several weeks. Heart rate did not increase and they were able to complete established maximum work loads without any loss of efficiency.

Many athletes require a certain amount of fat at the onset of training for a sport. Pre-season conditioning often requires more energy than the competitive season. In contact sports—football, soccer, hockey, and basketball—the fat deposits around the kidney and other organs are important to help prevent injury, so it is necessary to keep the weight up.

From a dieting standpoint, minimum caloric diets for early teenage athletes should be 1,500 calories per day.

When starting anyone on a program to lose weight, I think the most important point that parents need to realize is that the child should not be placed on a diet. Somehow, using the word "diet" creates unbelievable pressure on the child. A simple way to cut down on foods the child is consuming is just to reduce the amount of food that you give him at any of his meals. And remember that there is no specific program, diet or pill that can help anyone lose weight. If there were, whoever could come up with it would be one of the richest men in the world. Just a glance at the number of various diets and diet books shows that there is no such program. In fact, there are millions of programs, and basically any of them is sound if it provides one with proper nutrition while cutting down on the amount of food intake. By combining such a diet with a program of adequate exercise, anyone will lose weight.

I think it is important to mention that some individuals seem to be able to eat very little food and still continue to gain weight, while others can eat large quantities of food and not gain weight. This represents a difference in body utilization of food. It is advisable for anyone starting a weight-losing program to have a thorough physical examination and to continue the program under medical supervision if the problem of obesity is quite serious. It is extremely rare that the cause of obesity is of medical origin.

Generally, then, people gain weight because they take in more calories than they expend. Studies all over the country always come back to the same thing. The best way a dietary program can help a person lose weight is if (1) there is a decrease in the total caloric intake and (2) there is an increase in the caloric expenditure. That means, very simply, that we must eat less (that is, reduce the amount of calories that we take in) and we must burn up more.

There are two mistakes we often make when we start a reduction of calories: (1) eliminating breakfast or decreasing breakfast to the point where we then become hungry and continue to eat the rest of the day in an attempt to make up for breakfast, thus actually increasing our total caloric intake, and (2) cutting out foods to the extent that we have basically poor general nutrition program. Therefore, anyone on a reducing diet should take a good vitamin-mineral supplement. This will not provide any calories and at the same time will ensure an adequate supply of vitamins.

Since we've talked about weight control, perhaps a few words on height and growing might be in order.

On the average, Americans are taller than their neighbors in other countries throughout the world. Even children of Oriental extraction, when born in the United States, will tend to average almost six inches in height over the children of the Far East. As a nation we are the best fed in the world, plus we have an environmental advantage with health, sanitation, and such a variety of developmental activities.

To a great extent growth has a close relationship to heredity and there is nothing a child can do about the genes given him. If a youngster is to take full advantage of his genes he must practice the best of health habits.

For the growing athlete achieving full potential growth and development is an extra point. Research has pointed up several methods that will improve growth. First, during these important years an extra glass of milk will provide necessary nutrition so frequently lacking. Tests have shown that children will grow at a greater than expected rate when taking an extra glass of milk each day. Milk is probably nature's most perfect nutritional food.

Another tip is to sleep in a dark room. Medical studies have shown that light shining on the eyes while sleeping will cause the release of an anti-growth hormone. So sleep and bed rest are important to greater growth. Bill Walton, the great basketball player, stands 6 foot 11. He has tall parents and has brothers that are 6 foot 5. But he hurt his knee when he was 14 years old and had to have surgery. In 6 months of enforced bed rest Bill Walton grew 8 inches. He had plenty of sleep and plenty of good food and milk products while he was recovering from the surgery.

So during the growing period, drink an extra glass of milk a day, sleep in a dark room at night, and get plenty of exercise.

7

GENERAL HEALTH

Good health used to be thought of as "not feeling sick." We now know that illness can be present and sometimes not be felt. Later, good health was thought to mean that one was free from illness. That is a better definition, but the best one I think is the one that the World Health Organization formulated: "Health is a state of complete physical, mental, and social well-being and not merely the absence of disease or infirmity."

Throughout this book we have looked at the young athletes in the context of sports and training, conditioning and injuries. The young athletes are also concerned with their health apart from sports. Obviously, the young athletes have a better chance for good health because of their training and conditioning, but they also must be educated regarding good personal health as well as the dangers of alcohol and drugs. This chapter deals with general health habits and looks at some health and social problems facing our youngsters.

To determine the state of the youngster's general health, I strongly recommend a general physical exam by your family physician every year, no matter how sports-involved the individual is.

Care of the Teeth

Parents are constantly after their children to "brush your teeth," especially after eating. And this advice is very important. From the age of

180

six through thirteen, most of the child's baby teeth will be replaced by the permanent teeth. There are normally 32 permanent teeth. The wisdom teeth are the last to come in and they usually appear by the time the person is 21. However, sometimes the wisdom teeth never appear but remain impacted in the jaw.

There are three kinds of teeth: in the front of the mouth are the incisors. These are the sharp teeth that bite food into small pieces. Next are the canines or cuspids, which are used to tear the food apart. In the back are the molars or bicuspids, which are flat and are used to grind and crush the food.

The outside layer of the tooth is an exceptionally hard substance called the enamel. Interestingly enough, the color of one's teeth depends on the thickness of the enamel. Therefore no toothpaste can actually brighten or whiten teeth because toothpaste cannot add to the enamel of a tooth. But toothpaste can and does remove stains and film that adhere to the teeth and might be hiding the true color of the teeth.

Underneath the enamel is the dentine, a hard, bonelike substance that forms the solid structure of the tooth. Inside the dentine is the pulp, which is a soft tissue containing the blood vessels and nerves. Below the gum is the root of the tooth, which is held in place by cementum, a hard substance that is connected to the socket in the jaw.

The most common tooth problem for young athletes is tooth decay. Decay usually begins in the areas where most of the chewing is done and where usually the least brushing is done. These are the molars and the areas between the teeth. A sticky, translucent substance called dental plaque builds up and this plaque contains enough acid to destroy the enamel of the tooth. Once that enamel is destroyed and the bacteria get into the dentine, dental work is necessary. If the acid or bacteria get past the dentine and enter the pulp and the bone socket, an abscess can result with associated swelling, pain, and possible loss of the tooth.

The best way to avoid dental plaque is through constant, repeated brushing of the teeth. Normally, it takes food left in the cracks or spaces of the teeth about ten hours to decompose and form an acid. Not all foods form acids at the same rate. Vegetable acids form very slowly, whereas sugar is easily decomposed and can form acid in about five minutes. That's why dentists advise brushing after eating and caution against eating sweets. Acid buildup can be avoided by brushing teeth immediately after eating sweets or foods with high sugar contents. Attention should be paid to the crevices between the teeth. Brushing cannot get rid of dental plaque deposits between and behind the teeth, so the use of dental floss is recommended to supplement the brushing.

Halitosis. A lot of jokes have been made about halitosis and many a dental commercial is produced about the problem. But halitosis, or foul breath odor, can be a serious health problem. Eating onions or garlic or foods where they are present can cause temporary halitosis. A more serious form is caused by tooth decay, indigestion, infections in the mouth or throat, or diseases of the lungs or stomach. Hiding halitosis through a mouthwash or chewing gum does not cure it. If your child has halitosis, see your dentist or physician to find out the reason.

Gum Disorders: Here is a brief listing of some gum disorders and their symptoms. Treatment should come from your dentist.

1. *Gingivitis:* This is a disorder in which the gums become swollen, bleed easily, and are red and tender. Gingivitis is caused by deposits of decaying food, by misaligned teeth, or by dental plaque. It can also be caused by vitamin deficiencies or an allergy.

2. *Pyorrhea:* Sometimes called periodontitis, this is an inflammation of the membrane that covers the bony sockets of the teeth. Symptoms are loose teeth, persistent bad breath, and gums that bleed easily. It has the same causes as gingivitis.

3. *Trench mouth:* Also called Vincent's angina, this is a bacterial inflammation of the gums. The symptoms are the same as those of gingivitis except that the infection also spreads to the membranes lining the throat and the mouth. Trench mouth is an infectious disease and can be acquired by using the eating utensils of an infected person or even by kissing an infected person. People who smoke have a very difficult time getting rid of this disease. An antibiotic such as penicillin is necessary for the effective treatment of trench mouth.

Care of the Eyes

Probably no part of the body is as important to the athlete, or to anybody, for that matter, as the eyes. Yet we take them for granted most of the time and do little to protect them.

The most common abuse is eyestrain. This happens when the muscles of the eyes are overworked, and that usually is the result of reading or working in an area with inadequate light. Often youngsters will not take the time to turn on a light or move into the brighter part of the room when reading. Parents should always caution their young athletes about studying or reading without proper lighting.

Eye injuries can be prevented in the normal course of everyday activity if reasonable restraint is exercised. When out in glaring sunlight, one should wear sunglasses or have a cap with a sun visor on. If working out where there is a lot of dust, or in school in a shop or crafts class, the student should wear protective safety glasses or goggles. And if something becomes lodged in the eye and cannot be simply removed by rotating the eyeball or bringing the top lid over the lower one, one should cover the eye with some protective material like a gauze pad and get to the doctor.

A common eye disease is conjunctivitis. Conjunctivitis, which is characterized by the inflammation and swelling of the eyelid, is an eye infection that is the result of contamination of the eye. The most common sources are the hands, towels, and cough droplets. It can even be picked up by contact with infected clothing. So young athletes should not dry themselves off after a shower with towels that have been used by others. Most other eye diseases require medical attention and are difficult to prevent, as they are usually associated with advancing age.

Care of the Ears

A recent survey showed that there are about 13 million Americans with some kind of hearing disorder. That's a great number of people, and although it is true that most hearing disorders are hereditary, hearing impairment can develop from certain diseases such as chronic otitis media or meningitis. Other hearing disorders can result from simple carelessness.

Today we see many teenagers walking around carrying a radio blaring into their ear through an ear plug or headset. The music they are listening to is probably rock and the constant noise irritation from that music is harmful to the ear. Sitting in a room with the stereo blaring can also hurt the ear. Studies have shown that teenagers who constantly listen to loud music develop serious hearing problems as young adults.

When cleaning the ear, never attempt to clear the wax out of the ear canal—you may actually push the wax down further. A cotton swab may be used to clean the exterior of the ear. If the wax buildup in the ear becomes annoying, see a physician. Don't try to clean out the wax buildup yourself. To prevent wax buildup in the external canal, pour a capful or dropperful of hydrogen peroxide in the canal. Allow the peroxide to bubble and then to run out. Do this several times a week.

Be sure to see a doctor if there is any discharging of fluid from the ear, if there is any irritating noise in the ear that continues for a day, or if there is any suspicion of loss of hearing. And I recommend that with each yearly physical checkup, there be an examination of the youngster's hearing.

Care of the Skin

Everyone wants to have a good complexion, and sound health habits of proper diet, adequate rest, exercise, and cleanliness should help us attain this goal. However, teenagers are particularly prone to a skin disorder called acne. We used to think that acne was caused by eating too much candy and other sweets. Dandruff was also blamed on acne. But scientific research has shown that there is more to acne than what you eat.

Acne is caused by the action of a hormone called testosterone. This is a male sex hormone also manufactured by females, so both sexes can get acne. Testosterone causes the glands of the skin to secrete an oily substance into the skin follicles, which then become blocked; the oily deposits build up under the skin and lumps appear. If the skin is not properly cleaned, bacteria may feed on these deposits causing them to become inflamed. This action of testosterone usually begins around the age of 12 and progresses until about 16. Then it slows down and usually disappears when the person is about 21.

The physical effects of acne can be severe if the child tries to squeeze the pimples to get rid of them. All that does is spread the infection and possibly cause some permanent damage and scarring on the face or other areas.

But the greatest damage acne causes might be the psychological and emotional burden placed on the child. Some children withdraw from their friends, and even their family, thinking themselves ugly and somehow different. Parents can help by assuring the children that with proper medication and care the condition can be controlled. Also, emphasize that almost every teenager has some degree of acne at some point.

With use of a combination of cleansing agent and benzoyl peroxide, acne conditions can be controlled. The cleansing agent acts to remove the dirt and oily deposits in the follicles, while the benzoyl peroxide destroys the bacteria. At times antibiotics may be necessary to control more severe acne.

Another area of care of the skin deals with exposure to the sun. Extensive exposure to the sun can cause severe burning, tough, leathery, unattractive skin, and even cancer. Lotions that tan the body chemically may be harmful. Exposure to the sun should be done on a gradual basis, and lotion that screens out the ultraviolet rays of the sun should be used. Try to stay out of the sun between 10 A.M. and 2 P.M., when the sun is at its greatest strength. If a painful burn does occur, take a cool bath and then apply Alpha Keri to the skin.

Body Temperature

One serious health problem that few people seem to be aware of is that cold weather or water can cause serious injury, disability, or even death in extreme cases. Some years ago, in the late 1960's, a team of nine

Marines, all in top physical condition, were paddling their canoe across the Potomac River at Quantico, Virginia. It was early evening, toward the end of March. The canoe capsized, and within fifteen minutes all nine were dead. The cause of death was hypothermia, which is a deep loss of body heat. These tough, well-trained Marines, because of the loss of body heat from the cold water, quickly became exhausted, lost their sense of direction, and drowned. They were all strong swimmers and they were only about 10 yards from shore when they tipped over. But they weren't prepared for the cold.

This same lack of preparation is responsible for the death of hikers, hunters, skiers, campers, climbers, and many others in the outdoors.

What happens is that when the body temperature falls due to the cold, there is a great increase in the utilization of calories, causing fatigue; thus physical abilities fall off, and serious injury can result. Athletes who are participating in sports such as hockey, skiing, swimming, mountain climbing, football, or any outdoor activity must be careful of such heat loss.

Remember that the head carries a much greater proportion of the circulation of the blood than any other part of the body. Therefore, it is a good idea to make sure the head is covered in all of these activities. You'll notice on television that many swimmers wear stocking caps to competition. By keeping your head warm, you'll prevent a sharp heat loss and be able to compete at full speed while avoiding the ordeal of hypothermia.

Cooling of the body also results from evaporation of water and perspiration from the body. Your hands and feet can also lower body temperature if allowed to get cold. So proper gloves, socks, and shoes are very important in protecting the body temperature.

There is research that indicates that bacteria and viruses multiply faster in the cooler body. That's another reason to keep warm at all times. Wear those warm-up suits before, during, and after competition.

Alcohol

To most youngsters, alcohol is a stimulant. Actually, beer, wine, and "hard liquor" such as gin, vodka, bourbon, and whiskey are not stimulants but depressives. Alcohol is classified as a food and a drug. As a food, it has almost no virtues. It contains almost no vitamins, minerals, or proteins. And as a drug, it affects the nervous system to make the bodily functions slow down. Like any depressant, alcohol makes the person drowsy and dulls his senses. So people who think that a "drink will pick me up" are badly mistaken. There is no pickup; just the opposite effect takes place.

One of the things that makes alcohol so damaging to young people is that their systems are not mature enough to handle it. Children often think that because their parents can have a couple of drinks and not be affected, they can too. But in young, immature bodies, which in most cases have less body weight, there is more rapid absorption and higher concentration of alcohol in the system.

When alcohol is taken into the body, it does not have to be digested as other foods do. rather, the alcohol is absorbed directly from the stomach into the bloodstream, and is then carried to the liver. The liver oxidizes the alcohol or burns it up, and it does that to all the alcohol it can handle. The alcohol that is not oxidized by the liver then is carried throughout the body by the blood and reaches all the body cells. Eventually, all the alcohol is oxidized except for the small amount that leaves the body through the urine. Medical research shows that the body cells that are most immediately affected are those of the nervous system and the brain.

Youngsters drinking today have no idea of the physical and psychological effects that alcohol has on them. Since their young bodies cannot handle the alcohol, they quickly become drunk. If they take enough, they get sick, throw up, and sometimes fall and hurt themselves. But the psychological effects are often worse. They may do foolish things while intoxicated that they would not do sober. They can forget their moral standards, or drive too fast and end up a statistic on the highway accident charts. And it takes very little alcohol to get young children drunk. A couple of beers can do it, and the results can often damage a person for life.

Teenage driving accidents are a frequent result of alcohol. Safe driving requires control of the senses, good hand and eye coordination to handle the car, and a clear head to make the quick decisions necessary for driving. Booze impairs all the faculties needed to drive safely. And besides impairing the motor functions, alcohol has an even more deadly effect. It can make a driver do things that he would never attempt if he were sober. His sense of caution is reduced and his mental picture of his abilities becomes distorted. It is estimated that over 60 percent of the traffic accidents that take place each year in this country result from one of the drivers being under the influence of alcohol.

Alcohol can also harm the athlete by hurting his nutritional balance, his physical condition, his mental discipline so necessary in sports, and his work in school. Youngsters, including the athletes, are going to experiment with alcohol. But if they understand that it is an experiment filled with great potential for harm, maybe they will cut the experiment short and eventually stay away from alcohol.

If the young athlete sees his parents drinking and enjoying it, he quite naturally will think that it gives pleasure and is a sign of being grown up. So parents who drink should be very careful in their explanation of the dangers of drinking. It is a case of making sure that your actions are understood by the children. Remember, by and large, children will do what we do, not what we say.

Most important, as I have said throughout this book, the parent must be there to support and help the child. If there is a drinking problem or if the parent suspects that there might be one, hollering and screaming at the child will do no good. Scare tactics and stories about the horrors of drink do no good whatsoever to the children of today. Do not be patronizing either, because they can see right through that. Keep the lines of communication open, discuss alcohol and drinking in a calm manner, let the children know that you want to help, and most of the time you'll find the child will open up and talk.

This time of their life is most difficult and the adjustments that the children have to make, physically, emotionally, and socially, present terrific burdens for people so young and inexperienced. Sexual drives and the peer pressure are greatest now; these are very powerful influences on the teenager and cause frustration, tension, and worry. If the teenager turns to drink to get some relief from these problems, then a more serious problem can develop.

Research shows that half of the heavy drinkers in high school started drinking while they were in grammar school! Therefore, the best time for parents to talk to their children about drinking is around the ages of 11 through 14. This is when their ideals, values, and peer associations are being formed and there is still time to reach them. Once they are older and still drinking, then the problem will most likely be past the talking stage.

Interestingly enough, children of moderate drinkers seem to be less likely to develop a drinking problem than children of parents who condemn liquor and forbid it to their children.

Parents who understand the pressures of the peer group can help the child by showing them that they have only themselves to impress, nobody else, and that those who need alcohol to enjoy themselves are not basically confident in their own abilities. So drinking, the parents should stress, is not the mark of an adult, does not impress anybody, and only shows the person to be afriad of his or her own personality.

In summary, teenage drinking is a very serious problem. Parents and teenagers should face it in a calm, reasonable manner. Parents should talk to their children, explain to them the dangers of drinking for a young person, help them understand themselves by letting them know you understand their rush to grow up, give them your time and love, and make sure they know you want to help. With luck and hard work, your young athletes will pass through this time of their life and enjoy it.

Marijuana

Marijuana—also called "pot," "Mary Jane," "tea," or "weed"—is the most common form of drug abuse among teenagers today. In cigarette form, marijuana is referred to as a "joint" or a "reefer" or as "sticks." There are even special pipes for smoking marijuana. They are small silver bowls that are screwed into a stem and the whole contraption looks like a miniature of a moonshiners' still. The smell of the pipe bowl will tell you what has been in the pipe.

Marijuana is a mild, hallucinogenic drug. I use the term mild, advisedly because, though marijuana is not as powerful as some of the other hallucinogenic drugs, the long-term effects can be just as disastrous to the individual as harder drugs. The number of automobile accidents caused by smokers driving while they are "high" attests to the danger.

Marijuana comes from the top of a plant called an Indian hemp plant. The plant looks like any weed and it can grow anyplace, including your own back yard. The leaves and the flowers at the top of the plant are dried, then cut into fine pieces. Then the pieces are rolled into a cigarette or stuffed into a pipe.

Shortly after inhaling the smoke, the user notices a feeling of inner joy that is far out of proportion to the reality of the circumstances. This is described as being "high." The user's awareness and perception of time and space are considerably altered, and the coordination, especially that related to speed and accuracy, is also affected. Complex intellectual capacities that control dexterity are impaired.

The individual's basic personality is not appreciably changed, but his behavioral reactions may be different than normal. He may exhibit unwarranted self-confidence. Inhibitions may be lost to varying degrees. If a negative influence is insinuated, he may become slightly paranoid, anxious, and apprehensive. This experience is known as a "bummer" or a "downer."

Surprisingly, the individual will walk in an apparently normal state and be able to talk coherently, but sometimes with a slight hesitation or slur. But if placed under stress and required to react or behave with coordination, he'll usually fail.

Individuals using marijuana for the first time usually have little reaction to the drug. The effects are very unpredictable, but there is one thing certain: there are no beneficial results from using marijuana.

Although marijuana is not considered habit-forming, it is interesting to note that a great majority of those who use hard drugs such as heroin began their habit with the continual use of marijuana and then graduated to the habit-forming hallucinogens. Marijuana, with its mild effects, also serves as an introduction to drugs like LSD with their consequent terrifying harm and abuse.

Today there is a great deal of pressure across the country to legalize the use of marijuana. The President's ad-hoc panel on drug abuse had the following comment: ". . . the hazards of marijuana on a person have been exaggerated and that long criminal sentences imposed on the occasional user or possessor of the drug are in poor social perspective." Such statements as these, along with the great amount of material that whitewashes the use of the drug and that try to minimize its dangers, are a great disservice to the young user.

There is a great deal of money to be made with the legalized sale of marijuana. Whenever there are large profits to be made, people can find a way to minimize the hazards of almost anything. Much of the so-called evidence is full of half-truths and presented out of context to confuse the minds of the youngsters. People pushing the use and sale of marijuana say it is better than using alcohol. However, there is a clear-cut difference between the two.

To the brain or the central nervous system, alcohol is a depressant, that is, it slows down the activity of the brain cells themselves. Marijuana and the other hallucinogens create their effect by exciting the brain cells. When these cells become excited, overactive, they frequently die, so there is a good possibility that overexcitement following the use of marijuana will result in the death of some brain cells. This continual loss of brain cells produces the chronic changes that are so common among long-term users of marijuana. There is loss of social judgment and the loss of ability to have insight into their own problems. This loss of brain cells has been well-documented and proven in autopsy findings.

Note that it is not the prolonged use of marijuana that produced the death of the brain cells; it happens on the first time and every subsequent use. By contrast, it takes alcohol a long time to kill brain cells.

The next section deals with how to recognize the signs of drug abuse, and how you might help prevent it.

Drug Abuse

Taking drugs under a doctor's supervision or by prescription is the only way drugs should be given to the young athlete. Even the drugs from the medicine cabinet can be harmful if they are used in a way not prescribed or if an overdose is taken.

COMMON DRUGS AND NARCOTICS

Description	Street Name	Effects	Remarks
AMPHETAMINES: Stimulants; oral Source: Prescription, home medicine chest, illegal street market	Bennies Whites Uppers Dexies Beans Chalk	Talkative, excited, restless, reckless aggressive, shock, panic, confusion	Less control of muscles, coordination and judgment, runs down body
METHAPHETAMINE: Stimulant; injected, oral Source: Prescription, home medicine chest, illegal street market	Speed Meth Crystals	Up tight, confused, sick, loss of memory, insane, hallucinations	Can cause shock or death, brain damage
BARBITURATES: Depressants; oral Source: Prescription, home medicine chest, illegal street market	Reds, Blues Barbs, Pinks Rainbows Yellows Downers Stumblers Bullets	Slurred speech, staggers, wobbles, deep comas, suicidal tendencies	May be fatal when combined with alcohol
HALLUCINOGENS: Mind altering drugs Source: Illegal street market	Acid DMT STP Scramblers	Hallucination, panic, brain damage, suicide attempts, insanity	Unpredictable: users 'drop out of life;' effects may recur; seriously impairs brain functions
MARIJUANA: Mind altering drug Source: Illegal markets	Pot Grass Weed Joints Jays Hash THC	Hysteria, alters reality, impairs judgement, uncoordinated. distortion of senses	Effects vary with dose and quality; users cannot judge speed. distance, or time

HEROIN: Depressant; injected Source: Illegal street market	Stuff Smack Fit Kit	Blunts senses; causes craving sweets; always in stupor, violent behavior during withdrawal	Very addictive; difficult to cure; expensive
SNIFFING: Any volatile solvents Source: Anywhere	Glue, Gas Thinner Lacquer	Blurred vision, dizzy, sick headaches, nausea, weight loss	It is very dangerous

DRUG ABUSE INDICATORS: Eyes: very large or extremely small pupils, bloodshot, watery, red-rimmed
Skin: injection tracks, scars, sores
Odor: bad body odor and breath
Appetite: huge or very little. Craves sweets or liquids

We will not discuss the more dangerous drugs—cocaine, angel dust, heroin and LSD—and the harm they can do to the individual because there is already a great deal of information and knowledge about them and other hard drugs available.

There are behavioral clues that might tip you off to the fact that your children or one of their friends may be in some stage of drug abuse. Not any of the following is a definite signal that something is wrong; these are mainly signals that there is a possibility of a drug problem.

1. The youngster's lifestyle undergoes a drastic change.

2. The youngster demonstrates a radical change in personal appearance. Be especially suspicious when he or she takes to wearing long-sleeved shirts almost exclusively.

3. The youngster evidences loss of memory, confusion, or incoherence for no apparent reason.

4. The youngster becomes overly secretive about himself and acts suspicious of others when they deal with him.

5. There is a sudden need for money, usually demonstrated by the youngster's stealing or borrowing from friends or other members of the family or pawning items from his room.

6. The youngster begins to go off by himself into limited-access areas like a parked car or a cellar or storage room.

7. The youngster associates with people who are known drug users.

8. The youngster begins to wear sunglasses at odd times: he is trying to hide the condition of his eyes.

9. There are frequent outbursts of temper for no good reason.

10. The youngster deviates from his normal speech pattern with slang expressions like "cooker," "fix," "speed," "freaks," "spike," etc.

11. The youngster experiences frequent drowsy spells, or exhibits undue excitement patterns or demonstrates a distasteful attitude toward authority or people that he used to admire.

12. The youngster has in his possession any form of drug, bottle cap, or spoon with a bent handle, or syringe, eyedropper, or hypodermic needle.

If I had the answer on how to prevent drug abuse, I'd be a miracle man. Doctors, sociologists, psychiatrists, religious leaders, politicians, and parents have all tried and the problem is still with us. But I do have some thoughts, both as a doctor and as a parent.

First, present a clear and detailed explanation of all the facts related to the use of drugs. Secondly, do not preach. A factual discussion, built around the proper sources of authority, is very important. There are many publications about drugs and their effects. Information can be obtained from drug information centers, local narcotic centers, the local police, the hospitals, the schools, and magazines.

After you have had the discussion and everyone concerned has an understanding of the problem, you have to establish your policy concerning the use of drugs and the association with people who do use drugs. Your position must be clear and your children should know what steps you will take if there is any evidence of drug abuse. Be sure to make the position one that you and the youngsters can live with.

Finally, realize that drugs are around, that they are easy to get, especially marijuana. Also realize that your young athlete is going to be treated by a trainer and a doctor, so he might have drugs prescribed for him. Be very careful with these drugs and make sure they are used as prescribed.

If the child does have a problem, do not ignore it. It will not go away. The coach can kick the drug-using athlete off the team. That helps his problem but not that of the parent of the user. When there is a problem, get help immediately. Contact your family doctor and see what must be done to rehabilitate the youngster. Psychiatric care may be necessary. If so, get it.

The medications discussed in this section are, for the most part, available at the local pharmacy. Some require a doctor's prescription. All are intended as a help to the health of the athlete. Though some brand names will be mentioned, that in no way is a special recommendation for that brand.

Anabolics: These drugs have been used to promote physical growth and development. The more common ones are Dianabol and Winstrol. Although there have been some claims for their effectiveness, there has been no documented evidence that they in any way enhance athletic ability. The anabolics have many side effects which are frequently significant enough to counterindicate their use except under specific medical guidance. Because of the possibility of premature closure of the epiphysis (the growing end of the bone), which would interfere with normal growth and result in shortness of stature, these medications have no place in individuals who have not completed their growth.

Analgesics. This group of drugs relieves or suppresses pain in varying degrees. They do not interfere with an athlete's training and conditioning, but I recommend against the use of any analgesics right before practice or a game. The most commonly used analgesic is aspirin or the combination of aspirin with acetaminophen or phenacetin. For the milder discomforts of muscle aches and pains, the aspirin compounds can be very effective, especially during the preschool training period when the athlete is usually in a two-a-day workout and the muscles can become stiff and sore. Aspirin combined with caffeine, in such tablets as Empirin and Excedrin, can be very helpful in treating the simple headache. And aspirin combined with antihistamines, as in Coricidin, are helpful for the relief of the common cold. The more potent analgesics containing codeine, morphine, and other derivatives should always be dispensed by a physician and never taken prior to athletic competition.

Androgens. These are male hormones which are occasionally used for medical treatment of undescended testes. They should be used carefully, only under a physician's guidance.

Anesthetics. These drugs, used to deaden or kill pain, are always dispensed and used under the guidance of a physician. They should never be used to block the pain of an injury just so the athlete can play, especially a young athlete. Professional athletes use an anesthetic spray called ethylchloride, which is a cooling agent that provides a certain amount of numbness to the injured area and allows the athlete to continue. This is not to be used on young athletes, as the effects are temporary and the athlete allowed to continue might be seriously injured. Wrapping the injury in ice will numb the pain and also treat the swelling.

Anorexics. The preparations are mainly used for the suppression of appetite. The most common types are the amphetamines, which come in a variety of forms. These have too many stimulatory side effects to warrant their use for teenagers. The non-amphetamine anorexics, such as Ionamin, pondimin, saorex, and Tenuate, to name a few of the common ones, have certain advantages in controlling appetite, but should always be used under the guidance and prescription of a physician. The diet and eating habits should be modified not only to give immediate weight loss, but to develop prolonged beneficial eating habits to prevent a regaining of weight. For the most part the anorexics have side effects that can be very annoying, such as headaches, nervousness, and wakefulness at night.

Antacids. Antacids come in many forms, some of which can be purchased without a prescription and can be very helpful for mild stomach upsets. Some of the better preparations are Dicarbosil tablets or Gelusil. Should any abdominal pain persist, further medical advice should be obtained prior to the further use of antacids.

Antibacterials and *Antiseptics.* This medication is used mainly for infection and should be used under a physician's guidance. There are several preparations that are available for use topically, that is, on the skin. To prevent or treat mild infections, you can wash thoroughly with a good antiseptic soap and then apply one of the antibacterial ointments, such as Neosporin, Neo-Polycin, or garamycin. These can be purchased without a prescription. There is little to be gained from the use of hydrogen peroxide, H_2O_2, for cleaning wounds, but the H_2O_2 is valuable to irrigate and clean the external ear canal. Peroxide will prevent infection and also clean the wax. Minor infections in the mouth and the common and painful canker sore can sometimes be helped by the use of Gly-Oxide. Place ten to fifteen drops in the mouth for three minutes. Rinsing it over the sore area will sometimes provide an excellent antiseptic.

Antibiotics. The antibiotics are used to control and treat infections. They may be taken during athletic competition and not interfere with participation in sports; but the underlying condition should be thoroughly evaluated and should dictate when the athlete can return to full activity. Antibiotics should always be taken under a doctor's prescription, and in all cases the entire course of treatment should be completed. Athletes, by their nature and activity, seem to be susceptible to infections, but because of their generally excellent state of health, they seem to recover very quickly. There is often the tendency to cut short the treatment that has been prescribed. We should always be careful to see that the illness has been thoroughly cleared up before the athlete is allowed to return to competition, even though he may feel well. There has been some discussion that, since antibiotics interfere with the enzyme system, athletes taking them while competing in endurance or high-energy sports require additional Vitamin C. It is recommended that when they return in competition following the use of antibiotics, they take 200 to 400 milligrams of Vitamin C per day. Some individuals are hypersensitive or allergic to penicillin. In the case of athletes who have severe reactions to penicillin and who frequently travel or are away from home, it is advisable that they wear an identification bracelet or carry a card stating so. This, of course, is true for any allergic type of reaction, but it is particularly important in the case of penicillin.

Anticonvulsants. This medication is used to prevent convulsions or seizures. It should be used only under the control of a physician and the doses should be regulated to treat the underlying problem. Those athletes who are in good control and are under the guidance of their physician may participate in their sport. Some of the more common anticonvulsants are Dilantin, phenobarbital, and Valium. Each has its own particular effect, but in general they do sometimes cause a degree of interference with muscular coordination and cause sleepiness. The situation should be thoroughly reviewed in game-type conditions so that the athlete, and particularly his teammates and coach, will have confidence that there will be no difficulty during the game.

Antidepressants. Taking these drugs is not a reason not to participate in sports. Other than their very mild sedative effect, they do not interfere with performance.

Antidiarrheals. This medication can be extremely valuable in relieving the abdominal pain and cramping that accompanies diarrhea. The infectious diarrhea should not be confused with the frequent occurrence of a loose bowel movement prior to an athletic contest. Diarrhea before an event is usually very short-lived and requires no treatment other than keeping meals simple so as not to further complicate the picture. For simple abdominal cramps, a preparation such as Donnatal can be very helpful; if there is moderate to severe diarrhea with frequent or large, loose bowel movements, Donnagel, which combines the Donnatal with Kaopectate, can also be very effective. Should there be little abdominal discomfort and just frequent bowel movements, Kaopectate and control of the diet may be all that are required. If the diarrhea is more protracted, a preparation such as Lomotil can be very valuable in controlling it. Following a moderately severe bout of diarrhea, yogurt can be very helpful in returning the intestines to their normal bacterial content. For those who do not tolerate yogurt there is Lactinex, which helps provide the normal bacteria to the intestine.

Antihistamines. The antihistamines are used mainly to treat such disorders as hay fever, nasal congestion, hives, and other allergic reactions. The most common antihistamines are Benadryl (particularly useful for allergic reactions), Chlor-Trimeton (for hay fever), Phenergan, Pyribenzamine, Triaminic (which are used in cough mixtures), and Dramamine (commonly used for motion sickness and dizziness). The antihistamines are not a contraindication of participation in sports They do cause some degree of sleepiness, however; also they are often combined with the adrenaline-like compounds, which, because of their stimulating action, may reduce endurance and stamina.

Antinauseants. These drugs are used to prevent nausea and vomiting. The most common ones are Atarax and Compazine, taken orally, or the Tigan suppositories. Two others—Bonine and Dramamine—are used mainly for motion sickness. Children taking these can take part in athletic events but the underlying cause of the stomach upset or nausea and vomiting should be the primary consideration.

Antispasmodics. These medications are mainly for the use of upset stomachs or spasms and pain in the intestinal tract. The more common ones are Donnatal, Tamine, Pro-Banthine, and Sedadrops. They do often produce sleepiness because of their frequent combination with one of the phenobarbital-like compounds. Another side effect is some dryness of the mouth. There is no reason children cannot take this medication and continue to participate in sports. Donnatal is particularly useful in the liquid form calming and relaxing the stomach spasms without interfering with performance.

Bronchodilators: These preparations are used to relax and enlarge the bronchi or tubes into the lungs. They are helpful in treating asthma or asthma-like symptoms. Common preparations used are Asbron, Brondecon, Bronkotabs, Marax, Quadrinal, Quibron, Tedral, and other related preparations which contain theophylline. Any athlete with asthma will use these on a regular basis without any difficulty. These preparations are also frequently used in combination with adrenaline or ephedrine substances, which are banned in international competition. Therefore, they should be used with a certain amount of discretion. Consult a physician prior to continuing their use during athletic contests. All asthmatic compounds and preparations should be closely checked for the presence of adrenaline or ephedrine; the urine can also be tested for these substances.

Cardiovascular Preparations: There is very little use for most cardiac preparations in children, and certainly any child requiring a cardio-vascular preparation should be under the care of a pediatric cardiologist and should have extensive and thorough evaluation prior to participation in any sport activity. The most common preparations are the digital compounds and the hypotensives. Any athlete taking any of those preparations should have exercise tolerance tests to assure their safety.

Cough and Cold Preparations: There are many cough and cold prepara-tions, both over the counter and by prescription. Usually they are a combination of an antihistamine, a decongestant such as one of the ephedrine-like substances, and sometimes aspirin. More common cold preparations are Congesprin, Coricidin, Demazin, Dimetapp, Nova-histine, Sinutab, and Triaminic. There is no reason why these medications cannot be taken in proper dosages. However, the underlying cause of the cold or infection should be thoroughly evaluated prior to their use, and a physician should approve their use by an athlete taking part in sports.

Cough Preparations: The common ones are Benylin, Phenergan expec-torant, Robitussin, Novahistine, and Tuss-Ornade. Again, the medica-tions have little side effects and would allow for participation in athletics. However, the basic condition requiring their use should be the primary consideration.

Decongestants and *Expectorants:* Most of these have been mentioned elsewhere, for treatment of colds and the like. The more common ones are Allerest, Coricidin, Dimetapp, Naldecon, and Novahistine. Here again, they contain mainly a combination of antihistamine and ephedrine-like substances, which should not be used prior to athletic contests or practice. Nasal decongestants such as Neo-Synephrine and alcopheal-conephrine can provide some temporary relief for nasal congestion and are safe to use on a limited basis.

Dermatologicals: These are mostly in the form of cleansing lotions and topical creams and of course have no significant limitation during athletic competition.

Estrogens: Female hormones have been used for the regulation and cycling of menstrual periods, as well as for control of acne and as a contraceptive. Girls taking estrogens should realize that they do produce an accentuation of the female body build, which frequently will interfere with athletic performance. The enlargement of the breasts, the widening of the pelvis, and the increased fat deposition can cause a decrease in athletic performance.

Fungicides: Fungicides used to control athlete's foot are Desenex, Tinactin, and Lotrinin. They come in spray, ointment, and powder forms. The powder form is often used as a preventative.

Glucocorticoids: Cortisone preparations have a wide variety of use. The most popular ones are cortisone, decadron, medrol, and prednisone. Taken orally, for short terms, these do not have any significant effect on the body, but when taken over long periods of time they could interfere with the body's ability to react to stressful situations. Many of the cortisone preparations are injected into a joint or tendon to decrease inflammation; this does not produce any significant change in the body and would not interfere with athletic performance. Certainly the injections should be given under the guidance of a physician familiar with the problems of sports medicine.

Hemorrhoidal Preparations: These preparations provide some relief from hemorrhoids. The most common one is Anusol. Although some of them do contain pain medication or cortisone compounds, there is no contraindication to their use by athletes.

Hormones: Hormones cover a wide variety of substances that normally occur within the body. They are taken to increase or replace a body need. They should be taken under the daily supervision of a physician.

Laxatives: There are the bulk laxatives such as Metamucil, and the combination bulk and bowel stimulants such as Dialose and Peri-Colace. For short-term use in treating constipation these medications are of value; however, for longer periods it is better to concentrate on diet and the development of good bowel habits. Picking a regular time daily to relax and have a bowel movement, rather than the rush-rush of catch-as-catch-can, can be of tremendous value in relieving this problem. Frequently, it is necessary to use an enema. One of the simplest and easiest preparations is a Fleets disposable enema. This is preferable to the old type of enema because of its limited quantity of fluid and of pressure. For adults, mineral oil is extremely popular, but because it interferes with the absorption of the oil-soluble vitamins, it is advisable that mineral oil not be used without consulting a physician.

Mouthwashes: These preparations serve mainly as an astringent in the mouth and do very little to prevent dental caries or improve breath. The common ones are Lavoris, Cepacol and Listerine. Chloraseptic is a mouthwash that does have a certain antiseptic and may be useful for relieving pain of sore throats.

Muscle Relaxants: These are preparations to relieve the discomfort of sprains, where muscle spasm is a problem. A simpler combination for muscle relaxants is metprobamate (Miltown) and aspirin, which is the main medication of Equagesic and Norgesic. These preparations have their use following injuries but should not be taken to allow the athlete to participate in the presence of muscular discomfort.

Opthalmologicals: These are antibacterial eye ointments. Neosporin ophthalmic ointment is the most popular for the treatment of eye infections. For washing material from the eye, Dialose is popular; and for the simple correction of infection and irritation, Swimeye and Visine are also very useful. These preparations can be used for any simple infections or irritation about the eye and their early use may produce prompt relief.

Otic Preparations: There are several different types of eardrops. The simplest and best for pain are the Auralgan eardrops. For the prevention or intervention of swimmers' ear or chronic inflammation of the ear, Swim-Ear or Vo-Sol can be of great benefit. Should there be infection in the ear, the antibiotic eardrops such as Coly-Mycin Otic might be more advisable. Excessive wax in the ear is simply treated with hydrogen peroxide: pour directly or drop it into the ear canal and allow it to foam; then gently dry with a soft tissue. Using the hydrogen peroxide two or three times a week will prevent tremendous wax buildup.

Pediculicides and *Scabcides:* Both head lice and crabs plus scabies are more common than one might expect. The Kwell preparations are very effective in clearing up these conditions. However, good health habits are the best way to prevent their recurrence.

Sedatives: This group consists mainly of the barbiturates for sleep and for the control of convulsive disorders. The more commonly used barbiturates are Butibel, phenobarbital, Luminal, Nembutal, and Seconal. Most of these medications are somewhat short-acting; however, in some individuals their effects are more prolonged, producing a dopey or groggy condition that would interfere with athletic performance. Should the athlete have trouble sleeping the night before the game, there are some non-barbiturate preparations available. One is Phenergan, an antihistamine, which produces sleep without tremendous aftereffects. The chronic or prolonged use of any of the sedatives should be condemned, except under special conditions.

Vaginal Douches: There are many popular home douches and irrigants for young girls but it is best to seek advice from one's gynecologist. The popular douches are Massengill or Vagisec liquids, which come with clear directions for their use. Vaginal creams are popular for controlling infection and irritation about the genital area. Simple irritations can be treated with the cortisone creams. When a simple treatment is not effective, then diagnosis and treatment should be obtained from a physician.

Immunization Schedule

Tetanus. After initial immunization children should receive a diptheria-tetanus (DT) shot every five years. Following an open puncture wound, especially if it has been exposed to contamination by dirt, they should receive a booster tetanus shot.

The oral polio vaccine should be repeated every five years for the age group six through sixteen.

The athlete should also receive a single basic shot for rubeola (red measles or ten-day measles), rubella (three-day measles or German measles), and mumps.

When taking flu shots, there is a great possibility that the athlete will get a mild case of the flu. Remember that the flu virus given is for the flu that is expected that year. As a general rule, I do not recommend the flu shot for young athletes, unless they already have a diagnosed respiratory disease that would make flu prevention important.

Tobacco

In this country, and probably across the free world, more money is spent to sell cigarettes than to sell any other product that is consumed by the people. And there probably is almost as much money spent telling people how damaging smoking can be to the human body. It is a filthy habit. After entertaining at home, when all the guests have left, just take a look at the house. Ashtrays are filled with butts; glasses and cups, some still with liquid in them, usually have half-finished cigarettes floating in them; and the room probably reeks of foul cigarette odor.

Yet, there are more people smoking today than there were when the Surgeon-General of the United States first announced that smoking cigarettes was dangerous to your health. That happened in January 1971. Within a year, cigarette advertising was off television and radio, and each pack had to carry the warning that cigarettes were dangerous to the health of the user. Can you imagine a product that tells you it is dangerous and that is still being bought by people? Today, after more than a decade of research linking smoking to respiratory problems, heart disease, and cancer, cigarette sales are greater than they have ever been. On top of that, the price has almost doubled.

If that does not tell us something about the stubbornness of the smoker, nothing will. But the fact that millions smoke does not make it right. And when it comes to telling our young athletes how bad smoking is to their health, the lecture is usually given by a coach who lights up right after practice, or a health and hygiene teacher who can't wait to get to the teachers' lounge to get a smoke. Or, if the lecture is given at home, Mom or Dad probably is smoking while delivering the message. And, unfortunately, many of my colleagues in the medical profession are no great example of self-control when it comes to smoking.

Teenage smoking is part of the same problem that is evidenced in use of alcohol and drugs. It is the "in" thing to do. The peer pressure is too great. Smoking makes the youngsters feel more sophisticated, smarter, and older. There is no sound medical reason for smoking. Sucking in a breath of smoke is not an act of pleasure, and if it is held in the lungs long enough, it can cause pain, choking, or sometimes death.

Rather than list all the reasons why smoking is bad, I'll just explain medically what smoking does and why it should be stopped. First of all, two substances in cigarettes, nicotine and tar, are toxic, irritating to the body, and dangerous to your health. Further, smoking interferes with the air exchange in the lungs, reducing the amount of oxygen your system gets when you inhale a cigarette. This leads to cardiovascular problems, particularly coronary heart disease. In the lungs, the inhaling smoke increases respiratory problems, helping produce chronic emphysema as well as the great killer, lung cancer.

In the young athlete, a reduction of the amount of oxygen in the system causes shortness of breath after exercise. Oxygen is very important to the growing body of a youngster. Tobacco, by interfering with the oxygen intake into the bloodstream, reduces the general health of the body and makes athletic endeavors more difficult.

Years ago, there was little medical evidence for the claims that smoking was bad for the health. Today, all the warnings are based on sound scientific research and the relationship between smoking and heart disease, cancer, and chronic lung diseases is completely established. These problems may seem far removed from the world of the young athlete or any youngster. But soon they will be adults. The habit of smoking is tough to break. By keeping the youngsters aware of what smoking does to them internally and how it makes their athletic career more difficult, we may be able to keep them from smoking. If the parents smoke, they should not do it in front of the children. If they do not smoke, they should speak out against people who do, especially in public places like elevators, buses, or trains. Only by trying to show our youngsters that smoking is not smart or cool but a dirty, harmful habit, can we expect to keep them from smoking.

Coffee and Tea

Coffee and tea contain caffeine, which is a stimulant to the body. The caffeine is an artificial substance that acts on the body primarily to help keep people awake. These beverages produce no improvement in performance or any other helpful effects for the athlete.

Both coffee and tea are extremely poor sources of nutrition and they do not even contain enough salts to be an adequate substitute for water replacement. They are of no advantage to the young athlete. Ingestion of large quantities of either will increase the urinary output and therefore make less water available to the body.

Coffee or tea is no substitute for milk in the athlete's diet.

8

SOME FINAL THOUGHTS

In the opening chapter I talked about Marty Glickman's question to me about how he could go about getting his son interested in sports. The answer, in my case and in the examples of the other outstanding athletes we have talked to, seems to be relatively simple: accessibility and parental interest.

Obviously by accessibility I mean that your child has to have the chance to participate in sports through either the school program or the town organization, and the youngster has to have access to space, equipment, and other boys and girls who want to play.

As far as parental interest is concerned, I really feel that this is the key to getting your children into sports and keeping them interested. The athletes I spoke to in preparing this book each recounted the things their parents did to help them somehow along the way. With some, it was just coming to the game to watch them play, with others, building a backboard in the back yard or driving them many miles so they could compete. Whatever the duty, the parents made sure that they did what they could to help and encourage their child in his or her sport.

Today it is fashionable in some circles to criticize parents who are vocal in their encouragement to their children. Well, I don't feel that way. I don't approve of parents' berating their children in front of others, but I certainly understand that feeling of wanting success for their children.

And there is nothing wrong in wanting your child to be successful and nothing wrong in letting your child know how you feel. But if you have some constructive criticism of your young athlete, pass it along in the privacy of your home. Hollering at the child in front of his or her peers can only cause embarrassment and more often than not lead to resentment, which will be reflected in a loss of interest in sports.

We might be too organized in this country today in sports. One of the weaknesses of Little League programs and Pop Warner leagues and the soccer leagues that are springing up across the country is that the players really don't get that much chance to play. Sometimes I watch an hour of practice in baseball with the boys of the Little League, and most of the time few are really part of the game. Boys at the age of eight through fourteen should be playing baseball all the time, learning to hit, catch, field, and throw. It seems to me that the old sandlot pick-up games allowed for more of that than do the organized football, basketball, soccer, and other sports leagues for youngsters.

There is too much coaching, too. Kids eight or nine years old, just learning to play basketball, should not be so organized that their games are over-officiated, overcoached, and lacking in fun. The basketball is too heavy for them at that age and they should be playing at half court with each team getting the ball after each basket and all the boys getting a chance to dribble, shoot, and rebound. Some of the teams even play zone defense, so they never give the youngsters a chance to develop the skills of defense and offense that they will need as they grow older.

It is at this young age that the seeds of interest and the development of the skills take place. If a boy is made to stand in right field and never gets a ball hit to him, he gets bored. And when it is his turn to hit and the coach tells him "a walk is as good as a hit," he'll stand there, not trying to hit. The coach wants to win, naturally, but the boy will never learn to hit unless he takes his cuts, even if he strikes out.

I feel that it is the parent who can help these boys and girls get the chance to play more. Encourage your children to play after practice, to get involved in pick-up games. Play catch with them or jog with them or shoot some baskets with them. Make sure, when they come home after a game in which they did not get a hit, that you go back to the recreation field and let them hit some to you. The same principle applies to any sport. For it is only by the application through practice of the sport skills that the skills are developed and increased.

If you talk to the successful athletes, it becomes obvious that they made a commitment to themselves to be excellent in their chosen profession. But what of the thousands who played the same sport and never reached the level of excellence? Remember that these others make up the great majority of players. What matter if they did not go on to great careers in college or the pros. At least they played at some time in their life and had the real and lasting pleasure of competing. And if they gave it all they had when competing, that's all that can be asked.

I used successful athletes as examples in this book of what it takes to be outstanding. But what they told us is not unusual or impossible. They worked hard, practiced hard, and devoted themselves to being successful. Many of their teammates did the same growing up in grammar school and high school. And the dedication of those teammates, though they may not have been as talented in sports, has helped them in later life as businessmen, as professional men and women, and as parents. The boys and girls who play in the school band are just as dedicated to success as the athletes who are on the field—and many times they work even harder.

I mentioned that I see nothing wrong in stressing success, at any age level and in any endeavor. This attitude also holds true for studies, work, anything we do. This is a highly competitive society that our children are entering. There is tremendous pressure on them and on the parents and they are going to have to handle that pressure to be successful. Sports is a marvelous way for our children to learn to compete, to cooperate, to work hard for a goal, and to accept the teammates and opposition as they are.

In Chapter 1 we talked about the importance the late Vince Lombardi placed on winning. A lot of other coaches feel the same way. What they are talking about, though, is *making the effort* to win. It is through that effort to be successful that greatness is achieved. John Wooden of UCLA won as no college basketball coach has ever won, and he said his greatest joy was not in the victory itself but in seeing his players fulfill themselves as athletes with victories and as individuals who successfully completed the task.

You have heard the phrase "He gave 110 percent." Well, we know that no matter what your talent or physical abilities, the best you can give physically is 100 percent. Of course, one player's 100 percent can be better that the 100 percent of the opponent. But sometimes there is another factor in victory, and that is that extra 10 percent. Where does that come from? It is the mental effort the athlete makes that takes him past the 100 percent. The extra mental effort in sports often overcomes the physical abilities and talents of an opponent. We have all seen physically superior teams or individuals beaten by supposedly inferior teams or persons. Why? Any player or team can have an off-day, but more often than not, the winners had mentally prepared themselves to win.

Even at the level of sports we are concerned with in this book, the young athlete can develop the mental discipline to make himself a superior athlete, above and beyond his physical talents. Some coaches call it the "will to win." Others call it desire. Whatever term is used, what it really means is that the athlete mentally prepared himself or herself to win—concentrated on just what he or she had to do to win, focused on how it was to be done, and literally "willed" victory in the mind. When the event began, that athlete was already ahead of the competition because of this mental buildup.

Watch the athletes warming up before an event some time. Some of the participants are standing around joking with each other or waving to people in the stands or just acting in a casual manner. Then look at some of the others, quietly concentrating. They might be daydreaming, but most likely they are getting ready mentally for the competition. If you are any kind of handicapper, put your money on the athletes who are concentrating. Nine times out of ten, no matter what the physical superiority of the opponent, the one who is mentally preparing for the competition will win.

Obviously, if an athlete has little ability and is up against an outstanding athlete, all the mental will power in the world is not going to make up the difference. But the will to win can often be the determining factor that enables an athlete of average ability to overcome one of superior talent.

At the high school or grammar school level the most talented teams are going to win most of the time. But when upsets do take place, most often it is because the underdogs made up their minds that there was no way they were going to lose. At the professional level, where the skills are almost equal, the difference between winner and loser is often that mental toughness.

Now I don't want to give the impression that this mental discipline is painful or difficult. Players should not walk around with a scowl. Sports should be fun. The athlete should see himself as a winner, scoring the key basket, intercepting the pass, or striking out the top batter. He should know the strengths and weaknesses of the opponent. He should mentally program himself as to how to exploit weaknesses and what the result will be. This is enjoyment even if it sounds a little like daydreaming. It works. If the athlete sees himself in a winning way, concentrates on achieving what he mentally pictures, most often it will happen.

The parents can help their youngsters develop this mental attitude of winning by talking about the upcoming game or event, talking about the opposition, asking the youngster's analysis of what it will take to win. A positive attitude builds up confidence that the athlete is going to win, no matter who the opponent. All the great athletes and teams have that confidence. Their opponents can feel it when playing against them, and the spectators can see it from the stands. Parents can help build that confidence in their youngsters with their encouragement, comments, and interest.

The parent is coach, trainer, dietitian, confessor, bus driver, cheerleader, and fan all rolled into one. A lot is required from the parents, but the rewards of family closeness and pride the parents get from watching their children succeed can make it worthwhile.

There is one last thought I'd like to leave with both the parents and the young athletes: It is simply that sports are a wonderful part of life, so enjoy them; don't make sports more important than they are in the scheme of life. As the great golfer Walter Hagen said, "You only pass this way once, so stop and enjoy the flowers." Have fun.